DEEP ELLUM

John and Robin Dickson Series in Texas Music
Sponsored by the Center for Texas Music History
Texas State University–San Marcos
• Gary Hartman, General Editor

A list of other titles in this series is available at the back of the book.

DEEP ELLUM

THE OTHER SIDE OF DALLAS

ALAN GOVENAR AND JAY BRAKEFIELD

Texas A&M University Press
College Station

Library of Congress Cataloging-in-Publication Data

Govenar, Alan B., 1952–
   Deep Ellum : the other side of Dallas / Alan Govenar and Jay Brakefield. — 1st Texas A&M University Press ed.
       p. cm. — (John and Robin Dickson series in Texas music)
   Previously published under title: Deep Ellum and Central Track. Denton, Tex. : University of North Texas Press, 1998.
   Includes bibliographical references and index.
   ISBN-13: 978-1-60344-958-8 (pbk. : alk. paper)
   ISBN-10: 1-60344-958-2 (pbk. : alk. paper)
   ISBN-13: 978-1-60344-959-5 (e-book)
   ISBN-10: 1-60344-959-0 (e-book)
   1. Popular music—Texas—Dallas—History and criticism.   2. African Americans—Texas—Dallas—Music—History and criticism.   3. Deep Ellum (Dallas, Tex.)—History. 4. Dallas (Tex.)—Social life and customs.   I. Brakefield, Jay F., 1945–   II. Title. III. Series: John and Robin Dickson series in Texas music.
   ML3477.8.D35G68   2013
   781.6409764'2812—dc23
                                                                        2012041446

Frontispiece: Herbert Cowens, ca. 1926. Courtesy Herbert and Rubye Cowens Collection, Texas African American Photography Archive.

Contents

Preface

By the time we met at the funeral of blues pianist Alex Moore in 1989, Moore had finally received the recognition he deserved for his contributions to the Deep Ellum of his youth. Alan delivered a eulogy, and Jay was covering the event for the *Dallas Morning News*. That initial encounter led to a personal and professional relationship that has endured to the present day. As we talked and explored our common interests in folklore and music, particularly Texas blues, we returned again and again to Deep Ellum, the fabled Dallas district that lay between the offices of the *Morning News* and the East Dallas neighborhood where Alan had established his nonprofit Documentary Arts.

Alan had been researching Deep Ellum since he moved to Dallas in 1980. In 1981 he organized the Downtown Dallas Traditional Music Festival, and for that event he featured Moore, then eighty years old, and country blues guitarist and singer Bill Neely, as well as a group he assembled and called Dallas Jazz Greats, which included Buster Smith, Herbie Cowens, Boston Smith, Benny "Chops" Arredondo, and James Clay. The success of this festival led to others, and in 1983 Alan launched the Dallas Folk Festival on City Hall Plaza and wrote articles for the *Dallas Times Herald* and *Parkway* magazine on the musicians he presented. In addition, Alan began the development of *Traditional Music in Texas,* a thirty-nine-part radio series that he produced for broadcast on KERA 90.1 in Dallas. In 1984 he received a commission from the Dallas Museum of Art for *Living Texas Blues,* a project that involved writing a short book, producing an anthology cassette, and directing three short films, *Deep Ellum Blues, Battle of the Guitars,* and *Cigarette Blues.* In 1986 Alan released through Documentary Arts another anthology cassette, called *Deep Ellum Blues,* which contained many of his field and festival recordings of musicians who had started their careers during the heyday of Deep Ellum in the 1920s and 1930s and were still performing in the 1980s. That same year, Alan researched and produced the third Dallas Folk Festival, which attracted more than eighty thousand people to City Hall Plaza. This was followed by Dallas Folk Festivals in 1988 and 1991. While these festivals focused broadly on different styles of traditional music around Texas, the core local emphasis was the musical legacy of Deep Ellum; he changed the name of the Dallas Jazz Greats to the Heat Waves of Swing in honor of one of Buster Smith's greatest bands, which sometimes included T-Bone Walker. Over the years, Alan added musicians such as David "Fathead" Newman, who had gotten their start with Buster Smith when they were in high school in Dallas. Alan also featured the Light Crust Doughboys and worked with Marvin "Smokey" Montgomery in much the same way he did with Smith, encouraging him to include as many veterans of the band as possible.

In 1988 Alan's book *Meeting the Blues: The Rise of the Texas Sound* was published, and he recognized the need to do more. Impressed with Jay's skills as a researcher and his coverage of the Alex Moore funeral, Alan approached him with the idea of collaborating on a book on Deep Ellum. Time was growing short to conduct more in-depth interviews with those who recalled the area from the 1920s through the 1950s, when it died or at least went into a deep sleep until it was reborn in the 1980s as a hangout for artists and musicians and a launching pad for a new generation of bands such as New Bohemians and the Butthole Surfers.

When we commenced work in 1991, the first step was to identify those primary human sources and to find and interview them as soon as possible. Some of these we either knew or knew of; others, we found as we went along. One led to another. Each interview subject was asked whether he or she knew of others to talk to, and many did. These conversations with history were rich, rewarding, and often surprising. We talked to musicians who had started their careers during the heyday of Deep Ellum and returned to perform there in the 1980s, including Bill Neely, Buster Smith, Herbie Cowens, Jesse Thomas, Sammy Price, Eddie Durham, Marvin "Smokey" Montgomery, and Jim Boyd. We drew on interviews we had done before, sometimes years before, and, when possible, conducted follow-up interviews as new questions surfaced.

We talked to everyone we could find who had any firsthand knowledge of Deep Ellum. We are especially grateful to Dr. Robert Prince, Dr. Emerson Emory, James Thibodeaux, Homer "Bill" Callahan, C. W. "Gus" Edwards, Walker Kirkes, Ted Parrino, Masha Porte, Eddie Goldstein, Isaac "Rocky" Goldstein, Dora Goldstein, Louis Bedford, Theaul Howard, Quince Cox,

Herbie Cowens, Rubye Cowens, Jay McShann, Ernestine Putnam, Nick Cammarata, Anna Lois Cammarata, Anna Mae Conley, Lucille Bosh-McGaughey, and Johnny Moss.

While we depended heavily on primary sources, we also relied upon many people and institutions that provided us access to unpublished manuscripts and resource collections, including Eliana Pittman; Greg Jacobs; Zella Sobel; John Slate, who once worked for Documentary Arts at the Texas African American Photography Archive and went on to become an archivist for the city of Dallas; Geraldine Dunbar and Gaylon Polatti at the Dallas Historical Society; Jeanne Chvosta at the Dallas Museum of Art; the Dozier Foundation; Juliet George and Rose Biderman at the Jewish Community Center; Jimm Foster and Carol Roark at the Dallas Public Library; the Hogan Jazz Archive at Tulane University; the Institute of Jazz Studies at Rutgers University; and Kay Bost at the DeGolyer Library at Southern Methodist University.

In addition, we have benefited greatly from the work of other researchers and readers, including Kip Lornell, David Evans, Paul Oliver, Chris Strachwitz, Kate Fox, Sumter Bruton, Chuck Nevitt, Tim Schuller, Kevin Coffey, Danny Williams, Donald Payton, Allan Turner, Craig Flournoy, Larry Powell, Hank Wackwitz, Doug Seroff, Lynn Abbott, Thomas Riis, Christopher Wilkinson, and Tommy Löfgren.

Since the book was first published in 1998, a lot has changed. Many of those upon whose memories and expertise we drew have passed on. Deep Ellum itself has faded and come back. When we had an opportunity to publish a new edition, we embarked upon additional research that involved reconnecting with original sources such as blues musician Robin "Texas Slim" Sullivan, who shared memories of playing and hanging out with Alex Moore; former Deep Ellum and South Dallas businessman Herschel Wilonsky; and his son, longtime Dallas journalist Robert Wilonsky. And we found new ones, such as Western swing authority Jean A. Boyd; Austin music writer Michael Corcoran, who generously shared his research on gospel musicians Washington Phillips and Arizona Dranes; and Shane Ford and Anna Obek, who tirelessly researched gospel blues great Blind Willie Johnson and worked for the placement of state and privately funded memorials in Beaumont, where he lived the last years of his life.

Since 1998, too, the Internet has come into its own, providing a wealth of information at an astounding level of accessibility, and much new research has been published, including Boyd's three books; fresh work on Blind Lemon Jefferson by Alan and by David Evans and Luigi Monge; and

discographies such as Tony Russell's volume covering country music recordings from 1921 to 1942.

It's impossible to thank everyone who contributed, and we apologize for
any omissions. And of course we could not have done this work without the
support of our families, most notably, our wives, Kaleta Doolin and Shirley
Brakefield.

DEEP ELLUM

Deep Ellum

Fact and Fiction

Deep Ellum has been mythologized beyond recognition. Misconceptions about Deep Ellum abound, principally as a consequence of the lack of solid historical research. *The WPA Dallas Guide and History,* for instance, refers to Deep Ellum as the "survival of the Freedman's Town settlement of former slaves" and confuses the date of the Emancipation Proclamation, January 1, 1863, with the date that Texas slaves learned of their freedom, June 19, 1865.[1] Little documentation is provided in the *WPA Guide,* a valuable but flawed document researched and written by the Federal Writers' Project. Completed in 1940, the *WPA Guide* was not published in book form until more than fifty years later, though many researchers read it in manuscript form at the Dallas Public Library. Among those researchers was the widely respected Dallas historian A. C. Greene, who said, "Dallas became a mecca for former slaves, and several Freedmen's Towns, as the black communities were known, sprang up on its outskirts. One black community, called Deep Ellum because it was located along the farthest extension of Elm Street, created a separate universe and ultimately contributed more famous artists to folklore and music than did white Dallas."[2] Likewise, William L. McDonald stated, "The freedman towns that evolved in Dallas County just after the [Civil] war included . . . the Deep Ellum district, which reached its zenith in the 1920s and 1930s."[3] Retired Southern Methodist University professor Darwin Payne wrote, "'Deep Ellum,' that part of Elm Street just east of Central Avenue, had originated after the Civil War as a 'Freedmanstown.' Construction of the H&TC Railroad depot nearby had encouraged its growth and permanence."[4]

Indeed, several freed-slave communities were established in and around Dallas after the Civil War. The one called Freedmantown was a short distance north of Deep Ellum, in the historic area of the city once called State-

Elm Street theaters at night, 1925. Photograph by Frank Rogers. Courtesy of the Texas/
Dallas History and Archives Division, Dallas Public Library.

Thomas and now the Uptown neighborhood. This community extended to
the eastern edge of Deep Ellum, near present-day Baylor University Medical
Center. But Deep Ellum itself does not seem to have been a freedmantown.
Indeed, there could hardly have been a settlement called Deep Ellum immediately after the Civil War because the area was still wooded. In the early
1870s, with the coming of the railroads, the woods were cleared, and the
major east-west streets—Elm, Main, and Commerce—were extended.

The area has long been associated with music. This has considerable legit-
imacy, as we shall see, but this reputation has in many ways been obscured
and distorted. Larry Willoughby reported that:

> the hidden and forbidden clubs and speakeasies along the northern part of
> Elm Street were the center of the blues and jazz action. The area was seething
> with music—jazz combos, jump bands, bebop and boogie-woogie pianists,
> blues and jazz vocalists, and street-corner guitarists. It was a magnet for musi-
> cians of every racial and cultural background, and therefore, symbolically and
> in vivid musical reality, Deep Ellum was the most visible example of the inter-
> action of cultures that defines Texas music.[5]

Willoughby had the broad outlines right, but he succumbed to the temptation to exaggerate and romanticize the musical activity, not to mention significantly confusing several eras. Bebop didn't take hold until the 1940s, long after Dallas's black nightlife scene had moved away from Elm Street, for instance, and few nonblack musicians played in Deep Ellum because of the segregation of the time. For that matter, nightclubs in the modern sense didn't really exist in the twenties and thirties, when there was nightlife on Elm Street and in nearby portions of Central Track. Entertainment was presented outdoors on the streets and in parks, dance halls, theaters, and cafés, as well as in "chock houses" and "soft-drink stands" where bootleg alcohol was served. Writer Dave Oliphant described Deep Ellum as a red-light district and repeated an interviewer's misquotation of Buster Smith: "Ella B. Moore's theater" became "the L. B. Mose theater" because of Smith's Texas accent.[6]

The neighborhood has inspired other florid prose, such as this description from columnist J. H. Owens, "Old Ironsides," writing in a black weekly newspaper, the *Dallas Gazette,* in 1937:

Down on "Deep Ellum" in Dallas, where Central Avenue empties into Elm Street, is where Ethiopia stretches forth her hands. It is the one spot in the city that needs no daylight saving time because there is no bedtime, and working

Elm Street, Dallas, ca. 1907, Courtesy of the Texas African American Photography Archive.

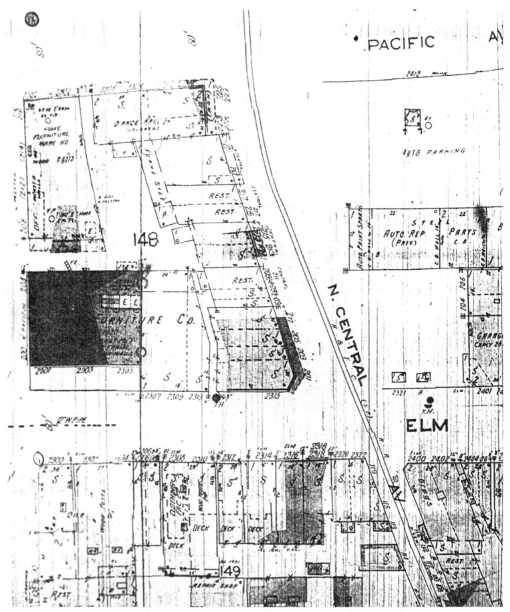

A 1920s Sanborn map of Dallas shows the intersection of Elm Street and Central Track. At the top and slightly left of center is the "Dance Hall (Colored)," which is the Tip Top dance hall. Courtesy of the Dallas Public Library.

Deep Ellum, Dallas, 1922. Courtesy of the Texas/Dallas History and Archives Division, Dallas Public Library.

hours have no limits. The only place recorded on earth where business, religion, hoodooism, gambling and stealing goes [*sic*] on at the same time without friction. . . . Last Saturday a prophet held the best audience in this "Madison Square Garden" in announcing that Jesus Christ would come to Dallas in person in 1939. At the same time a pickpocket was lifting a week's wages from another guy's pocket, who stood with open mouth to hear the prophecy.[7]

Compounding Deep Ellum's aura of mystery, the very origin of its name is uncertain. But from its beginnings as a Wild West saloon district near the railroad station of the 1870s, this part of town was far from the center of Dallas life; hence the "Deep" designation. "Ellum" (or "Elem"), on the other hand, was a phonetic spelling for a colloquial pronunciation of "Elm" by African Americans or Eastern European Jews or both, who did business there and lived in neighborhoods nearby. Likewise, it is not certain when the term "Deep Ellum" was coined; some veterans of the area said they had heard it all their lives. Others swore they had never heard it until the 1980s revival. It doesn't seem to have appeared in early Dallas newspapers. There is a reference to "Deep Elm" in a 1918 edition of the African American newspaper *Chicago Defender*. Certainly, however, the term was in wide use by the time of a 1925 *Dallas Morning News* article headlined, "Hidden Nooks: 'Deep Ellum' Has Its Renown But After All It Is Merely the Darkies' Parade Ground." Readers were informed in an overtly racist tone:

> Of course, "Deep Ellum" is the Broadway of the Dallas Black Belt. Venture up there any Saturday night and you will see thousands of Negro merry-makers parading the streets in the gay life of a care-free race. Venture a little farther into the Black Belt and you will find that North Central Avenue is the Coney Island of the Negro district. It is on "de tracks" that the Negroes go to have a good time. Thousands of them parade the Central Railway tracks in the evenings and it is there that most of their amusements are staged.[8]

It can also be difficult to define precisely what Deep Ellum was. Visual representations of its street life are scant. Aside from a 1922 photo of streetcar track being laid on Elm Street and numerous photos of Jewish shopkeepers, there are at least two images of blacks walking along Central Track. In 1932, Dallas artist Otis Dozier completed a painting called *Deep Elm* that shows African Americans carrying watermelons past a pawnshop.

Central Track, 1926. From the *Dallas Morning News* Collection, DeGolyer Library, Southern Methodist University. #Ag84.294.3.123.

Shotgun houses in Dallas, 1927. Baylor Hospital is in the background. Courtesy of the Dallas Public Library.

Little has been found to give any sense of the musical activity that occurred in Deep Ellum and Central Track. There are, however, several photographs of musicians who started their careers in Dallas and were, to varying degrees, associated with Deep Ellum and Central Track. Some of these are publicity stills, while others come from private sources. For this book, many people made their collections available, including Alex Moore, Marvin Montgomery, Walker Kirkes, Ted Parrino, Rudolph McMillan, Louis Bedford, Eddie Goldstein, and C. W. "Gus" Edwards. Additional images are reproductions from the *Chicago Defender,* as well as from numerous public institutions: the Dallas Public Library, Southern Methodist University, the Jewish Community Center of Dallas, and the Texas African American Photography Archive.

The *WPA Guide,* in a section called "Deep Ellum: Harlem in Miniature," states:

> Deep Ellum is the colloquialism used by both Negroes and whites for the congested Negro shopping district and amusement center lying on both sides of Elm Street between Preston and Good Streets, and the section about it for two or three city blocks to the north and south. The police department regards the real Deep Ellum as that area between Central Avenue, where run the all-but-abandoned railroad tracks, and Hawkins Street to the east in the 2500 block.[9]

Surviving white merchants and their families said the real Deep Ellum was a few blocks of Elm Street, and really just the south side of the street at that. But as the *Morning News* article and the *WPA Guide* indicate, nearby Central Avenue, or Central Track, could be considered a part of Deep Ellum as well. Businesses owned and patronized by African Americans lined the H&TC tracks from Freedmantown, or North Dallas, south to Main Street. These included shoeshine stands and cafés, which often featured gambling, drinking, and music, as well as dance halls and movie and vaudeville theaters. A few of these businesses spilled onto the north side of Elm near the railroad crossing, which could help explain why white merchants felt that only the south side was significant.

It's also important to remember that street names have changed since the WPA book was written. Preston Street no longer exists and should not be confused with Preston Road. The former Preston Street is now Central Expressway at street level. And Good Street has become the Good-Latimer Expressway.

White merchants may have made a distinction between Deep Ellum and Central Track, but it's clear that the African Americans who frequented both the businesses along the track and those on Elm made no such distinction. A strong indication of this is found in a poem, "Deep Ellum and Central Track," published in 1936 by the African American folklorist J. Mason Brewer, who once taught Spanish at Booker T. Washington High School in Dallas:

> *Talk about Harlem ef yuh wants tuh,*
> *An Lennox Avenue*
> *But Ah got sumpin' now, Baby,*
> *Ah kin talk about too.*
> *Harlem's got hits browns an' hits yallers*
> *And sealskin mamas in black.*
> *But 'tain't got nothin' on Dallas,*
> *Deep Ellum and Central Track.*
> *Harlem's got hits gin and hits whiskey*
> *Uh li'l penthouse o' two;*
> *But Ah'm still telling you, Baby,*
> *Dallas got sumpin,' too.*
> *Now hit mought not be no apartment*
> *Mought be uh 'shot-gun' shack;*
> *But de gals sho makes you 'member*

The Fair Store, owned by David Fair, Elm Street, 1905. Courtesy of the Jewish Community Center, Dallas.

> *Deep Ellum and Central Track.*
> *Done been all eroun' yo' big State Street,*
> *Uh way up dere in Chi;*
> *An hits uh pretty good hang-out—Baby, dat ain't no lie.*
> *Gals up dere do de snakehips,*
> *On de streets fuh uh fac';*
> *But gimme my gal an' de Jig Saw*
> *Deep Ellum an' Central Track.*[10]

In effect, Deep Ellum became known as the "black downtown" Dallas. As lawyer and former judge Louis Bedford, an African American, said:

It [Deep Ellum] was centrally located. So, since people came from every section . . . you didn't have shopping centers and all the satellite places to go; it was right down there. So, it seems logical to me that if whites had a downtown section that was convenient for everyone, blacks would need the same thing. People rode streetcars, wasn't a whole lot of cars. People had to come to town anyway to pay their utility bills and things of that nature. They had to come to City Hall; they could walk a few blocks. If they wanted to have a bite to eat and they had no place to eat because of the segregated atmosphere, there was Deep Ellum. They had to go to the restroom, there was Deep Ellum. It was someplace central where people could go. It was the heart. There were people living in Oak Cliff, people living in South Dallas, people living in North Dallas, but Deep Ellum was the core.[11]

Deep Ellum was not a neighborhood, strictly speaking. Few had residences there, at least after the turn of the century, though rooming houses endured for several decades. It was primarily a business district—more accurately, the confluence of two business districts, one white (mostly Jewish), one black. When you talk about Deep Ellum, you're really talking about Deep Ellum and Central Track, as Brewer did. For brevity's sake, in this book, "Deep Ellum" will include Central Track, formally called Central Avenue.

The white-owned stores on Elm served both black and white patrons. On Saturdays, Deep Ellum evoked the State Fair of Texas, thronged with people shopping for furniture, groceries, clothing, and other staples at reasonable prices. It was in a sense the outlet mall of its day. Many places, pawnshops in particular, stayed open late on weekends. Some merchants lived in or above their stores. "Probably the liveliest place in the city of Dallas was Deep Ellum," said Herschel Wilonsky, born in 1944, whose father and uncles owned businesses on Elm Street. "That was the most busy place you'd ever see. Looking back at it now, it was kind of like a city sidewalk in New York at 12:30 in the afternoon. On whatever street you're walking up, people just walking into you. That's what Deep Ellum was. Everything happened, I mean nightclubs, black nightclubs, white nightclubs. The place was hopping. You could go downtown any night of the week. People were down there shopping at H. L. Green's or any of the department stores, Titche's," closer to downtown.[12]

Although Deep Ellum was never officially a red-light district like Fannin Street in Shreveport or Storyville in New Orleans, other hotbeds of musical development, it was a place where such vices as gambling and prostitution flourished, often in return for payoffs to the authorities. Black musician Sammy Price, speaking of the teens and early 1920s, said there were plenty of Deep Ellum drinking establishments run by women called "landladies." Asked whether whites were seen around these places, he replied, "If there were any whites down there, they were running a foot race."

"In Deep Ellum, there was an alley called 'death row,' where someone would get killed every Saturday," Price continued. "And there was a stool pigeon for the police, and his name was 'Yellow Britches.' If someone came

A 1932 painting, *Deep Elm* by Otis Dozier. Courtesy of the Dallas Museum of Art.

into town that he didn't know, he put some chalk on the back of [the stranger's] pants so that police could identify him."[13]

Pawnbroker Isaac "Rocky" Goldstein, speaking of the 1930s and 1940s, exaggerated the murder rate even more: "There was a killing every day. There were fights on the corner of Central and Elm all the time, and they had these Holy-Roller women trying to convert these guys."[14] In fact, in 1936 Dallas had 102 homicides; 79 percent were black-on-black crimes. Despite the hyperbole that pops up in such personal reminiscences, Deep Ellum was certainly prone to the violence that follows poverty, drinking, prostitution, and gambling.

For decades, the area's biggest retail establishment was Sam Dysterbach's department store at Elm and Pearl streets, run by a second-generation Deep Ellum merchant, whom blacks sometimes referred to as "Sam Dustyback." Goldstein recalled that the store still had hitching posts out front and a nineteenth-century system of pulleys to move money around the place in a basket. Dysterbach was prosperous, in part because of lucrative contracts to sell uniforms to everyone from the police department to high school bands. He sold to farmers on credit and gave food away at Christmas.

Like many others, Goldstein remembered a legless man called Wagon Willie, who got about on a skateboard. "He came in one day and said, 'Mr. Rocky, I need ten bucks; hold my wagon for me.' I says, 'Okay.' I give him a ten, he's going out of the store, swinging his body. I say, 'Willie, come on back here. You owe me ten dollars whenever you got it. Take your wagon with you.' I couldn't see him moving his body like that."[15]

According to several accounts, Wagon Willie was a skilled gambler and pickpocket who bootlegged out of his home on the edge of Deep Ellum and once went to prison for stealing a car and driving it to Oklahoma. Willie wasn't alone in pawning odd items. Goldstein said one woman hocked her mother's ashes.

White singer Bill Neely recalled the area in the 1930s. He'd pick cotton all week in McKinney, then hitchhike into town and make for Deep Ellum. One of his regular haunts was a place he called "Ma's"—probably Mother's Place in the 2800 block of Elm—run by Lucille Cortimillia. "Ma's apron was so slick, even the flies slid off," Neely said. "She wore a .38-caliber pistol, and when she said, 'Hop,' they hopped. And the kind of people who went there weren't much better: gangsters, gamblers, people like Raymond Hamilton, Baby Face Nelson, and Bonnie and Clyde." One night at Ma's, Neely recalled, he was singing when a man rose and told the noisy crowd to shut up. A hush fell over the place. The man was Raymond Hamilton, a member of the Barrow gang.

By that time, Neely said, Deep Ellum had become legendary for its music, gambling, and street life but also had degenerated into "a skid row, where all the hoboes landed. It was where the drunkards and winos and people trying to roll one another hung out. There were all kinds of people: cowboys, Mexicans, blacks, and down-and-out farmers."[16] Deep Ellum generally seemed to attract people who were offbeat. Rocky Goldstein once employed the black sheep of a wealthy Chicago family. The man was such a skilled salesman that he would often take a watch from the shop with him and sell it to another patron in the café where he ate lunch. The man eventually died of a drug overdose in his room at the rundown Campbell Hotel down the street.

Goldstein also recalled a salesman who was covered with tattoos, including one of a pig. He would pull out one of his body hairs and hand it to someone saying, "Here, I'm giving you a hair out of the pig's ass." When things were slow, he'd strip to his underwear and do a handstand in the middle of Elm Street.[17]

The strip along Central Track featured not only offbeat characters and gambling but prostitution as well. Women would sit outside on posts along Central Track, selling themselves for a quarter in the 1920s. Several walk-up hotels such as the Powell became notorious by the 1940s. "If you weren't movin' in that Powell Hotel," recalled Willard Watson, who later achieved fame as a folk artist, "them bedbugs would be movin' you."[18]

Black historian Dr. Robert Prince recalled the history of racial violence in Dallas and his horror at seeing documentation of the 1910 Elks Arch lynching. As a teenager, Prince remembered the gamblers and the women. Among the characters was a dark, muscular man called "Blue," who served as the lookout, or "good eye," in a gambling joint, and a gambler called "Six-Toed Willie."[19]

Anna Mae Conley, born in 1919, attended J. P. Starks Elementary, which backed up to the tracks in Freedmantown, before she went to Booker T. Washington High School:

> It was a long ways. But to get there, all we had to do was walk out Central Track. And we did that. Most of 'em, from the time they started high school until they finished high school. But after I had gone down Central Track about two months, I could see all those bad places. Now nothing was happening during the daytime, but you knew what was happening. And I found another way to get home. I came out Ross Avenue and came on to St. Paul, or either I walked to Ervay.

Front page of the *Dallas Dispatch*, March 3, 1910. Courtesy of Hal Simon.

Conley's friend Lucille Bosh McGaughey, born in 1918, recalled that this route took them down San Jacinto Street near the high school. According to McGaughey, white prostitutes sat in the windows of houses and lured men, who would pay them fifty cents.[20]

During its heyday, from the early part of the twentieth century through the late twenties or early thirties, Deep Ellum was filled with contradictions: It was a business district that became legendary for violence and sin. As the song "Deep Ellum Blues" says, one went "down" on or in Deep Ellum, down to a world where people broke the accepted norms of behavior. Deep Ellum was a real place that provided a variety of services, legal and illegal, and came to represent the uncertainties and dangers associated with the growth of Dallas as a city. Indeed, several prominent and successful individuals and companies got their start in Deep Ellum.

As firsthand accounts attest, Deep Ellum once really did ring with music, from the street blues of Blind Lemon Jefferson and others to the orchestras that played in the theaters. Some musicians who played in Deep Ellum had quite an impact. Jefferson was the first country blues singer to achieve commercial success as a recording artist. He became very popular in his brief recording career and influenced a wide range of musicians, including another Dallas guitarist, Aaron "T-Bone" Walker, and Mississippian B. B. King. Jazz saxophonists Budd Johnson and Henry "Buster" Smith moved on to jazz centers such as Kansas City and New York, where they played major roles in shaping swing and then bebop. And the black music played in Deep Ellum was a force in the development of Western swing.

Deep Ellum, then, was a crossroads, a nexus, where peoples and cultures could interact and influence each other in relative freedom. A lot of interesting people filtered through an area of just a few blocks centered around a railroad crossing. Along Central Track and in North Dallas, African Americans created an amazingly rich, layered society.

In this book, we investigate what Deep Ellum was and what it meant socially, historically, and musically and as a kind of metaphor for the underside of the city of Dallas. We explore the growth of Deep Ellum and focus on the groups of people who migrated there and the business activity and cultural life they generated. Music encouraged the interaction between cultures, especially with the advent of commercial recordings and radio. By the turn of the twentieth century, rudimentary styles of blues, jazz, and early country music were being performed in Dallas. Insofar as Deep Ellum is a metaphor for the interplay of these groups, our treatment is wide ranging and interdisciplinary. To establish the overall significance

Elks Arch lynching of Allen Brooks, photo postcard, Dallas, March 3, 1910. Courtesy of the Dallas County Heritage Society.

of Deep Ellum, we examine its relation to the broader context of Dallas history and to the settlement patterns and commerce of African Americans and Eastern European Jews. In so doing, we elaborate on the lives and careers of seminal musicians and others who played vital roles in the area.

Given the lack of substantive documentation of this period of Dallas history, we found it necessary to bring together disparate sources, including oral history, scholarly articles and books, and anecdotal evidence. Many of these sources were identified in the vast collections of the nonprofit organization Documentary Arts and its Texas African American Photography Archive, cofounded by Alan Govenar and Kaleta Doolin. We assessed the relative merits of each source on a case-by-case basis. Articles and books were checked for their accuracy; in some cases we discovered errors that had been repeated so often that they were assumed to be fact, such as the freedmantown origins of Deep Ellum. Oral history and anecdotal evidence were authenticated through city directories, maps, and other public records. Of necessity, we integrated these accounts to present the most comprehensive description of people and events. In instances where primary and secondary sources simply did not exist, we were forced to extend the bounds of our discussion beyond Deep Ellum proper to incorporate relevant information about other areas of Dallas and Texas history. This also helps to provide a context for the events we describe.

Deep Ellum has provided an alternative to Dallas's image of itself as a staid and proper place modeled more after the great cities of the East and the Midwest than those of Texas or elsewhere in the South or the Southwest. Indeed, upon hearing that Fort Worth advertised itself as "where the West begins," humorist Will Rogers is said to have added, "And Dallas is where the East peters out." The reality of Dallas, of course, was quite different from the image it sought to portray.

"Deep Elem Blues"

Song of the Street

The best-known song about Deep Ellum, "Deep Elem Blues," is still performed more than eighty years after it was first recorded. The lyrics may recall a past that is romanticized and distorted, but they are nonetheless evocative of a time and place where one had to be ready for anything. The Shelton Brothers sang in their 1935 recording:

> When you go down in Deep Elem
> To have a little fun
> You better have your fifteen dollars
> When that policeman comes.
> Oh, sweet Mama, Daddy's got them Deep Elem blues.
>
> Once I had a sweetheart
> Who meant the world to me,
> But she hung around Deep Elem
> Now she ain't what she used to be.
>
> When you go down in Deep Elem,
> Keep your money in your shoes
> 'Cause the women on Deep Elem
> Got them Deep Elem blues.
>
> When you go down in Deep Elem,
> Keep your money in your pants
> 'Cause the redheads in Deep Elem
> Never give a man a chance.

Shelton Brothers (Bob and Joe),
"Deep Elem Blues," Decca 46008 B.
Courtesy Documentary Arts.

Shelton Brothers (Bob and Joe),
"Just Because," Decca 46008 A.
Courtesy Documentary Arts.

(Chorus)
Oh, sweet Mama, Daddy's got them Deep Elem blues
(sung twice)

Once I knew a preacher
Preached the Bible through and through
But he went down in Deep Elem
Now his preachin' days are through.

(Chorus)
Oh, sweet Mama, Daddy's got them Deep Elem blues
(sung once)

When you go down in Deep Elem,
Keep your money in your socks
'Cause the women in Deep Elem
Will throw you on the rocks.

(Chorus)
Oh, sweet Mama, Daddy's got them Deep Elem blues
(sung twice)

Although Deep Ellum is usually associated with African Americans and their music, this song isn't really a blues at all but an up-tempo, string-band number. Its numerous versions seem to have been recorded exclusively by white musicians, though anecdotal evidence suggests that it was performed with more of a bluesy tone by African Americans. The first recording of the song, bearing the name "Deep Elm Blues," was made in 1933 for the Victor and Bluebird labels by the Lone Star Cowboys. The band, which was called the Lone Star Rangers on some discs issued on the Regal-Zonophone and Twin labels, included Leon Chappelear, Joe Attlesey, and Bob Attlesey. The song was recorded again as "Deep Elem Blues" in 1935 for Decca by the Attleseys, who by that time were calling themselves the Shelton Brothers, and was followed by "Deep Elem No. 2" and "Deep Elem No. 3" and other variants, such as "Just Because You're in Deep Elem" and "What's the Matter with Deep Elem."

The lyrics and music to "Deep Elem Blues" were based on a 1927 OKeh recording, "The Georgia Black Bottom," by the Georgia Crackers, a group that featured Paul Cofer on fiddle, Leon Cofer on banjo, and Ben Evans on guitar.[1] The tune is virtually identical to that of "Deep Elem Blues," and the lyrics are essentially the same:

> If you go down in Black Bottom
> Put your money in your shoes.
> The women in Black Bottom
> Got them Black Bottom Blues.
> Oh, good mama, your daddy's got them black bottom blues.
>
> If you go down in Black Bottom
> Just to have a little fun,
> Have your sixteen dollars ready
> When that police wagon comes.
>
> Well, I had a good little woman
> And I taken her to the fair,
> She would have won the premium
> But she had bad hair.
>
> Well, I went down to Black Bottom
> Just to get a little booze,
> And now I'm on the chain gang
> Wearing them brogan shoes.
>
> If you've got a good little woman
> Better keep her by your side,
> That old [band member name]
> Take your baby and ride.[2]

The Sheltons, who moved from East Texas to Dallas and became radio celebrities, claimed authorship of "Deep Elem Blues." Perhaps this was simply a case of theft, but the songs' themes are complex and revealing. "Black Bottom" referred to both a number of African American communities throughout the South and to a popular dance. The theme of both the Georgia and the Texas songs is white men going to a black neighborhood in search of illicit pleasure. In addition, the word "deep" seems to have had a widespread association with sin. Houstonians referred to "loose" women as "deep Congress floozies," a reference to the street in the old part of the city that was once notorious for prostitution, and the Western swing band

Shelly Lee Alley and His Alley Cats recorded a song called "Deep Congress Avenue" in 1937.

Whatever the truth of its authorship, "Deep Elem Blues" seems to have evolved in the manner of a true folk song. "Everybody who sang it added something to it," said Bill Neely, a white songster and guitarist from McKinney, Texas, who emulated a blues style. Neely hitchhiked to Dallas in the 1930s and performed at the legendary Ma's Place on the fringe of Deep Ellum.

This song, however, was not the first to use the phrase "Deep Elm Blues." It apparently first appeared in "Deep Elm (You Tell 'Em I'm Blue)," which was recorded by several dance bands in 1925. These bands included Paul van Loan and His Orchestra; Peck Mills and His Orchestra; Herb Wiedoeft and His Cinderella Roof Orchestra; Busse's Buzzards, a unit of

Unidentified street musicians, magazine clipping, n.d. Courtesy of Documentary Arts.

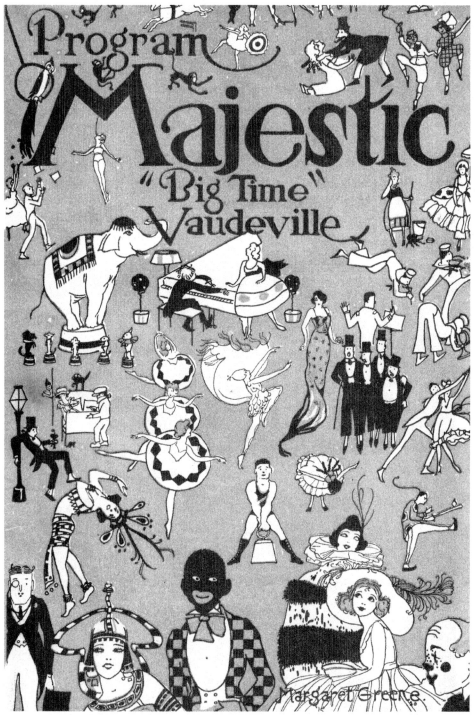

Program, Majestic (Theatre), "Big Time" Vaudeville, August 29, 1920. Courtesy of the Texas African American Photography Archive.

Inside the image:

Jack Keasler   Slim Harbert   Bob Shelton

Season's Greetings

The Sunshine Boys

Joe Shelton
Gene Sullivan

Leon Hall
Harry Sorensen

MANY FOLKS NOW SAY

NEW PE-RU-NA

The Great New Cold Fighter often

WINS FIGHT WITH A COLD

By Helping to Build Up Cold Fighting Resistance

1938

Joe Shelton, Gene Sullivan, Jack Kessler, Slim Harbert, Bob Shelton, Leon Hall, and Harry Sorensen, 1938. Courtesy of Cary Ginell.

Slim Harbert, Joe Shelton, Bob Shelton, Wiley Walker, Gene Sullivan, and Harry
Sorensen, ca. late 1930s. Courtesy of Cary Ginell.

Prairie Ramblers, "Deep Elem Blues,"
Melotone 5–11–51 A. Courtesy of Cary
Ginell.

Shelton Brothers (Bob and Joe),
"Deep Elem Blues," Decca 5099 A.
Courtesy of Cary Ginell.

Shelton Brothers (Bob and Joe), "Deep Elem Blues No. 2," Decca 5198 A. Courtesy of Cary Ginell.

Shelton Brothers (Bob and Joe), "What's the Matter With Deep Elem," Decca 5898 A.

Shelton Brothers, "Deep Elm Boogie Woogie Blues," King 660-A. Courtesy of Cary Ginell.

Dick Stabile and His Orchestra, "Deep Elem Blues," Decca 716 B. Courtesy of Cary Ginell.

Texas Wanderers, "Deep Elm Swing,"
Decca 5775 A. Courtesy of Cary Ginell.

Wilburn Brothers (Teddy and Doyle),
"Deep Elem Blues," Decca 29887.
Courtesy of Cary Ginell

Paul Whiteman's orchestra that included the song's composer, Willard Robison, on piano; and The Little Ramblers. Of those who recorded the song, The Little Ramblers, a small contingent from the famous California Ramblers, was probably the best known. It featured Tommy Dorsey on trombone. The recording by the Tennessee Tooters was also issued on British labels under the name of Pete Massey's All Black Band, which, despite its name, apparently had no black members.

In 1927, "Deep Elm (You Tell 'Em I'm Blue)" was recorded by Robison, who had written the song with William R. Clay. Originally from Shelbina, Missouri, Robison was leading his own band by 1917, and his high, sweet singing voice was popular among the musicians of his day. While the 1925 recordings of "Deep Elm" had a jazz orchestration, Robison's arrangement was much simpler; he sang in a nostalgic style reminiscent of the popular songs of the period and accompanied himself on piano. Robison had a deep interest in black music and culture and led a band he called the Deep River Orchestra. But whether he—or any of the other musicians who performed the song, for that matter—ever set foot in Deep Ellum is unknown. By the time he wrote the number, Robison may have passed through Dallas by train or met performers from Texas who, like him, had traveled around the country and gone to New York looking for commercial success. Clearly, Robison's composition, in addition to referencing Deep Ellum, focuses on

the loneliness of traveling and the longing for home, although its overall
affect is more reflective of the popular sentimentality of Tin Pan Alley:

> You've heard 'em sing about Beale Street,
> Way down in Memphis, Tennesee [*sic*].
> You've heard 'em say that Broadway
> Was the only place to be.
> I want to take exception
> to tell you 'bout a place I've found.
> Now just a street where they don't cheat
> Down in Dallas town.
> Deep Elm, you tell 'em I'm blue
> All the time that, that I'm away from you
> For I can see my "used to be"
> One sweet woman who cared for me
> Waiting for the news,
> Just any old thing to cure Deep Elm Blues.
> I've made up my mind that I'll go
> Back home in Dallas, I'll never roam no more.
> I've been around more than I should
> I never done nothin' to do me no good, so
> I'm catchin' a rattler today
> Hey, hey, hey, hey, hey,
> To keep Deep Elm Blues away.
> I'm catching a rattler today
> Back home in Dallas, I'm sure I'm headed that way
> Now I been around more than I should
> And I've never done nothin' to do me no good, so
> I'm catching a rattler today,
> Hey, hey, hey, hey, hey, hey,
> To keep Deep Elm Blues away.

The line about "a street where they don't cheat" seems ironic used in reference to a street well known for its wheeling and dealing. Whether the irony
is intentional or simply the result of an easy rhyme is unknown. Unlike
Robison's, the Sheltons' later record referred to the neighborhood as "Deep
Elem." Why they chose this spelling over the generally accepted "Ellum" is
unknown; perhaps it was a record company snafu, or perhaps they wanted
to differentiate their version from others. Though there appears to be no

Jimmie Revard and His Oklahoma
Playboys (singing by Adolph Hoffner
[Hofner]), "Daddy's Got the Deep Elm
Blues—Fox Trot," Bluebird B-7061-A.
Courtesy of Cary Ginell.

Lone Star Cowboys, "Deep Elm Blues,"
Bluebird B-6001-A. Courtesy of Cary
Ginell.

black recording of "Deep Ellum Blues," it's known that at least one black
musician performed it: Booker Pittman, a grandson of educator Booker
T. Washington and son of two key figures in the history of black Dallas.
Hank Wackwitz, a Dutch-born musician and jazz collector living in retire-
ment in North Texas, recalled playing in the 1950s in a cruise-ship band
that included Pittman, a saxophonist and singer. When Pittman sang "Deep
Ellum Blues," said Wackwitz, the other musicians, all Europeans, "hadn't
the slightest idea what he was singing about."[3]

"Deep Elem Blues" quickly spread beyond Dallas. Trumpeter Harry
James, who had grown up in Beaumont, persuaded his boss, band leader
Ben Pollack, to record an instrumental called "Deep Elm" in 1936. The
song and various follow-up versions such as "What's the Matter with
Deep Elem" and "Just Because You're in Deep Elem" were recorded by the
Sheltons and other bands. Subsequently, "Deep Elem Blues" has been performed and recorded by a number of other bands, including Hank Thompson and the Brazos Valley Boys, Jerry Lee Lewis, the Grateful Dead, and in
recent years by the Wronglers, with Jimmie Dale Gilmore.

In many ways, the song encapsulates a reality that has been embellished
through the process of folklore and oral history. The extent to which the
lyrics of "Deep Elem Blues" project an accurate portrait of the neighborhood is certainly debatable. Nonetheless, this song, probably more than

anything else, has made Deep Ellum one of the best-known and least-understood sections of Dallas. "Deep Elem Blues" embodies the values of a city in transition. Certainly, within the lyrics a sense of irony and humor is associated with the foibles of those who went there. The allusions to women, preachers, and police cut across cultural boundaries and reflect a shared experience among the people of a particular time and place. "Deep Elem Blues" is a window on music and life in Dallas, from its earliest years as a city through its heyday and its ultimate demise and redevelopment.

The Railroads Create
Deep Ellum

D allas was founded in 1841 by a Tennessee lawyer, John Neely
Bryan, who settled on a bluff about where the former Texas
School Book Depository now stands. Then, long before the
Trinity River was rechanneled for flood control, Bryan's bluff sloped down
to a natural ford where travelers, first Indian, then white, often crossed.
Bryan knew that the Republic of Texas had selected the spot for the junction of two major highways, one of which survives as Preston Road. Bryan's
earliest plan apparently was to found a trading post and to do business with
the Indians.

Thus the Trinity River played a vital role in the establishment of Dallas.
But despite attempts that continued into the twentieth century, it stubbornly
resisted navigation. It became obvious that if Dallas was to become a business center, another means had to be found to bring this about. That development was interrupted by the Civil War. Dallas served as a regional food
distribution center, and the county's slave population swelled from around
900 to 2,500. The city was relatively untouched by the conflict. At war's
end, it was a town of about 2,000 poised for growth. Its strong business
leadership included men such as William Henry Gaston, a former Confederate army officer who became a banker and major landowner in Dallas.
Sarah Cockrell, the widow of one of the city's founders, Alexander Cockrell,
also wielded considerable power, but because of the male domination of the
time, she worked quietly behind the scenes.

These leaders concluded that railroads were Dallas's route to commercial
success. In this, of course, they had considerable competition; railroad fever
was sweeping the nation. But they had an uncommon determination and
were not above a bit of trickery—some would say ruthlessness.

After the war, the Houston & Texas Central Railroad (H&TC) resumed
its northward progress. Its projected route would have brought the line eight

Union Station in Dallas, 1905. The tall building across the tracks, the railroad hotel, later housed the Tip Top dance hall. Courtesy of the *Dallas Morning News*.

miles east of Dallas County's courthouse, too far away to do the city much good. Here, Gaston's land holdings saved the day. His home was more than a mile east of the courthouse square—then considered so far from city life that he once attempted to recruit neighbors by offering land free to anyone who would build on it. Gaston offered the railroad right of way, and he and the other businessmen sweetened the pot with $5,000 in cash. The railroad accepted the offer. In anticipation of the laying of the track and construction of a station, the city cleared the wooded area and extended the major east-west streets: Elm, Main, and Commerce. News of the railroads' coming triggered a boom. "Dallas is improving rapidly," lawyer John Milton McCoy, later Dallas's first city attorney, wrote to his brother in Indiana in December 1871. "The prospects are very flattering indeed. Everything points to the crossing of two great roads here. Property is at exorbitant prices. The people are crazy, talking about Dallas being the Indianapolis of Texas for a railroad center. Emigration pouring in and everybody talking about the town."[1]

The first train steamed into town on July 16, 1872, and Dallas went crazy. As Robert Seay, a young lawyer recently arrived from Tennessee, wrote: "Men whooped, women screamed, or even sobbed, and children yelped in fright and amazement. As to that, there were some grown folks there who had never seen a railway train before, and I think the chugging of

North Dallas house with watermelon garden, near Thomas Avenue and Hall Street, ca. 1920s. Courtesy of Nick Cammarata.

the log-burning furnace and the hissing of the steam startled them, a little."[2] An estimated five thousand to ten thousand people turned out to hear hours of self-congratulatory speeches by city leaders and railroad officials and to feast on free buffalo steaks.

The civic leaders also turned their sights on the Texas & Pacific Railroad (T&P), which had been chartered by Congress in 1871 to extend its line to San Diego. The railroad planned the line along the 32nd Parallel, fifty miles south of Dallas. But a local legislator attached to the right-of-way bill a seemingly innocuous rider requiring the T&P to cross the H&TC within a mile of Browder Springs. It did not mention, of course, that Browder Springs, south of town, was Dallas's water supply. When railroad officials learned this, they threatened to run the line south of the springs, so it would still miss Dallas. But Gaston kicked in 142 acres for the right of way plus the 10 acres for the station. The city came up with $200,000 in bonds and $5,000 in cash and offered to let the railroad run on Burleson Street, which would be renamed Pacific Avenue. The T&P reached Dallas in February 1873, just in time for a panic, or depression, which halted its growth for several years at the community of Eagle Ford, about six miles west of town.

A resident named Wood Ramsey wrote that, when he came to Dallas in 1875, "The Union Depot building was a squatty, one-story structure. The farmers, cowboys, loafers and loungers who crowded the platform and opened a way for us to get from the train as it pulled up with a clanging bell, broke up into squads and leisurely gravitated back to the domino tables in the adjacent saloons from which the whistle of the locomotive had jerked them."[3]

Within a year of the H&TC's arrival, between 750 and 900 new buildings were erected in the city, including a $75,000 courthouse. Dallas was virtually starting over; the wooden buildings downtown had been destroyed in 1860 by a fire that was blamed (falsely, many believe) on a slave revolt. In fact, three slaves were hanged, and all the other slaves in the county were ordered whipped. The post-railroad boom brought the terminus merchants, so-called because they had followed the H&TC north, where they set up stores in the railhead towns: Millican, Bryan, Hearne, Calvert, Kosse, Bremond, Groesbeck, and Corsicana. Because they had last stopped in Corsicana, many were called the "Corsicana crowd" once they reached Dallas.

The new arrivals, many of whom were Eastern European Jews, erected portable buildings with amazing speed. As the young lawyer Seay wrote:

The merchants, professional men, gamblers and floaters who had followed the terminus all the way to the north moved from Corsicana to Dallas in a body. Up to that time the town had been confined to the courthouse square. The newcomers bought on the road now known as Elm Street, between Jefferson and Griffin, and began to set up their portable houses which in sections they had brought from Corsicana. Almost overnight they built a new town. It was all so sudden and amazing that the natives could liken it to nothing but the fic-

The Cammarata family's grocery store near Central Track, ca. 1940s. In front of the car is one of the Cammarata brothers. Courtesy of Nick Cammarata.

Issy Miller's café at Elm and Central Track, 1932. Issy is standing behind the cash register. Courtesy of the Jewish Community Center.

tion they had read in "Arabian Nights." But to most of them it was woefully lacking in the pleasures that went with the perusal of Aladdin's performances, for it looked very much as if the railroad and the people who had come with it were bent on killing the old town . . . the old town began to put up its dukes for a fight . . . but the town had started to wander from the square and there was no bringing it back—and by the time the towns had met at Jefferson and Market, everybody had become friendly, for it was plain that after all the two towns were only one.[4]

Some of the terminus merchants stayed and became major business and civic figures. The Sanger brothers, Alex and Philip, and E. M. Kahn established successful department stores downtown. The Sangers settled in the Cedars, a fashionable neighborhood south of downtown.

Dallas did not become another Indianapolis. It many ways, it was a typical frontier settlement. In the 1870s, cattle were driven through downtown Dallas to cross the Trinity at the ford below Bryan's cabin. Buffalo were shot in the nearby countryside, and Dallas became a center for the trade in their hides. Amusements included several red-light districts, dance halls, beer halls and gardens, boxing matches, cockfighting, rat killing, and an occasional

Looking north on Central Track, Dallas, 1947. Photograph by Alexander H. Moore.
Courtesy of Documentary Arts.

bear baiting. John Henry "Doc" Holliday practiced dentistry in Dallas for
three years before he was asked to leave town following a saloon shooting.
The outlaw Belle Starr also spent time around Dallas, where she lived in the
community of Scyene, now part of the eastern suburb of Mesquite.

People kept pouring in. Historian Philip Lindsley wrote of the city in
1875: "The flood tide of emigration was now on. Every train on the Texas
and Pacific Railway was literally packed with emigrants from the older
states. In addition there were regular emigrant trains with special rates, and
these overflowed with men, women and children."[5] The city's population,
which had been 775 in 1860, reached 2,000 in 1865 and 3,000 in 1870 and
passed 10,000 by 1880.

In the 1870s, soon after the railroads came, the future Deep Ellum was
a ragtag collection of pastures, cornfields, cattle and hog pens, restaurants,
lodging houses, and saloons, an area where people went about armed and

gambling flourished at all hours. Cowboys whooped and fired their pistols as they rode up and down the unpaved streets—sometimes right into the saloons. Variety theaters often featured musicians, female dancers, and other performers, and alcohol heightened the patrons' fun.

Meanwhile, northeast of the city limits, another community was growing, one founded by freed slaves. It was called Freedmantown and referred to as such in the city directories of the period; later it became known as North Dallas. The intersection of Thomas Avenue and Hall Street became the heart of Freedmantown, whose growth, like that of the rest of the city, was fed by the railroads. The lines provided work for many black men and housed some of these men and their families in narrow rental houses along the right of way. This strung-out community became known as Stringtown. The houses were called "shotgun houses" because, it was said, a shotgun shell fired through the front door would travel out the back without hitting anything (presuming, of course, that no one was unlucky enough to be standing in the way). South of downtown near the H&TC track was another black community, a sprawl of unpaved streets called the Prairie.

Black men also found jobs in the industrial area that grew up near the railroad junction, in planing mills, meatpacking plants, oil works, waste mills, and dairies. The black influx was fed, too, by the boll weevil, which began devastating the Texas cotton crop in the early 1890s. Some African Americans continued to pick cotton after moving to Dallas, waiting near the railroad station to be hired. Farmers, first in wagons, later in trucks, hauled laborers to fields around Dallas or farther into East or West Texas. This continued until after World War II.

Many black women worked in white homes. Some lived with their families in servants' quarters, others in houses purchased by their employers, who deducted the mortgage payments from their pay. Thus, segregated housing emerged, though the city would not codify it into an ordinance until the early twentieth century.

Gradually, black businesses were established along Central Track, where they replaced the shotgun houses of Stringtown and the white-owned businesses. By the turn of the twentieth century, the pattern was set: Central Track was predominantly black, and Elm Street was mostly white owned but catered to customers of both races. For blacks and whites alike, Dallas was a city of opportunity, and Deep Ellum, near the railroad station and relatively far from the main business district, was a place to get started.

William Sidney Pittman

Architect of Deep Ellum

W illiam Sidney Pittman was one of those who took advantage of the opportunity Dallas had to offer in the early years of the twentieth century. He was a brilliant man who became a hero to his people and something of a monster to his family. Born in 1875 to former slaves, he attended Booker T. Washington's Tuskegee Institute and, with Washington's backing, studied architecture at Drexel Institute in Philadelphia. He graduated in 1900 and returned to Tuskegee to teach. But after quarreling with an official, he departed to establish a successful architectural practice in Washington, DC. In 1907 he married Washington's daughter Portia in a ceremony that was the height of the social season at Tuskegee.[1]

In 1913 the Pittmans and their children moved to Dallas. Pittman designed a comfortable two-story house in North Dallas on Germania Street, which was renamed Liberty Street during World War I. Their neighbors were other African Americans and Italian immigrants who manufactured dolls. For many years, Italian Americans operated a number of businesses, including bakeries and groceries and liquor stores, in North Dallas. Several cafés that served African Americans were owned by Greek immigrants.

Portia Pittman was a talented musician who taught music at Dallas Colored High School, which was renamed for her father in 1922, and she gave private lessons as well. Sammy Price, who later became a well-known jazz and blues pianist, did yard work for the family and took lessons from Mrs. Pittman. "Sammy," she told him, "you will never learn to read music, but you have a wonderful ear."[2]

Pittman's architecture included several African Methodist Episcopal (AME) churches in Texas, including Allen Chapel in Fort Worth, Joshua Chapel in Waxahachie, and Wesley Chapel in Houston, all of which have been designated historic structures. Joshua and Wesley chapels remained in

Architectural rendering of the Pythian Temple by William Sidney Pittman, 1916.

use in mid-2012; Allen Chapel was hit by lightning late in 2011 and was repaired so it could be returned to use. Pittman also designed the St. James AME Church in Dallas, which was purchased in 1998 by the Meadows Foundation and renovated. In 2012 it housed the Mental Health Association of Greater Dallas and the Conference of Southwest Foundations.

The architect's greatest Dallas achievement was designing the state headquarters of the Grand Lodge of the Colored Knights of Pythias[3] in the 2500 block of Elm, completed in 1916. It was, from an architectural standpoint, the most distinctive building in Deep Ellum. It was made of red brick and featured tall, arched windows and a neoclassical façade. On the first floor were a barbershop and a drugstore. The second and third floors included office space for many of Dallas's black professionals, including Dr. P. M.

Sunday and agricultural agent Cedar Walton, father of the jazz musician of the same name. In addition, Drs. Richard. T. Hamilton and E. E. Ward, as well as the noted dentist Dr. A. H. Dyson, had offices in the Pythian Temple. The Negro Business Bureau had headquarters in the building, as did the Standard Life Insurance Company, the American Mutual Benefit Society, and the notary public W. M. P. Walleck.[4] The Golden Chain of the World, an organization similar to the Pythians, also had offices there. It advertised in the *Dallas Express:* "Join to-day. Die today. Pay to-day!"[5]

The fourth-floor ballroom, complete with an elaborate chandelier, was used for dances, performances, and other community events. In March 1919 the Fisk Jubilee Singers, who had done much to popularize black sacred music, performed "classics, songs and old plantation melodies" in the ballroom. General admission was a quarter; reserved seats, fifty cents.[6] That October, Sgt. Neadham Roberts, described in the *Express* as "Our First Colored Hero of the World's War" and "the Hell-Fighting Hero," lectured there under the auspices of the NAACP. Admission was fifty cents.[7] Black nationalist Marcus Garvey spoke at the temple on June 19, 1922, and spawned local interest in his back-to-Africa movement. A card distributed in North Dallas reads: "I have heard the call—I have need to go to Africa!" In January 1923, George Washington Carver demonstrated sweet potato products at the Pythian Temple for an audience of eight hundred.[8]

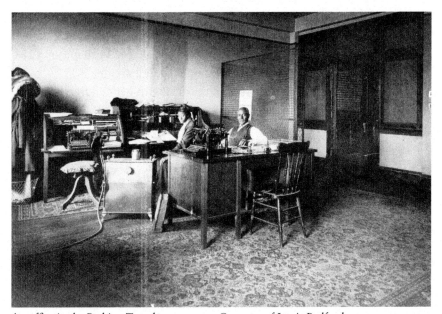

An office in the Pythian Temple, ca. 1920s. Courtesy of Louis Bedford.

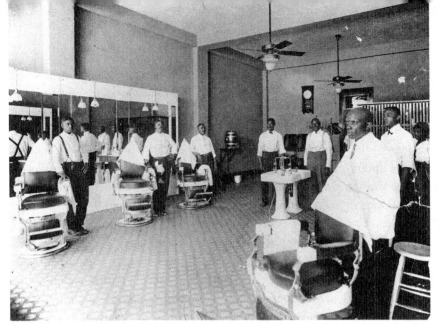

A barbershop in the Pythian Temple, ca. 1920s. Courtesy of Louis Bedford.

During the 1920s Pittman was not only successful as an architect but was also president of the Brotherhood of Negro Building Mechanics.[9] Despite the Pittmans' contributions to their community, their home life was troubled. Portia was, by all accounts, warm and caring, while he was dictatorial, angry, and abusive. His children, Booker, Sidney, and Fannie, called him "Big Pitt." Booker Pittman later wrote that his father sometimes beat his children until he was exhausted and they were semiconscious.[10] According to one account, Portia Pittman decided to leave her husband in 1928 after he struck Fannie across the face during a heated argument.[11]

Whatever the details, Portia Pittman returned with her children to Washington, DC. She lived there until 1978, having outlived her husband and all her children. Booker Pittman was a poor student who felt self-conscious about being known as Booker T. Washington's grandson. He became a jazz musician and lived much of his life in Brazil, where he died in 1969. His stepdaughter, Eliana Pittman, a singer and actress, said her father never discussed his father at all.[12]

After his wife left him, William Sidney Pittman became increasingly embittered. In 1929 he founded a weekly paper, the *Brotherhood Eyes,* with offices in his home. Its masthead pronounced it "A Newspaper That Doesn't Cross the Color Line." Pittman called his anonymous contributors "The Eyes." Headlines from a surviving copy dated July 28, 1934, identify his targets: "Black (Rev) 'Dillinger' and Sis 'Rev' Healer Vie in Skinning Saps";

NEGRO BUSINESS

BULLETIN

A Monthly Magazine devoted to Better Business
Among Negroes of Dallas

Published by
THE NEGRO BUSINESS BUREAU

Room 210, Pythian Temple
DALLAS, TEXAS

FEBRUARY--1925

Cover of *Negro Business Bulletin*, Dallas, Texas, February 1925. Courtesy Texas African American Photography Archive.

Are You Protected Under This?

Comp'ete protection for all. We insure from 2 Years to 60 Years

Policies from $30.00 to $575.00

JOIN TODAY

THE GOLDEN CHAIN OF THE WORLD

Room 210, Pythian Temple
Dallas, Texas   Phone Y-2302

W. I. Dickson, Supreme Knight   R. L. H. Rice, Supreme Secretary

Analyze, Systematize and Advertise. If you can't do it, see The Negro Business Bureau.

NOTICE

Colored people must come to understand that they ought to employ the services of an architect when they do any building of any kind. He saves them a lot of worry and a great deal of money.

W. Sidney Pittman, the architect, and President of the Brotherhood of Negro Building Mechanics, will give any information along this line.

Phone H-3078

Address: 1018 Liberty St., Dallas, Texas

Phone Y-2701

VOLNA PRODUCTS

Hair Straightener and Grower.   ::   Drug and Toilet Sundries   ::   Fountain Syrups and Bottled Sodas   ::   ::   *Refined and Pure*

West Texas Mfg. Co.

Cor. Duncan and Taylor Streets

All Financial Members in good standing of the

Interior page of *Negro Business Bulletin*, Dallas, Texas, February 1925. Courtesy Texas African American Photography Archive.

William Sidney Pittman (back row, second from right) and the Drexel Institute architecture class of 1900. Courtesy of the Drexel University Archives.

"Negro Murderers Hurt Dallas; Pulpit Wolves Not Having It Easy Any Longer." The slangy stories were really diatribes. A Waco-datelined story under the "Dillinger" headline on July 28, 1934, proclaimed,

> My friends, the Baptist 'so'sation [association] No. 2 is now on the screen here and we assure you that the fine change is coming in from all parts and old brer "rev" moderator "Dillinger" is one happy soul. He carries his "machine gun" in the Master's Holy Bible and when he cocks his machine gun of hypocrisy, and smiles, the saps drop their change. The poor, starved church folks freely give up their last dime to 'so'sations and lodges, to insurance companies and undertakers and preachers (male and female) and then go home and choke their "chiterlins" slim because they roll over and growl and beg for food. Old parson "Dillinger" knows where they are hungry. He knows the white people can't use them. He knows they are blind to depression. And he knows they are weak in every way. Yet he and others take their little money from them because the poor saps want the moderator to see and love them best, and say great and good things about them after they are dead and can't even hear what "de pahsons" have to say about them. They know that's why the poor

creatures go hungry to pay 'so'sation dues. Old brer "Dillinger" can sure look through a Negro, and he has kept him snoozing for lo, these many years. He had fleeced, and "skint" the Race dead poor until now he has plenty of money for his wife and boys and he himself is styled as one of our great men. In fact, he is too great to visit his sleepy bunch. Does this man love his Race? Or is it just their pocket he's after?[13]

In the 1940s, Pittman was charged with mail fraud. Testimony at his trial, heavily covered in the *Express* and other black papers, alleged that he had sometimes attempted to shake down business owners by offering positive coverage in return for advertising. He denied the charges but was convicted and spent two years in federal prison.

Upon his release, he returned to Dallas and campaigned for former vice president Henry Wallace, a left-wing candidate for president, in 1948. Pittman often ate lunch at the Pride of Dallas Café on Allen Street, owned by longtime restaurateurs Quitman McMillan and Daisy McMillan. Their younger son, Rudolph, who grew up working in the café, recalled Pittman years later: "He stepped on too many people's toes. When he came out [of prison], he was a very, very bitter man, but he was brilliant. Oh, he was brilliant. . . . He was a broken man. . . . He was very feeble."[14] Pittman died in 1958 and lies buried in Glen Oaks Cemetery on Hatcher Street in South Dallas. His grave was initially unmarked, but he got a grave marker in 1985, thanks to the efforts of County Commissioner John Wiley Price and the Dallas Historical Society.[15] A street in that section of town once was named for him, but it is now called Bethurum Avenue.

Time was not good to the Pythian Temple, either. In 1939 a Robertson County woman sued the Pythians after the organization failed to pay her husband's death benefit. Under new leadership, the statewide group struggled to regain its financial health and resumed paying death benefits. However, the building went into receivership and in 1946 was sold to Ben Ackerman, a local Jewish businessman. In 1956 Ackerman sold it for $100,000 after a local lodge sued him. They were awarded $16,557 by State District Judge Sarah T. Hughes, who later became well known for swearing in Lyndon Johnson as president after John F. Kennedy was assassinated. For a time, local Pythians maintained an office across the street, above a pawnshop owned by Rubin "Honest Joe" Goldstein.

Sergeant Roberts, the black World War I hero, also came to a sad end. He and his wife hanged themselves in their New Jersey home in 1949 after he was accused—falsely, it seems—of fondling a white girl in a movie theater.

Have Heard the Call - I Have Need to go to Africa!

Miss Beatrice Savannah Lott, 3410 Lafayette, Da...°

Back to Africa handbill. "I Have Heard the Call—I Have Need to Go to Africa! Miss Beatrice Savannah Lott, 3410 Lafayette, Dallas," ca. 1922. Courtesy of the Texas African American Photography Archive.

For a number of years, the former temple housed Union Bankers Insurance Company. By the early 1980s, the red brick building had been redone in a dreary gray, as had the adjoining one, which housed various businesses, including Goodwill Industries and the Blue Cross/Blue Shield insurance company. In the early 1980s, Union Bankers began covering up the "Knights of Pythias" name lettered on the façade. Historic preservationists got a court order to preserve the lettering, in an effort indicative of the black community's initiative to reclaim an era when blacks, against great odds, achieved considerable success in business in Deep Ellum. In 1989 the building was designated a local historic landmark. Sadly, though, efforts to restore it to its former glory have failed to materialize.[16]

Black Dallas

African Americans in Dallas advanced rapidly during Reconstruction. The 1911 *Business and Professional Directory of Colored Persons* in Dallas, chronicling the growth of black Dallas during the previous twenty-five years, attests to the strides made in education, religion, health care, business, and politics:

During the last twenty-five years the American Negro has made his most substantial progress along material lines. Inspired by the teachings of Booker T. Washington, and those men who hold similar views, the Negro has boldly launched out into almost every line of commercial activity. Along the line of his advancement beyond doubt may be observed the wreckage of many a meritorious business venture; but withal he has achieved some successes of which he may boast with pardonable pride.

The Dallas Negro, catching the spirit of the times, has gone forth into the marts of trade and sought, with more or less success, to win a place and to make himself and his race a potent factor in the commercial life of his city. Many of his efforts have met with failure but not all of them. On every hand are to be seen evidences of his success. Successes that are small perhaps when viewed in the light of the achievements of his white fellow citizen, but looming large when viewed from the standpoint of the difficulties and the obstacles he has had to overcome.

The limited space at our command will not permit an exhaustive review of the commercial activity of the Negro of Dallas. Nor shall we be able to give a detailed account of all the various business enterprises now being conducted in this city by our people. We shall content ourselves with directing attention to a number of the more successful enterprises, with the hope that those who have had a less measure of success may find encouragement to strive more diligently and that an increasing number of our young men may be encour-

The Gypsy Tea Room on Central Track, ca. 1930s. Courtesy of the Dallas Public Library.

aged by these examples to take advantage of the opportunities open to them in this direction.[1]

Many did take advantage of opportunity despite horrific incidents such as the March 3, 1910, lynching of Allen Brooks, an African American accused of raping a white girl. A mob dragged him from a courtroom, threw him out a courthouse window, and hung his stripped and stabbed body from the Elks Arch, which had been constructed downtown for a lodge convention. A photo of the lynching was used on a postcard. The incident generated nationwide news coverage and outrage among members of the National Association for the Advancement of Colored People (NAACP), established a year earlier.

The Harlem Theatre on Elm Street, ca. 1940s. Courtesy of the Dallas Public Library.

Black-owned businesses flourished around the city, interspersed with white-owned establishments, although the "separate-but-equal" principle, upheld by the United States Supreme Court in *Plessy v. Ferguson* (1896), codified racial discrimination. In Dallas, as in other cities around the country, segregation was enforced by custom and later through the passage of laws that restricted African American access to public facilities and to virtually every conceivable place where whites and blacks might have social contact. Dallas enacted its segregation ordinance in 1916. Increasing racial tension pushed many of the downtown black businesses into the area originally known as Freedmantown and subsequently as North Dallas. "Central Track," the neighborhood along the Houston and Texas Central Railroad line, connected North Dallas to Deep Ellum.

In 1899 educator John Paul Starks came to Dallas from Georgia and established a weekly newspaper called the *Bee*. Later renamed the *Dallas Express,* it survived into the 1960s. Other papers, such as William Sidney Pittman's *Brotherhood Eyes,* came and went. The black community was seldom covered in the mainstream white newspapers, the exception being news of a violent nature that seemed to back up racial stereotypes, as when *Express* editor W. E. King was slain in 1919 by a woman named Hattie Burleson.

Restaurant owner Quitman McMillan, 1925. Courtesy of Rudolph McMillan.

Restaurants were established by entrepreneurs such as Quitman McMillan, who was born around 1880 in the East Texas town of Quitman. Never fond of farm work, McMillan moved to Dallas in 1907 and found work as a bartender. Then he went into partnership with a man named Watson in a café in the 100 block of North Central Avenue, between Main and Elm, but Watson could not stomach the backroom gambling that was essential for success and soon left the business. Within a few years, McMillan had established McMillan's Café in the 2400 block of Elm, a few doors from the black-owned Penny Savings Bank, originally established in 1903 by Maggie L. Walker in Virginia.

African Americans had their own variety—or vaudeville—theaters in Dallas by the 1890s. These included the Black Elephant, which occupied several locations around Central Track and was described as "notorious" in newspaper accounts. It appears that many such theaters, black and white, offered sexually alluring women who entertained beer-swilling male patrons, and the Black Elephant's real distinction may have been simply that it was a black establishment. Some other similar (white) theaters at the time included Thompson's Varieties, the White Elephant, Hanlon's Varieties, Mascott (Varieties), and the Camp Street Variety.

"Negro Troops," corner of Elm and Akard, ca. 1910–1915. Courtesy of Luc Sante and the Texas African American Photography Archive.

Ads and announcements from an African American newspaper, the *Dallas Express*, during the 1920s.

A July 1890 *Dallas Times Herald* article probably exemplified the white attitude toward such venues: "Two months ago, Robert Giles and Ed Watson, two *mokes* [a disparaging term for African Americans], were star performers at a Negro dive on Camp Street known to the public as the 'Palace Theatre.' Two Lang, a Chinaman in the vicinity, was robbed one night of $1.90 and identified Giles and Watson as the men who held him up and deprived him of one day's receipts of his 'washee-washee' house."[2] A few months later, the city council passed an ordinance stiffening regulation of such theaters and drove several, including the Black Elephant, out of business.

Despite this setback, black show business flourished in Deep Ellum soon after the turn of the twentieth century, paralleling the growth of theaters

Abe and Pappy's club on Elm Street, ca. 1940s. Courtesy of the Texas African American Photography Archive.

Two unidentified children, Abe and Pappy's club on Elm Street, ca. 1940s. Courtesy of the Texas African American Photography Archive.

offering films or high-class vaudeville entertainment or both in cities all over the country. In Dallas in 1908, John "Fat Jack" Harris opened the Grand Central Theater in the 400 block of North Central, near its intersection with Swiss Avenue. Everyone called the place "Fat Jack's." Harris often sat outside in overalls, smoking cigarettes, chatting with passersby, and selling tickets at 17 cents for adults, 11 cents for children. His leadership of

Funeral procession on Second Avenue, ca. early 1940s. Courtesy of the Texas African American Photography Archive.

the house band drew praise in the *Freeman,* a black-owned weekly paper in Indianapolis that devoted considerable coverage to black show business nationwide. In January 1910 Harris scored a coup by presenting a film of the great black heavyweight boxing champion Jack Johnson doing battle with a white fighter named Stanley Ketchel.[3]

Also by 1910, the Swiss Airdome Theater (described in an *Express* ad as "managed by colored people for colored people, and all the performers are colored") had been established on Swiss Avenue near Central. The Star opened in 1913 at 2407 Elm, and the Mammoth the following year in a building that had once been a white saloon. Another theater, the Circle, was replaced by the Palace, which started showing movies and added vaudeville in 1920. By the late teens, a movie house had also come to North Dallas— the High School Theatre at 3211 Cochran Street. The Park Theater in the 400 block of Central opened in March 1912. Two years later its management was assumed by vaudevillians Chintz Moore and Ella B. Moore, who came to Dallas from Charleston, South Carolina, where they had operated the Maceo Theater. Both had been popular performers. He was a comedian who hailed from Galveston, Texas; she, an actress described in the *Freeman* as a "character and novelty soubrette." Advertising in the *Dallas Express,*

Pinkston Clinic, Dallas, ca. 1930s. Courtesy of the Dallas Historical Society.

they said the Park offered "High class vaudeville and moving pictures. Visit the Park lawn, nicest place in town."[4] Ella B. Moore is generally described as warm and friendly; her husband as hot-headed. This is borne out by a 1920 *Freeman* article noting that he had been wounded by a theatrical company manager after taking five shots at the man.[5]

As more theaters were established, theater owners began organizing circuits, or "times." Fred Barrasso of Memphis founded the Tri-State Circuit, which was cut short by his unexpected death in 1911. The first successful black circuit is thought to have been the Dudley Circuit, founded by Sherman H. Dudley, a comedian born in Texas—probably Austin—around 1880. Dudley became known for bringing a mule named Patrick onstage in his act. He bought a theater in Washington, DC, in 1913, and by 1916 had almost thirty theaters in the South, East, and Midwest, but none in Texas.

The Moores advertised that they booked their shows through another circuit, the Colored Consolidated Vaudeville Exchange. Chintz Moore also seems to have booked shows on his own in Paris and other Texas towns. Dallas theaters obtained national recognition by advertising in the *Freeman* and the *Chicago Defender*. Both these papers had contributing writers in Dallas and regularly published news from the city and elsewhere in Texas.

Vaudeville entertainment, with deep roots in minstrel shows dating to

Lone Star Restaurant Association sign, Dallas, Texas, n.d. Courtesy of the African American Museum, Dallas, Texas.

Unidentified store, North Dallas, Texas, ca. 1930s. Courtesy of the Texas African American Photography Archive.

slavery, took various forms, including the "tab" or "tabloid" show, a shortened version of a musical comedy, lasting about an hour and featuring a reduced cast. Overall, shows reflected the original name of the form, "variety," but a much higher-class, more family-oriented entertainment than the rowdy joints of a few years earlier. Dallas's black theater patrons enjoyed touring minstrel and stock companies; novelty acts, such as the five-hundred-pound Cleo-Cleo and Jack Rabbit, the hoop contortionist; comedians such as Little Jimmie Cox, a Charlie Chaplin imitator; duos such as Butterbeans and Susie; beautiful, high-kicking dancers; and musicians and singers.

With the national success of Mamie Smith's 1920 recording of "Crazy Blues" (which was not truly a blues at all), theaters in Dallas, as elsewhere,

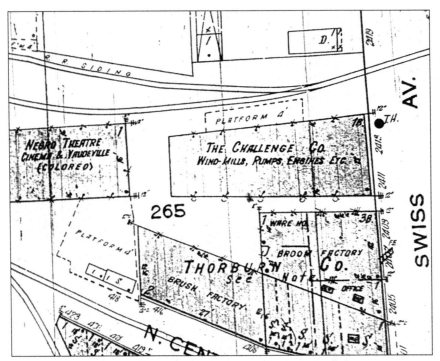

A 1920s Sanborn map of Dallas showing the area between North Central and Swiss avenues. Courtesy of the Dallas Public Library.

often featured her and other female "classic blues" singers, including Trixie Smith and Clara Smith and the "Empress of the Blues," Bessie Smith (all of these Smiths were unrelated, as far as is known), and Ida Cox. Locally, singers such as Bobbie Cadillac, Lillian Glinn, and others became so popular that they attracted the interest of record companies in Chicago and New York.

Blues historian Paul Oliver speculates that many of the women blues singers of this period were "street-walkers, who sang with the brothel pianists before turning tricks."[6] There is little evidence to substantiate this, other than in the lyrics to the songs themselves, which recount the harshness of life on the street.

Bobbie Cadillac, in her recording "Carbolic Acid Blues" (released in 1928 with an unidentified piano accompanist), reiterates the themes of betrayal and violence:

> I told her I loved her man,
> grave will be her resting place.
> (Repeat)

She looked at me with burning eyes,
threw carbolic acid in my face.
In my bed, my face burned to the bone.
(Repeat)
If carbolic don't kill me,
penitentiary gonna be my home.

Of all the women blues singers in Dallas during the 1920s, Lillian Glinn was certainly the most famous. She performed first at the Park Theater and later toured to theaters around the South. In an interview with Paul Oliver in 1970, Glinn said that she did not know her exact birth date but thought that it might have been in 1902 in a small town about thirty miles east of Dallas. In her early twenties, she moved to Dallas, where she was heard singing at a local church by the respected though little-recorded Texas singer Hattie Burleson. (Whether this Burleson is the woman who shot *Express* editor King is unknown.) Through Burleson, Glinn was introduced to Ella B. Moore, and the two women persuaded her to sing blues and vaudeville songs.

Glinn's popularity at the Park Theater in Dallas prompted R. T. Ashford, who owned a shine parlor and record shop at 409 N. Central Avenue on the corner of Elm Street, to contact the Columbia label. As her manager,

McMillan Sanitarium, Dallas, ca. 1920s. Left to right: Dr. McMillan, Dr. Pinkston, Nurse Starks. Courtesy of the Dallas Historical Society.

Shotgun house, Dallas, 1920s. Courtesy of the Texas/Dallas History and Archives Division, Dallas Public Library.

Ashford facilitated a recording contract. Ashford was a shrewd entrepreneur who was involved in establishing the Dallas Negro Chamber of Commerce. He had come to Dallas from Nacogdoches and worked at a succession of jobs, including doorman at Sanger Brothers' department store. Ashford was to play a pivotal role in the export of Dallas music.

In Lillian Glinn's first hit record, "Doggin' Me," she sang in a strong contralto voice and displayed originality in composition, though she used traditional blues lyrics and themes. Although she rarely created her own blues verses, she was especially talented at restructuring them. She sang that her "daddy's love is like a hydrant, he turns it off and on" and that "men are like street-cars, runnin' all over town." In several of her songs, Glinn addresses other women, offering warnings about the unreliability of lovers or advice on how to keep a man. In "Cravin' a Man Blues," she sings:

> There's one man I love, one man I crave,
> one man I'm wild about.
> (Repeat)
> The one man I crave, he knows what it's all about.
> Someday, I'll get every man I love.
> (Repeat)
> Just as sure as I kneel,
> and the stars shine up above
> Will there ever be a time
> when a woman won't need no man?
> (Repeat)
> And when that day comes, I want to die if I can.
> I'm gonna tell you people something,
> as true as the stars above.
> (Repeat)
> Now pretty ain't worth nothing,
> If you ain't got the man you love.
> (Repeat)

Glinn's singing was direct, and her lyrics were easy to understand, underscored sometimes by half-spoken, half-sung passages in a preaching style and sometimes, as in "Front Door Woman" and "All the Week," by a hummed stanza. Some of her songs are poignantly sexual with a yearning sound, such as "Wobble It a Little Daddy," with its traditional door-key image, or "Packing House Blues," which opens with these lines:

> A bucket of blood,
> a butcher's knife is all I crave.
> (Repeat)
> Let me work in your packing house, daddy,
> while I am your slave.

One of Glinn's last recordings was "Atlanta Blues," which swings lightly and was apparently composed about her experiences in that city at the 81

Jimmy Bell and the Bombshells, Rose Room, Dallas, 1940s. Courtesy of the Texas African American Photography Archive.

Theater on Decatur Street, where she decided to give up professional blues singing and return to the church. In the late 1930s she moved to California, where she later married Rev. O. P. Smith in Oakland. During her relatively short career, Glinn had a national reputation as a singer. Although her singing had a distinctive Texas sound, her accompaniment often consisted of a New Orleans–style band with banjo, tuba, and piano.

"Race records" was a catchall categorization of all styles of African American music at this time and included blues, jazz, gospel, novelty tunes, and popular songs. The term "race," however, was also commonly used in the black press as a means of distinguishing African Americans from others. Both male and female performers were also known as "race" musicians, and generally the male theatrical acts were as eclectic in nature as those of their female counterparts, catering to the demands of promoters and the ever-changing tastes of their audience. Typically, each half of the show featured an "olio," a short act performed outside the curtain, and included a number of different musical acts and comedy routines. One of the most popular and influential male performers of the twenties was Lonnie Johnson, who had a crooner's voice and a light, jazzy touch on guitar.

This was a heady time for black show business in the United States, and the Moores' ads in the *Express* brimmed with racial pride: "Controlled and managed by colored people, catering to nothing but colored people . . . Last year's books showed $50,000 paid to colored people," proclaimed an ad on March 13, 1920. Actually, however, the black theaters did cater to whites to some extent. Many offered a Friday-night "midnight ramble," a late show for white patrons, who paid a bit more than black theatergoers did. White musician Bill Neely recalled: "They let white people in for the midnight shows, and it was rowdy. The girls took most of their clothing off. They had blues singers, hoochie-koochies, and the girls did whatever they were big enough to do."[7] Black musician Sammy Price said the rowdiness had been exaggerated, that the midnight rambles were simply shows for whites and that the admission price was a bit higher.

The regular admission price at the Park was thirty cents for adults, twenty cents for children. The theater opened at six in the evening and featured a Sunday matinee. On June 26, 1920, an *Express* ad touted "a seven-day colored street fair. Big brass band every day. Park Theater Lawn, 424 Central." According to a May 8, 1915, *Freeman* article, "Mrs. Ella B. Moore has secured the whole first regiment K of P [Knights of Pythias] band to give concerts on the Parklawn every night, where great crowds of strollers can find ease and rest between acts." The *Freeman* and the *Defender* sometimes referred to "the Central Avenue Stroll," likening it to the Chicago black entertainment district called the Stroll.

Unidentified dancers, Abe and Pappy's club on Elm Street, ca. 1940s. Courtesy of the Texas African American Photography Archive

In 1920 Chintz Moore and about thirty other black Southern and Mid-western theater owners established the premier black vaudeville circuit, the Theater Owners Booking Association (TOBA), which grew to more than eighty theaters. Performers joked that the acronym stood for "Tough on Black Acts" or "Tough on Black Asses" because contracts heavily favored management, and conditions were often crude. A 1924 *Freeman* column called the Park "another barn, no toilets, water nor any other accommodations backstage." It said the Palace Theater in Memphis "has four dressing rooms; very nasty."

Entertainment wasn't limited to theaters. In November 1919, *Express* publisher Starks's sons Clarence and F. E. opened the Green Parrot Jazzland, at 2413 Elm. Admission was thirty-five cents, "including war tax." The owners advertised that their third-floor establishment had "the prettiest girls, the jazziest dancers." It was over the Buffalo Club and, at street level, the Royal Café. The Royal was replaced by Whittaker's Café, which advertised: "Call our rent cars, day and night." This spot, a few years later, became McMillan's Café. In addition to R. T. Ashford's Music Shop, the 1925 *Negro Business Bulletin* listed four other music stores in the area: the Ajax Music Shop (705 N. Central Avenue), Black Swan Music Shop (1717 Hall Street), Brashear's Music Shop (1727 Hall Street), and Jordan's Music Shop (Hall and Central). Many of the traveling entertainers stayed at the Del Monico Hotel, established in 1918, at the corner of Central and Swiss avenues. The 1925 *Bulletin* also identifies three other hotels (Frazier Hotel, Lincoln Hotel, and Waukesha Hotel), as well as numerous private residences that offered furnished rooms for rent.

The *Bulletin* highlights the increasing concentration of African American businesses in "black" areas and the existence of an essentially self-sufficient community. The 1925 directory lists a range of businesses, including carpenters, cement workers, blacksmiths, painters, decorators, a bricklayer, contractors, landscapers, auto repair shops, a carpet renovator, plumbers, a cooper, accountants, a private detective agency, moving businesses, attorneys, undertakers (two of which provided ambulance service), doctors and dentists, hospitals, taxi services, dressmakers, cafés and restaurants, barbershops and beauty parlors, furniture stores and repair businesses, a dairy, real estate agencies, shoe shops, shine parlors, a newspaper and a magazine, a dry cleaner, notions and dry goods stores, tailor shops, dancing schools, grocers, drugstores, and ice dealers. Such communities sprang up across the country and were a great source of pride among African Americans, who were also acutely aware that their achievements could make them a target.

Unidentified dancer, Abe and Pappy's club on Elm Street, ca. 1940s. Courtesy of the Texas African American Photography Archive.

In 1921, for instance, when lynchings and attacks on black communities were sweeping the nation, the Greenwood area of Tulsa, Oklahoma, known as the "Black Wall Street," was virtually destroyed by mobs of whites who killed an estimated three hundred black people. In Dallas, the Tip Top dance hall on Central was a popular spot for music and dancing in the twenties. It was on the second floor of a former railroad hotel at Central Track and Pacific. The dance hall was also known by other names, including the Central Dance Hall and the Royal Social and Amusement Club. Its nickname of Tip Top apparently came from the Tip Top tailor shop downstairs. Bands often played outside on weekends for the shop's customers. "Tip Top was tailors," recalled drummer Herbie Cowens, a Dallas native. "Tip Top was where I played every Saturday in front of that place, and they made clothes. . . . We played out in front, and people would come out to hear the music."[8] Booker Pittman remembered the Tip Top from working nearby at a shoe shine stand and record store that he doesn't name but was probably Ashford's. T-Bone Walker recalled playing at the Tip Top. New Orleans trumpet player Don Albert praised the music but described the hall as "the raggediest and worst place in Dallas."[9]

Juneteenth parade, 1947, at Thomas Avenue and Hall Street. Photograph by Alexander H. Moore. Courtesy of Documentary Arts.

Asked about the musicians who played outside, Cowens referred to another New Orleans musician who frequented Dallas: "Most of the time it was Frenchy, who was a trumpet player. He had the band, and he had three or four different [instrumental] pieces on it. . . . He was kind of a heavyset fellow, and he could blow his horn; they say you could hear it from Elm Street to far North Dallas. His name was Polite Christian. I don't know how he spelled it, but he was from New Orleans."[10] Albert's assessment was similar but less charitable: "Frenchy wasn't a good trumpet player, but he was loud." In any event, Frenchy was well known as universally liked. The young Budd Johnson played drums with him, and clarinetist Jesse Hooker recorded with Frenchy's String Band in Dallas.

In October 1924, to national fanfare in the black press, the Moores opened a second theater, the Ella B. Moore, in the same block as the Park, with a performance of the Lafayette Players Stock Company. The theater was the showplace of the Southwest on the TOBA. It was described as

modern in every particular. It has a ground floor, which could accommodate 600 persons, a balcony that seated 500, loge seats for 100 and four boxes.

It also had an office, an automatic entrance gate operated from the office, a reception room, and an office for the use of traveling managers. The structure was topped with a roof garden, and there were seven dressing rooms and an orchestra room. There was also a shower bath for the artists backstage."[11]

The year after opening the new theater, the Moores closed the Park.

Although black business owners in Dallas were essentially self-sufficient and able to meet the needs of their community, they did, by necessity, interact with Jewish shopkeepers in Deep Ellum. Shopkeepers were generally sympathetic to the plight of African Americans,

"Rouse, Ye Klansmen," sheet music by Thos. F. Ewton, Dallas, 1922.

who, like them, were immigrants to Dallas and subjected to social discrimination and racism. Jewish businessmen in Deep Ellum encouraged blacks to patronize their shops and offered not only credit and loans to their black customers but also the opportunity to try on clothing at a time when this was forbidden in stores in downtown Dallas.

Jewish Pawnbrokers and Merchants of Deep Ellum

Many of the pawnbrokers and merchants of Deep Ellum emigrated from Eastern Europe, fleeing oppression and seeking opportunity. Some landed at New York's Ellis Island and later went south and west to cities such as Dallas. Others were among the ten thousand Jews who entered through the port of Galveston, Texas, between 1907 and 1914 under the "Galveston movement" or "Galveston plan," organized and funded by New York financier Jacob Schiff. A relocation agency helped them find work.[1]

Among the Ellis Island immigrants was Volf Soltes, a native of Austria. In 1916, when he was about twenty-one, he moved to Dallas, where his sister Jenny lived. He recalled arriving with "a black derby, red mustache and all that makes one look like a New Yorker." Soltes also brought a toughness learned on the streets of New York, where he had learned to fight to protect his father from hoodlums who pulled his beard and called him a "Christ-killer" as he sold vegetables from a pushcart.

Among Volf Soltes's early employers in Dallas was Commercial Metals, which later grew into a giant company. In the early 1920s, he went into business with Sam Goldberg, and the two operated Uncle Sam's Pawn Shop on Elm Street. Within a few years, Soltes, who had Americanized his name to William, or Willie, bought out his partner but didn't change the name of the shop. Uncle Sam's became a kind of training ground for most of the pawnbrokers who followed.

Willie and his wife, the former Sarah Rachovsky, lived on Caroline Street, in a Jewish neighborhood just north of downtown known as Short North Dallas or Frogtown because it was inundated with frogs fleeing to higher ground when the nearby Trinity River flooded. By some accounts, the area had once been called "Little Jerusalem" or "Goose Valley" because many of its

The Goldstein family, 1930. Courtesy of Eddie Goldstein.

early residents raised geese. In 1925 the Solteses bought a house on Park Row in South Dallas, which had become the city's primary Jewish community.

One of Willie's nephews, Dave Goldstein, came from New York for a visit and worked in the pawnshop. Dave was a tall, good-looking young man, and one day in 1923 he caught the eye of fifteen-year-old Dora Abramson as she was walking to school. Her friend Max Utay also worked in the store, and she asked him about Dave. The fact that Dave didn't have

Deep Ellum grocer Nathan Rosen, ca. 1930s. Courtesy of the Jewish Community Center.

much money and that his widowed mother had sold goods from a push-cart and worked in a factory in New York didn't deter Dora at all. But her budding romance enraged her father, Itzhak "Issie" Abramson, a Russian immigrant who had never had much success in the United States. His wife, Necha, known as "Annie," was pregnant with Dora when they sailed from Bremen, Germany, in the winter of 1907, headed for Galveston. Issie was fleeing service in the czar's army. His shoemaking trade brought him and his family to Dallas, where he started working in a Deep Ellum shop. The Abramsons initially stayed with the Utays, who lived in a run-down area south of downtown, then moved to a house on Cora Street on the edge of black North Dallas. Issie disliked the confinement of working in the shoe shop and had a variety of other jobs. For a time, he drove an oversized taxi called a jitney between Dallas and Fort Worth, about thirty miles away. He tried running his own store. And he worked with B. Schwartz, a wheeler-dealer who owned the Day and Night Pawn Shop in the 2400 block of Elm and invested in rental properties. Schwartz, a former New Yorker, also bought up quantities of goods for resale, and Issie accompanied him on buying trips to businesses that were failing or had overstocks.

Issie was determined that his eight children would do better than he had, and he had decided that Dora would marry one of B. Schwartz's sons, Hymie. So when Dora decided to marry Dave Goldstein, she told her mother but not her father. Dave and Dora wed on New Year's Eve of 1924 at a friend's home in Fort Worth and spent the night in a hotel. The next day, when they returned to Dallas and stopped by to see Dora's parents, Issie threw them out. Dora returned the next week to help her mother, who had broken her leg and still had young children to care for. But Issie Abramson and Dave Goldstein never spoke again.

A 1920s *Dallas Express* ad for Sam Dysterbach's store.

The first years of the marriage were hard. Dave and Dora worked at a dry-goods store in Deep Ellum. In 1930 Dave borrowed $2,000 from a bank and established a new dry-goods store. With the Depression on, people kept asking about pawning things, so the couple added a small pawnshop operation. Eventually they phased out dry goods and established a pawnshop. Among their customers in the early 1930s were Bonnie Parker and Clyde Barrow. "They were just a couple of young kids in love," Dora Goldstein recalled. "He'd buy her a little gingham housedress for $1.98."[2]

Gradually, more of Dave's family moved to Dallas. When the stock market crashed, his brother Isaac was an eighteen-year-old law student in New York. Forced to discontinue his studies, he migrated to Dallas and went to work for his brother Dave. First he lived with his brother's family, then got a room in South Dallas. "I worked like a slave," Isaac "Rocky" Goldstein said years later, "eight in the morning until ten at night; Thursdays and Saturdays until midnight. Half a day on Sunday—until 3 p.m."[3] Many of the pawnshops stayed open late, and hard work was common, but relations between the brothers were strained. "He mistreated me, pushed me around," Isaac Goldstein said, "so I quit him and went to work for Klar and Winterman," an established, relatively upscale pawnshop at 2308 Elm. "I was supposed to get a commission, but there was no money, so I went to work for my uncle, William Soltes." He said he stayed with his uncle for ten years, then left, he said, when Soltes failed to deliver on his promise to give him part of the business. Goldstein established his own pawnshop, Rocky's, in the 2200 block of Elm.

Dave and Isaac's mother moved to Dallas, too, as did their sister Molly. In 1931 the third brother, Rubin, came for a Passover visit. He lived in New York, where he was in the scrap-metal business with Leonard LaRosa, uncle of singer Julius La Rosa. Rubin liked Dallas and soon returned to stay. He bought a stock of hardware from the old Starr Harness Company, which was going out of business, and opened a store at 2510½ Elm, next to a fish market. A few years later, he merged his store with Joe's Gun and Lock Shop, run by his sister Molly and her husband, Joe Doerner. When Doerner ran off with a woman from the produce market across the street, Rubin took over the business and helped his sister start another, Molly's Tool Shop. About 1936 Rubin moved to the location at 2524 Elm, which he would occupy for the rest of his life as "Honest Joe," Deep Ellum's best-known pawnbroker. Honest Joe's son Eddie Goldstein said his father got his nickname in the thirties when a drunken house painter called Little Jimmy was waiting to hock his brushes for enough money to go over to Sigel's liquor store and get a bottle of cheap wine When the woman ahead of him in line asked for a receipt, Little Jimmy reassured her, "Don't worry, lady, this is Honest Joe," and the name stuck.[4]

There are many stories about Honest Joe, who was a publicity genius. He was always in the papers. His shop eventually was on the Gray Line bus tour of Dallas. Texas Utilities Company chairman John W. Carpenter loved his store and would come by to don a pair of overalls and browse through used tools. Retired Dallas police officer Joe Cody recalled that a captain once wanted Honest Joe arrested for something. Cody went to the shop and found Honest Joe in the back, playing dominos with Carpenter and Mayor Robert Thornton. "Arrest him yourself," he told the captain.[5] Honest Joe once saved a pickpocket called "Hook" from the penitentiary by testifying that the man's prosthetic hands were in hock when the crime was committed.

The store was festooned with signs: "Honest Joe, Loan Ranger" and "YCMMSOYA," which stood for "You can't make money sitting on your Afghanistan." There was even a sign proclaiming "Emmes Joe"—"Honest Joe" in Hebrew. An equally gaudy station wagon parked outside the store

Klar and Winterman Pawn Shop, ca. 1920s. Courtesy of the Jewish Community Center.

featured a nonfunctional machine gun. Joe Cody recalled that when things got slow, Honest Joe would drive the wagon downtown, park it illegally near the courthouse and stage a shouting match with whatever hapless officer showed up to ticket the vehicle. Anything for publicity.

Honest Joe's featured an amazing array of junk that extended to tables on the sidewalk in front. Max Wyll, who served for years as secretary-treasurer of the Dallas Pawnbrokers' Association, was always trying to get the papers interested in a picture of Klar and Winterman, a "nice clean store. But no, they wanted that slimy place."[6]

Dora Goldstein did not get along with Honest Joe, but she had to walk past his store on her way to work. Once when she was involved in a minor auto accident, Honest Joe taped a newspaper story about the incident in his window and hung a shrunken head over it. Herschel Wilonsky, whose father and uncle ran S&W Auto Parts, across the street from Honest Joe's at 2515 Elm, recalled being in Honest Joe's one day when he was about eight years old. A woman came in to return a .25-caliber pistol that she had bought. She angrily complained that the weapon lacked stopping power: "I

Rocky Goldstein in his store in the 2200 block of Elm Street, ca. 1940s. Courtesy of the Jewish Community Center.

shot him three times, and he didn't even fall." Unfazed, Honest Joe told her, "I've got a bigger gun. Size is no problem."[7]

Herschel Wilonsky's father, Harry, had come to Dallas from Lithuania and joined three brothers who were already in the city. He worked at various jobs and went to night school to learn English. In 1932 he and a brother-in-law, Harry Shay, opened the auto parts store. Shay soon left the business and was replaced by Harry Wilonsky's brother Eli, who had been a partner in Cobbel and Wilonsky, a clothing store and tailor shop in Deep Ellum. The brothers also owned a wrecking yard next door to the store and a nearby building that was leased out for a restaurant operated by Milam Fertula. Another brother, Jake, and his wife, Rebecca, owned the Dallas Pawn Shop at 2020 Elm.

Pawnshops served a real need. For poor blacks and whites alike, the pawnshop operated as a bank by lending money and giving credit and selling merchandise at reasonable prices. Musician Marvin "Smokey" Montgomery, a longtime member of the Light Crust Doughboys, bought his first good banjo for $50 at Uncle Jake's Pawn Shop on Elm. His friend guitar player Jim Boyd said one of his band members once asked him for the time, and he jokingly replied, "Well, I'll have to go by Uncle Jake's Pawn Shop and look at my watch."[8]

All the pawnshops were owned by Jews, and for years virtually all were in Deep Ellum. Most made their money primarily on small loans at 10 percent per month interest. People hocked, or "soaked," virtually everything: shoes, suits, guns, musical instruments, artificial limbs. Eddie Goldstein said his father regularly did business with a little Hispanic man called Hot Tamale, who wore an overcoat even in the summer and made his living selling hot tamales from a pushcart. Hot Tamale regularly pawned his teeth for $5 with Honest Joe, then rented them back for a dime so he could eat lunch.

"You got to meet a lot of funny people in the pawn business," Dora Goldstein recalled. "We knew Jack Ruby just like he was a brother, went to his nightclub. Everybody liked him. His employees loved him. If my girls went to his club, he'd leave his business and take them home.

"I would say that 90 percent of our customers were black. Very few Mexicans. We had a few bigshot white customers. . . . I would say that 75 percent of our black customers were in every week. They'd get it out on Friday and pawn it back on Monday. Suits, pants, jackets, wristwatches, rings, radios, TVs. One guy worked for a funeral parlor, and he'd pawn the ends on the caskets. One of them pawned his false teeth."[9] Deep Ellum in some ways was a self-contained little world. Shoe repairman Max Grabstald had a deal with Klar and Winterman. He would pay one month's interest, 10 percent, on unredeemed shoes, which he would then repair and sell.

Though the area was generally thought of as rough and dangerous, robberies and muggings of business people were almost unheard of before the 1950s. Merchants walked to the bank with $1,000 or $2,000 in their pockets, right past the throngs of African Americans around Central Track, with no fear at all. "It was respect," Eddie Goldstein said. Of course, a black person who was caught committing a crime against a white would have been in serious trouble. The shops were required to keep items ninety days, though sometimes these rules were bent. Wyll recalled that one pawnbroker sold a suit to a black man moments after another had pawned it. "What will you do if the man wants his suit back?" Wyll asked. "I'll get him another one," the broker replied.

Sometimes exploitation was more overt. Businessman Sam Luterman was visiting a friend in his Deep Ellum pawnshop one day when a black man came in to pay on a loan. The clerk told the owner in Yiddish that she couldn't find a card on the customer. "Schlep da gelt," the owner replied: Get the money. After the black man left, Luterman told his friend, "Well, I guess you'll make sure the money gets to the right pawnshop." "We're not in the habit of turning down money," his friend said.[10]

Sylvia and Label Feldman, Label's Pawn Shop, ca. 1940s. Courtesy of the Jewish Community Center.

To some extent, this hard-nosed attitude may have come from the merchants' own hard-knocks background. Wyll's father, Issie, an immigrant from Warsaw, could not afford to live in the Cedars, south of downtown, like the Sanger brothers and other rich merchants. They lived in Frogtown, north of downtown, near the area that became known as Little Mexico. Issie Wyll had a Schepps Bakery route and often woke his son at 4:00 a.m. to accompany him on his rounds. Max would hide under the bed, but his father would roust him, saying, "Come on, I know you're under there."[11] Television producer Aaron Spelling's father was a tailor in Deep Ellum, and Spelling recalled running for their South Dallas home to avoid a viciously anti-Semitic group of boys called the Purple Gang.

Pawnbroking was not the only occupation open to Jewish immigrants in Deep Ellum. Sam Stillman's father, Hyman, for example, was a cabinet maker who had come from a town near Kiev in 1908. Two years later his wife, Gertrude, and three-year-old Sam joined Hyman in Dallas, where they lived in Frogtown for a while. In 1920 the Stillmans joined the movement of Dallas's Jewish community to South Dallas, where Sam graduated from Forest High School. In 1926 he went to work for The Model Tailors, a prestigious clothing shop in Deep Ellum that was located in space leased from Klar and Winterman.[12] "We were sort of the queen of the block,"

Tommie Schwartz (left) and Morris Silverberg, Day and Night Pawn Shop, ca. 1940s. Courtesy of the Jewish Community Center.

recalled Masha Porte, who worked at The Model Tailors from 1932 to 1941, "because we were a two-story building with a little balcony, which is where our office was on one side and the cutting room on the other, and everything else was just pawnshops and one-story, mostly, clothing stores and that sort of thing." She recalled walking to Oatis drugstore at Elm and Central. "I used to walk down there all the time without any fear whatsoever, to buy cigarettes and whatnot. That's another thing I remember, never being afraid down there. And a lot of white gamblers and gangsters were there. In fact, Benny Binion was a customer. He used to have his clothes custom-made at The Model Tailors."[13]

Willard Watson was a street hustler and pimp around Central Track in the early forties. He recalled that he would buy a suit for $21 and have a friend sew a Model Tailors label in it. He'd wear it a few times, then pawn it for at least as much as he paid for it.[14] Sam Stillman, who worked at The Model Tailors until the early fifties, said they never charged more than $65 for a tailor-made suit.

Generally, the relations between Jews and blacks in Deep Ellum were more progressive than in other areas of Dallas, where blacks could not shop at all or were not allowed to try on clothes. "They were customers," said Joe Freed of Freed Furniture, which his father started in Deep Ellum, "and

Honest Joe's Pawn Shop, ca. 1950s. Courtesy of the Texas/Dallas History and Archives Division, Dallas Public Library.

there was a certain warmth."[15] That warmth, though, seldom if ever led to socializing outside the workplace. And even the friendliest relations were often infused with the paternalism of the time.

"I got along with the blacks better than I did with the whites," Dora Goldstein said. "White people, even the cheapest ones, always want to be the big shots." But she admitted that it was also sometimes difficult dealing with blacks. "It was rough. Very rough. I wouldn't call it exactly fighting, but a lot of harsh words and dirty words and sometimes a slap or two. You had to be tough with them. You could not be soft with them. They respected you more if you were tough, if they couldn't get away with something. They had a relationship with us because we were good to them; we were kind to them."[16] She recalled using a long iron bar to ward off several large, angry, drunken black customers. However, she also fondly remembered walking uptown for exercise and, on the way back, accepting rides from black cabbies who hollered out, "Mrs. Dave, you need a ride?"[17]

Label Feldman, one of the last of the old-time pawnbrokers, remained in business on Commerce Street west of Harwood until 1997, when he sold out to a chain operation. Some of Feldman's black customers had their checks mailed there for safekeeping and drew out money as they needed it.[18]

"The pawnshop was their bank," said Eddie Goldstein, Honest Joe's son. "Credit grocery store, the credit clothiers, they were all in Deep Ellum. Deep Ellum in its heyday was pawnshop, pawnshop, pawnshop, dry goods store; pawnshop, pawnshop, pawnshop, grocery store; pawnshop, pawnshop, pawnshop, shoe store. There wasn't competition. Everybody complemented one another. Everyone works together to get the customers there, then you cut the other guy's throat to get the customer away. It's just the exact same theory as they use today in the franchise locations."[19]

Some saw a special relationship between blacks and Jews because of a shared heritage of suffering and discrimination. Sam Stillman said, "Jewish people having been persecuted for hundreds of years, when they came to this country and they were accepted, in general . . . they felt that, after all, the black is a human being. We had black maids or yard men. We always invited them in and had them sit at our table and eat with us . . . we never thought anything about it." Others, like Eddie Goldstein, saw the relationship differently. "It wasn't because they were both minorities or anything like that; it was business," he said.

Honest Joe's Pawn Shop, ca. 1950s. Courtesy of the Texas/Dallas History and Archives Division, Dallas Public Library.

It is undeniable, though, that both blacks and Jews were victims of discrimination in an overtly racist era. The Ku Klux Klan wielded great political power in Dallas and Texas in the 1920s. In the early twenties, Klan membership in the state may have reached 100,000, and the organization controlled the governments of both Dallas and Fort Worth and probably had a majority in the state House of Representatives when it convened in January 1923. In 1922 a Klan candidate, Earle B. Mayfield, was elected to the US Senate. Ku Klux Klan Day at the State Fair of Texas in October 1923 drew about 75,000 Klansmen and their families to Fair Park. Fort Worth Klansmen were believed responsible for the 1927 flogging of businessman Morris Strauss. In 1921 Klansmen dragged black bellhop Alex Johnson from the Adolphus Hotel in downtown Dallas and branded the letters "KKK" on his forehead with acid. A field near the South Dallas black community of Joppa was reportedly used for torture and hanging of African Americans who were deemed troublemakers.[20]

Though the political power of the Klan was essentially broken by the late 1920s, the ideology of white supremacy continued as a force in Dallas until the 1950s and 1960s, when federal legislation and court rulings began the process of desegregation and integration. However, by that time the housing and business patterns of blacks and Jews had changed, and so had Deep Ellum. South Dallas, which had been a Jewish area, became a residential and commercial district for African Americans. Many Jews relocated in the areas north of Highland Park, where the Dallas Country Club excluded them from membership. In their new neighborhoods, Jews established homes, synagogues, and businesses.

Blind Lemon Jefferson

Downhome Blues

The Model Tailors in Deep Ellum was where the black and white worlds of Dallas converged. The customers included underworld characters Benny Binion and his number two man, Harry Urban; George "Machine Gun" Kelly; and Joe Civello, a local Mafia boss. But a cross-section of upstanding Dallas men bought clothes there as well, including prominent blacks: civil rights leader A. Maceo Smith and blues musician Blind Lemon Jefferson. To many blacks, clothing from The Model Tailors was a status symbol. "They had to have a Model Tailors suit," Isaac Goldstein recalled. "Good slides [shoes], a good hat, and a Model Tailors suit."[1] The suit Blind Lemon Jefferson was wearing in the only documented photograph of him was likely from The Model Tailors, and for him it was emblematic of his newfound success in the mid-1920s. By then, Jefferson had become the most significant blues singer to perform in Deep Ellum. His life and career epitomize the downhome blues of his generation.

Lemon Jefferson was born September 24, 1893, to Alec and "Classy" Banks Jefferson on a farm in Couchman, a small community near Wortham, which was a stop on the Houston & Texas Central (H&TC) line seventy-five miles south of Dallas. The H&TC carried the crop from Wortham's cotton gins to market in Dallas. Little is known about Jefferson's early life, though he probably heard songsters and bluesmen, such as Henry "Ragtime Texas" Thomas[2] and Alger "Texas" Alexander. Both Thomas and Alexander traveled around East Texas and performed a variety of blues and dance tunes. The cause of Jefferson's blindness isn't known, or whether he had some sight. Why would a blind man wear glasses, as he does in the only known publicity photo of him?

Jefferson came from a large family that included children from his mother's first marriage. How he learned to play guitar is still not entirely clear, but

Blind Lemon Jefferson, ca. 1927. Courtesy of Documentary Arts.

two of his childhood friends, Hobart Carter and Quince Cox, said that his parents bought him an instrument when he was child. Reportedly, he did get some schooling and was especially astute at listening to others. Carter attributed Jefferson's songwriting prowess to his almost uncanny ability to "keep in mind" what he heard around him. Clearly, the far-reaching thematic range of Lemon's songs attests to the breadth of his understanding of the cultural traditions of the world in which he lived.[3]

Jefferson showed an aptitude for music at an early age and learned to get around the nearby little towns of Wortham, Kirvin, Streetman, and Groesbeck. "Lemon started out playing his guitar on these streets, and I was on those same streets," said Quince Cox, born in 1903, who once served as caretaker in the Wortham cemetery, where Jefferson is buried. "I pitched quarters and nickels to him, and he'd play his guitar at any time of night. He used to play at Jake Lee's barbershop every Saturday, and people from all over came to hear him play. Then he'd get on this road at ten or eleven o'clock, and he'd walk to Kirvin, seven or eight miles. He'd play and keep walking, but he knew where he was going."[4]

Alec Jefferson told writer Sam Charters that his mother wouldn't let him go to the country suppers where his cousin Lemon was playing. "They was rough. Men was hustling women and selling bootleg, and Lemon was singing for them all night. They didn't even do any kind of dancing, just stompin'." Hobart Carter said that Lemon often played "breakdowns out in the woods near Couchman" and that he was sometimes accompanied by a fiddler named Lorenzo Ross. "They had a hallelujah time. We had our suppers and things. Saturday nights and things like that. All through the winter, we'd have some cold nights and some rainy nights. We had plenty of chock houses at that time. You get some sugar, put it in a crock. Let it set three days and go to drinking it. Chock houses were everywhere at that time."[5]

Quince Cox maintained, "Lemon played anything he had to play. And he played pretty good, too. What did we call them songs? Reels. . . . He could play anything you asked him to play." In addition to dance tunes, Cox remembered that Jefferson sometimes "howled" or "squealed" when he performed in public. "You hear one of them around a wolf or a possum or a coon or something on the track, he could do that good, too. Sure would . . . oh, yeah, he'd squeal just like a dog. Make it sound good, too."[6]

Carter said that Blind Lemon's family belonged to the Shiloh Baptist Church in Kirvin and that the young Lemon was highly regarded for his ability as a singer of spirituals as well as blues.[7] "He didn't play for a church," Carter remembered, "but he sang church songs." Former blues

Blind Lemon Jefferson race record ads from the *Chicago Defender* during the late 1920s. Courtesy of Documentary Arts.

A 1920s *Dallas Express* ad for The Model Tailors. Courtesy Dallas Public Library.

singer Reverend Rubin Lacy told blues historian David Evans that Jefferson once refused an offer from two men to pay him $10 each to play "Blues Come to Texas Loping like a Mule" because he had promised his mother that he'd never play a blues on Sunday. Wortham postmaster Uel L. Davis Jr. told a *Waco Tribune-Herald* reporter, "That was one thing about Lemon. He'd be singing in church one day, singing at a house of ill repute the next."[8]

Carter described Jefferson as a man who was "about halfway quiet," who was "almost business all the time." Although he apparently had more than one wife, Carter and Cox saw him as a Christian kind of man who preferred to "play in nice places, in front of hotels or barbershops, at house parties and country dances, and sometimes at local churches and Saturday night suppers."[9] Physically, Blind Lemon Jefferson was imposing. He was usually well dressed, wearing "good clothes"—Stetson hats and blue serge suits.

The 1920 census shows Jefferson living in Freestone County with an older half-brother, Nit C. Banks, and his family. Jefferson's occupation is listed as "musician," and his employer as "general public." The details of his personal life around this time are largely unknown. Hobart Carter said that Jefferson had "so many wives" but was unable to name them. Quince Cox said that Lemon might have had as many as four wives, but he, too, could provide no names. In any event, it is known that sometime after 1920, Jefferson met Roberta Ransom of Mexia in neighboring Limestone County, who was rumored to be ten years his senior. They married in 1927, the year that Ransom's son by a previous marriage, Theaul Howard, died. Howard's son, also named Theaul, remained in the area and retired in nearby Ferris, Texas. He recalled that when his father was laid out before the funeral, Blind Lemon held him up and told him to touch the body so he would never fear the dead.[10]

Theaul Howard and several longtime residents of Mexia said Jefferson and Roberta Ransom lived in a house on West Hopkins Street and that Jefferson performed on "the Beat," a nearby strip of black businesses that included a movie theater, cafés, and honky-tonks and apparently was a small-town version of Deep Ellum. According to Charlie Hurd, who was 101 years old and living in a Mexia nursing home in 1993, Jefferson also played in a string band with the Phillips brothers, Wash, Tim, and Doc. This Wash Phillips may have been Washington Phillips, who recorded in Dallas in the late 1920s, singing religious songs and accompanying himself on a small, autoharp-like instrument.[11]

In his teens, Jefferson also began spending time in Dallas. Sam Charters, who interviewed Jefferson's family members and friends in the 1950s, said that Jefferson "wrestled for money in Dallas theatres. Since he was blind, he could be billed as a novelty wrestler. He weighed nearly 250 pounds, so he was never hurt, but it was a rough way to make a living. As soon as he started making a little money singing, he left the theatres."[12]

About 1912 Jefferson met Huddie Ledbetter, better known as Lead Belly, in the Deep Ellum area of Dallas, and over the next few years the two became friends. Huddie Ledbetter was born in 1889 on the Louisiana side of Caddo Lake, which spans the Texas-Louisiana border. His wild and reckless youth in that frontier country foreshadowed the trouble that would keep him in prison for much of his life. His musical talent was evident early, too. Lead Belly first played a small concertina called a windjammer. He soon learned other instruments, including guitar, and played for country dances, or "sukey jumps." All his music had a strong, pulsing rhythm that reflected this background.[13]

Lead Belly married in Kaufman County, Texas, east of Dallas, in 1908, and it is believed that he and his wife, Lethe, moved to Dallas about two years later. They alternated between doing farmwork in outlying areas and living in the city, where Lead Belly worked as a musician. He said later that in Dallas he heard his first jazz band. In Dallas or a nearby community, Lead Belly discovered the instrument that became his favorite, the twelve-string guitar, at that time associated mostly with Mexican musicians.

Blind Lemon Jefferson, "Sunshine   Blind Lemon Jefferson, "Lonesome
Special," Chicago, October 1927,   House Blues," Chicago, October 1927,
Paramount 12593. Courtesy Documen-   Paramount 12593. Courtesy Documen-
tary Arts.   tary Arts.

In the extensive interviews he gave later, Lead Belly provided various dates for his initial meeting with Jefferson, sometimes placing it as early as 1904. But he mentioned 1912 most consistently, and that seems plausible. Jefferson would then have been eighteen or nineteen years old.[14] The two became musical partners in Dallas and the outlying area. Lead Belly learned much about the blues from Blind Lemon, and Lead Belly had plenty to contribute as a musician and a showman. He was a dancer, too, and he'd often break into a "buck and wing," a kind of flat-footed shuffle, as the two performed on the street and around Union Depot near Central and Elm.

Lead Belly said they were so popular that "the women would come running, Lord have mercy. They'd hug and kiss us so much we could hardly play. He was a blind man, and I used to lead him around. When him and I go in the depot, we'd sit down and talk to one another."[15] Sometimes the two strolled through white neighborhoods "serenading" for tips. They also performed on the Interurban, the electric railroad that ran from Dallas north to Denison and south though Corsicana to Waco. "I'd get Blind Lemon right on," Lead Belly recalled. "We get out two guitars; we just ride ... anything. We wouldn't have to pay no money in them times. We get on the train, the driver takes us anywhere we want to go. Well, we just get on, and the conductor say, 'Boys, sit down. You goin' to play music?' We tell him, 'Yes.'"[16]

Another favorite haunt was Silver City, a wide-open place where Lead Belly said they went by bus. There were several Texas towns named Silver City, and it's not known which one the duo frequented, but the one in Navarro County, not far from Wortham, seems a likely candidate. The partnership broke up about 1915 when Lead Belly left Dallas. In 1918 he was sentenced to prison for murder. The two apparently never saw each other again, though Lead Belly often talked about Blind Lemon after he was released from his second prison term in 1935 and went on to become internationally famous as a folk singer who recorded classics such as "Goodnight, Irene." Lead Belly died in 1949.

It's unclear how much time Jefferson spent in Dallas and whether his wife moved there with him. Musician Sam Price said Jefferson was married to a woman named Roberta and that the musician would play and sing daily around Central and Elm until about ten at night, then walk back to his home in the Prairie, south of downtown Dallas. "He was a bootlegger," Price said, "and when he'd get back home he had such a sensitive ear. He didn't want his wife to drink. Well, when he'd go away, she'd take two or three drinks out of the bottle, and she'd think he wouldn't know it. But he'd take the bottle when he came home and say, 'How you doin', baby? How'd we do today?'

"'Nobody bought no whiskey,' she'd answer.

"Well, he'd take the bottle and shake it," Price said, "and he could hear that there were two or three drinks missing. And what he'd do, he'd beat the hell out of her for that."[17]

It may be that Jefferson traveled back and forth from Dallas to Mexia. His name does not appear in Dallas city directories, although in 1929 and 1930 there is a listing for an Alex Jefferson, farmer, and his wife, Classie, on Beal Street in South Dallas. Jefferson played up and down Central Track outside and in the honky-tonks and cafés. He was often seen around the intersection of Elm and the track. Willard Watson, who later became well known as the folk artist the Texas Kid, recalled seeing him playing at the Tip Top dance hall. Sam Stillman, who worked for years at The Model Tailors in Deep Ellum, said Jefferson bought his clothes there but seldom if ever performed on Elm Street.[18]

Bluesman Sam "Lightnin'" Hopkins first encountered Blind Lemon at a Baptist church picnic in Buffalo, Texas, in 1920. Hopkins, then eight years old, watched Jefferson intently all day, then attempted to play along. Hopkins recalled that Jefferson, displeased, shouted, "Boy, you've got to play it right!"[19] When Jefferson realized that he was talking to a child, though, he had Hopkins hoisted onto a truck so the crowd could watch him play.

Navasota songster Mance Lipscomb told biographer Glen Myers, "When we got to Dallas, we hung around where we could hear Blind Lemon sing and play . . . there were hundreds of people up and down that [Central] Track. So, that's where I got acquainted with him, 1917. He hung out 'round the Track, Deep Ellum. And people started coming in there, from 9:30 until six o'clock that evening, then he would go home because it was getting dark and someone carried him home."[20]

Lipscomb's description of Jefferson is similar to that of others who saw him: "a big, loud songster . . . a big, stout fella . . . and he played dance songs and never did much church song. He had a tin cup wired on the neck of his guitar. And when you pass to give him something, why, he'd thank you. But he would never take no pennies. You could drop a penny in there, and he'd know the sound. He'd take it and throw it away."[21]

Others recalled Jefferson's putting his hat down in the street for contributions rather than using a cup. Several accounts attest to his skill in identifying the money given him. Singer Victoria Spivey, who knew him in Texas, said Jefferson often used the expression "Don't play me cheap" and that he meant what he said. When Blind Lemon was in Atlanta for a recording session, he asked producer Tom Rockwell for a five-dollar advance. As a joke, Rockwell handed him a dollar bill, but Blind Lemon seemed to recognize it and complained. "You could hand him a dozen bills," bluesman Thomas Shaw commented. "He'd tell you just that fast whether it's a five- or a one-dollar bill."[22]

Accounts of Blind Lemon's ability to get around are somewhat contradictory. Any number of other musicians claimed to have led him through the streets when they were young, but others who knew him were astounded by his sense of direction. In an interview with Sam Charters, Lightnin' Hopkins said, "He didn't allow no one to lead him. He say then you call him blind. No, don't call him blind. He never did feel like that. He was born like that."[23] Researcher Mack McCormick said Blind Lemon's sister talked of his independence and said that when she'd visit him in Dallas, he'd show off how well he could get around unaided. It is possible that Blind Lemon suffered from macular degeneration and retained some peripheral vision.[24]

Bluesman T-Bone Walker said that when he was growing up in Dallas, "I used to lead him around, playing and passing the cup, take him from one beer joint to another. I liked hearing him play. He would sing like nobody's

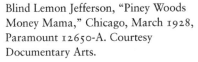

Blind Lemon Jefferson, "Piney Woods Money Mama," Chicago, March 1928, Paramount 12650-A. Courtesy Documentary Arts.

Blind Lemon Jefferson, "Low Down Mojo Blues," Chicago, June 1928, Paramount 12650-B. Courtesy Documentary Arts.

business. He was a friend of my father's. People used to crowd around him so you couldn't see him."[25]

Walker was born in 1910 in Linden, Texas. His nickname derived from his mother's pet name for him, "T-Bow," from his middle name, Thibeaux. When he was two, he moved with his mother to Dallas and lived there and in Fort Worth until 1933, when he joined the black migration to Southern California. In 1929 he made his first recordings, "Trinity River Blues" and "Wichita Falls Blues," under the name "Oak Cliff T-Bone," accompanied by Doug Finnell on piano. On those early recordings, Walker's playing reveals the clear influence of Blind Lemon Jefferson.

Josh White, a singer who spent much of his childhood as a lead boy for blind beggars, told blues historian Paul Oliver that he took Blind Lemon into the streets around noon, when the crowds were thickest, and that sometimes he accompanied Jefferson with a tambourine, tapping a loud rhythm on his knee to draw a good crowd. Then he would turn the tambourine over and cry, "Help the blind, help the blind."[26] James Thibodeaux, a Dallas photographer and painter, substantiated that and remembered seeing Jefferson and White walking together on Thomas Avenue in North Dallas. Perhaps Blind Lemon used a lead boy at some times, particularly when he was in unfamiliar surroundings, and not at others. Some of those who claimed to have led him could be embellishing their own stories. Or perhaps the stories are true, and Blind Lemon simply liked the company or enjoyed serving as a mentor to younger musicians.

Jefferson's ramblings often took him by the shine parlor and record shop operated by R. T. Ashford (1883–1976) near the corner of Elm Street and Central Avenue. The February 1925 *Negro Business Bulletin* lists the business as the R. T. Ashford Record Shop, located at 409 Central Avenue. However, Ashford's daughter Lurline Holland (1910–1999) maintained that her father started the first black shining parlor at 408 North Central in Dallas as early as 1920, that he had "sixteen chairs, one for each man," and that it became the "first black record shop" with "all the black and white artists—mostly black blues singers—the records, Columbia, Paramount, OKeh—the singers were Ethel Waters, Bessie Smith, Ida Cox, and Sara Martin. In the music shop were three soundproof rooms—called booths or cubicles—to play on the Victrola before buying the records. Two or three people could sit in and hear. They always bought three or more records, at the cost of seventy-five cents each. These were people who worked and got their pay weekly—professionals got paid by the month and bought one [record] every once in a while."[27]

Sam Price said that he worked at Ashford's and told his boss the singer should be recorded; others have questioned that claim. At any rate, Ashford talked to Paramount Records about the singer, and the Wisconsin-based company invited Jefferson to make race records in Chicago. Ashford accompanied him on his first trip, in 1925. Holland recalled that her father "would carry people [Blind Lemon and others] with talent on the train to Chicago to audition."

When commercial recording scouts came to Texas, they discovered that field recordings usually posed a variety of technical problems. Portable equipment was large and unwieldy, and sound engineering and acoustics were hard to control. In some areas in the South, carbon microphones, introduced in 1925, had to be kept on ice because hot weather and humidity made them crackle. In addition to technical problems, suitable locations were difficult to find. According to historian Samuel Charters, "During one company's trip to Dallas, they first tried to rent a room in a hotel but were refused: The management would not allow blacks on the premises. Next they tried setting up in a church, but that led to a near riot when the congregation found out what kind of music they were performing and the gear had to be scrambled out the back door. The next day they tried their luck in a roller-skating rink. It was the noisiest damn place in the world, and when drunken skaters started brawling with the musicians and forcing the engineers up against the wall at knifepoint it was clearly time to move on again. They eventually used a banquet hall."[28]

In the 1920s and 1930s, after Blind Lemon's initial success, numerous commercial blues recording sessions were held in Dallas in various downtown locations. The exact sites, however, remain unknown, except for 508 Park Avenue, where Robert Johnson recorded in 1937. Jefferson, who was the most successful blues performer to come from Dallas, apparently never recorded in the city, though an unverified story has it that an early session took place in the rug department of a furniture store. Jefferson was taken instead to Chicago, where studio facilities were available.

His first recordings, though not the first released, were "Old Rounder's Blues" and "Beggin' Back." Later in 1925 or the following year he also recorded, under the pseudonym Deacon L. J. Bates, the spiritual songs "I Want to Be like Jesus in My Heart" and "All I Want Is That Pure Religion." In February 1926 Jefferson recorded "Got the Blues," followed in May by "Long Lonesome Blues," which became his first national hit. Other gospel material was released under the pseudonyms Elder J. C. Brown and Deacon Jackson. All his recordings were made for Paramount except for eight songs recorded for OKeh in Atlanta in March 1927, only two of which were released.

Many of the songs that Blind Lemon recorded were personalized versions of traditional folk blues from East Texas and utilized proverbs and other elements of African American folk speech. These songs included "Jack O' Diamonds Blues," about the perils of gambling; a rendition of "Two Horses Standing in a Line," which he renamed "See That My Grave Is Kept Clean"; "See, See Rider," which he transformed into "Corinna Blues"; and "Boll Weevil Blues," a legendary song about the creature that devastated the cotton fields of his homeland.

In his songs, Blind Lemon identified himself with the experiences of his audience—suffering and hope, economic anxiety and failure, the breakup of the family and the desire to escape through wandering, love, and sex. In "Shuckin' Sugar Blues," he sang:

> I've got your picture, and I'm goin' to put it in a frame
> I've got your picture and put it in a frame, shuckin' sugar,
> Then if you leave town I can find you just the same.

In "Sunshine Special," though, his attitude toward travel was less opti-
mistic:

> Gonna leave on the Sunshine Special,
> gonna leave on the Santa Fe
> Leave on the Sunshine Special,
> goin' in on the Santa Fe
> Don't say nothin' about that Katy
> because it's taken my brown from me.

In Blind Lemon's songs, travel was a means of achieving freedom and
escape from the burdens of day-to-day life, but wandering also led to sepa-
ration from loved ones and to loneliness. This ambivalence toward "leaving" and "settling down" was a common theme in his music and was rein-
forced in one of his best-known songs, "Matchbox Blues":

> I'm sitting here wonderin' will a matchbox hold my clothes
> I'm sitting here wonderin' will a matchbox hold my clothes
> I ain't got so many matches, but I got so far to go.

Here again, the advantages of traveling outweighed the pleasures of "settling down," though the message was not completely despairing. Jefferson's
music expressed the emotions many African Americans of his generation
must have felt, especially those who were leaving the rural towns of East
Texas and moving to the city of Dallas looking for work and a place to live.

Humor was a very important element in Blind Lemon's blues, and it was
expounded with a wry irony and an almost blustery exuberance about sexuality and sexual relations. In "Baker Shop Blues," he declared,

> I'm crazy about my light bread and my pig meat on the side
> I say I'm crazy about my light bread with my pig meat on the side
> But if I taste your jellyroll, I'll be satisfied
> I want to know if your jellyroll is fresh
> I want to know if your jellyroll's stale
> I want to know if your jellyroll is fresh,
> I want to know if your jellyroll's stale
> I'm gonna haul off and buy me some if I have to break it loose in jail.

Overt sexual references were often combined with humorous metaphors and analogies. In "Oil Well Blues," he underscored his own sexuality with an almost self-mocking tone:

> Ain't nothin' to hurt you, sugar, ain't nothin' bad
> Ain't nothin' to hurt you, honey, ain't nothin' bad
> It's the first oil well that your little boy ever had.

In "That Black Snake Moan," Blind Lemon was even more obvious about his sexual allusions and accentuated his lascivious sense of humor:

> Mmmm-m, black snake crawlin' in my room
> Mmmm-m, black snake crawlin' in my room
> Some pretty mama better come and get this black snake soon.

In "That Black Snake Moan, No. 2," he reiterated his desires with greater emphasis:

> I woke up this morning, black snake was makin' such a ruckus in my
>   room
> Black snake is evil, black snake is all I see
> Black snake is evil, black snake is all I see
> I woke up this morning, black snake was moved in on me.

In contrast to this sexual humor was Blind Lemon's ambivalent attitude toward women. In some of his songs they were called "good gal," "sugar," "baby," "honey," and "high brown," but in others they were scorned as "wild," "dirty mistreaters," and "deceitful."

In "Elder Green," Blind Lemon expressed his attraction for his woman with enthusiasm:

> I've got a high brown, and she's long and tall
> Lord, Lord, Lord, she'll make a panther squall.

But in "Got the Blues," he was both intrigued and repulsed by his "good gal":

You can't ever tell what a woman's got on her mind
Man, you can't ever tell what a women's got on her mind
You might think she's crazy about you; she's leaving you all the time.

In "Piney Woods Money Mama," his antagonism was directed toward a woman's scheming mother:

Lord, heavy-hip mama, she's done moved to this piney wood.
Heavy-hip mama, she done moved to this piney wood
She's a high-steppin' woman, she don't mean no man no good.
She got ways like the devil and hair like an Indian squaw.
She got ways like the devil and hair like an Indian squaw.
She's been tryin' two years to get me to be her son-in-law.

In general, the women in Blind Lemon's songs were revered for their sexuality and allure but condemned for their unrequited love and manipulative personalities. In "Pneumonia Blues," he held his women responsible for his illness; in "Prison Cell Blues," for his incarceration; in "Deceitful Brownskin Blues," for robbing him; and in "Peach Orchard Mama," for cheating on him. The details of Blind Lemon's actual relationships with women and his family life are sketchy. Sam Price said he and Roberta had a child soon after they married in the 1920s. The reference book *Blues Who's Who,* citing a 1970 booklet called "Blind Lemon Jefferson" by Bob Groom, says Blind Lemon and Roberta had a son named Miles, who was a musician. However, Theaul Howard, Hobart Carter, and others who knew Jefferson said he had no children.

By casting women into such a wide range of roles in his songs, Blind Lemon was able to more fully identify with the experiences of his audience, an identification that carried over into other areas of life and suffering. In "Mosquito Moan," he recounted the displeasures caused by a common insect but retained his sense of humor:

Now I'm sittin' in my kitchen, mosquitoes all around my screen
Now I'm sittin' in my kitchen, mosquitoes all around my screen
If I don't arrange to get a mosquito bomb,
I'll be seldom seen.

Blind Lemon's songs also talked of many of the pests and animals found in East Texas farming communities, including mules, cows, horses, snakes, and rabbits. These references conveyed a sense of time and place, but animals also served as references to travel, sexuality, and despair. In "One Dime Blues," "Broke and Hungry," and "Tin Cup Blues," Blind Lemon commented poignantly on the poverty and oppression rampant among African Americans. In "Tin Cup Blues" he lamented:

> I stood on the corner and almost bust my head.
> I stood on the corner, almost bust my head.
> I couldn't earn enough to buy me a loaf of bread.
> My gal's a housemaid, and she earns a dollar a week.
> I'm so hungry on payday, I can hardly speak.
> Now gather round me people, let me tell you a true fact.
> I said gather round me people, let me tell you a true fact.
> That tough luck has struck me, and the rats is sleepin' in my hat.

In addition to the personal hardships of his audience, Blind Lemon sang about the ravages of natural disaster in "Rising High Water Blues" and about the injustices of the criminal-justice system in his songs about prison life, though there is no record that he actually spent time in jail. In "Hangman's Blues" Blind Lemon demonstrated his ability to project himself into another man's hopelessness:

> Well, mean old hangman is waitin' to tighten up that noose.
> I have a mean old hangman waitin' to tighten up that noose.
> Lord, I'm so scared I am tremblin' in my shoes.
> Jury heard my case and said my hands was red.
> Jury heard my case and said my hands was red.
> And judge he sentenced me to be hangin' till I'm dead.
> The crowd is around the courthouse, and time is goin' fast.
> And the crowd is around the courthouse and time is goin' fast.
> Soon a good for nothin' killer is goin' to breathe his last.

Blind Lemon recorded two versions of this song. The first was more dramatic, with a fast, pulsating guitar accompaniment that simulated the rapid heartbeat of the convicted man. In "Hangman's Blues," as well as in "Prison Cell Blues," "'Lectric Chair Blues," "Lockstep Blues," and "Blind Lemon's Penitentiary Blues," he depicted jail life as grim and cruel and criticized the unfairness of the court system. The bluesman's songs about prison and the longing for freedom were not his most popular, but they nonetheless reflected the social conditions of the times and expressed themes that were vital to the country blues tradition.

During the zenith of his brief recording career, between 1926 and 1928, Blind Lemon often commuted between Dallas and Chicago, where he had a South Side "kitchenette" at 37th and Rhodes. But he continued to travel around Texas and to other states, including Oklahoma, Georgia, and Mississippi. Mississippi Delta bluesman Houston Stackhouse remembered seeing Jefferson in his hometown. "He came to Crystal Springs and was playin' in some little show for a doctor. . . . They had it in Freetown, there at the colored school. There was plenty of people there. It was a big school and crowded all indoors, people couldn't get to see him. They had to bring him out to the front, on the porch."[29]

Blind Lemon's producer for Paramount, Mayo Williams, who was African American himself, marveled at the appeal of his songs. In appreciation of Blind Lemon's earning power, Williams bought him a $725 Ford, and the singer hired a chauffeur to drive it for him. Blind Lemon also owned a 1923 or '24 Dodge, which he mentioned in his performances of "D. B. Blues." According to Hobart Carter, Lemon's chauffeur was a man named Papa Sollie, who came from Mexia. "People would come from everywhere to hear Blind Lemon sing. If they put that money there heavy, he'd sing heavy, but if the money was light, he'd tell Papa Sollie they got to leave from there."[30]

Quince Cox remembered another (or perhaps the same) chauffeur with the nickname of Stingaree, also from Mexia, who apparently died before Lemon did. It is likely that Lemon, given his frequent travel, had more than one chauffeur and depended on a number of people for transportation and other services. Mayo Williams said that Jefferson's royalties accumulated so quickly that he was encouraged to open a savings account, which reached a balance of $1,500. For a black performer to receive royalties at all was extraordinary for the time. In an interview with Stephen Calt, Williams called Jefferson "a soul singer, naturally," but he doubted that Blind Lemon could have originated all of his song themes. "He was just as cool and calm and collected as any artist I've ever seen," Williams said.[31]

Blind Lemon's guitar style and singing were distinctive. His vocal range was unusual, too, comfortably spanning two octaves. He knew how to play slide guitar but did so on only one record, "Jack O' Diamond Blues." He recorded seventy-one blues, five spirituals, and two ragtime pieces.[32]

Jefferson made extensive use of single-note runs, often apparently picked with his thumb, and played in a variety of keys and tunings, including open G, banjo tuning. He held the guitar almost perpendicular to his chest, which some have attributed to his girth. Musicologist David Evans, however, thinks it had to do more with Jefferson's style of playing and notes that the position was favored by two electric guitarists much influenced by Jefferson: T-Bone Walker and Charlie Christian. Jefferson, like other blues players, relied on a stock of musical figures, or "licks," but could also improvise, brilliantly at times. Moreover, his rhythmic sense was fluid, even quirky, making him difficult to emulate. As Evans says, "He knew how to 'whip' the guitar, push the beat, and accelerate the tempo. At times the underlying pulse is implied but not stated on the guitar or is kept by Lemon's foot patting."[33]

Some other blues musicians have criticized Jefferson for breaking time, but Evans feels that this was a conscious technique rather than a failing. Some of Jefferson's songs, he writes, "are highly rhythmic and seem to be dance-related. In others, Jefferson breaks time or displays a flexible approach to tempo. It seems quite clear that he wanted at least some of his blues, if not all, to be listened to with careful attention."[34] Among Jefferson's fans is the legendary B. B. King, who has called him "majestic" and has said, "It was unbelievable to hear him play. And the way he played with his rhythm patterns, he was way ahead of his time."[35]

As Evans points out, Jefferson made use of harmonic substitutions and other devices that were unusual for a solo blues guitarist of his time, including long, sustained notes, extreme string bending, and tremolo passages like those used by mandolin players. Evans writes, "Although Jefferson may have been the first to adapt many of these ideas successfully to solo guitar for accompanying blues singing, most of them were around already in the lead lines and solos of jazz horn players and in ragtime, jazz, and blues piano playing,"[36] influences that Jefferson may well have been exposed to through live or recorded performances. Many of the innovations credited to Robert Johnson in his 1936 and 1937 recordings, Evans and others feel, should rightly be attributed to Jefferson.

Some have seen a decline in Jefferson's performance late in his recording career, but Evans disagrees, pointing out that Jefferson seems to have concentrated increasingly on being a composer and conveying the message of his songs. His early recordings between 1925 and 1927 were heavily rooted in the folk blues tradition, incorporating lyrics and verses that were then in circulation. By 1928 and 1929 Jefferson was clearly more aware of recordings that were being made at that time. Starting in 1927, several of his records featured piano accompaniment, including "How Long, How Long," which echoed elements of Leroy Carr's popular "How Long, How Long Blues." Overall, by this stage in his career, Jefferson appears to have consciously made his lyrics less derivative, and his songs demonstrated more thematic development and internal consistency.

Evans and Luigi Monge have examined written versions of several Jefferson songs that were either unissued or never recorded. One of these, "I Labor So Far from Home," is a reworking of the traditional English folk song "Our Goodman," which was recorded by Coley Jones as "Drunkard's Special." Their extensive analysis of documents in the Library of Congress found a recurrent theme of "violent attacks and outbursts, either suffered or perpetrated by the blind singer. Another is the theme of blindness itself. As explained in an earlier article by Monge, the many cryptic references in Jefferson's lyrics unveil a psychological preoccupation with his blindness and constitute the sub-theme underlying the whole of his lyrical output."[37]

No one knows what would have happened to Blind Lemon Jefferson's career if he had lived. But in late 1929 he died in Chicago. The circumstances and even the date of his death are unclear. No official record has been found, and the oral accounts are contradictory. Arthur Laibly, who had succeeded Williams as Blind Lemon's producer, said the singer died of a heart attack—based on a report from Laibly's office assistant. Laibly heard that Blind Lemon died during a blizzard, an account reiterated by Williams, who added that the singer had collapsed in his car and had been abandoned by his chauffeur. According to other accounts, someone failed to pick Blind Lemon up at the train station, and he tried to walk to his hotel and froze after losing his way in the snow, which disoriented him by muffling sounds.

The *Wortham Journal* of Friday, January 3, 1930, reported, in an article headlined "Lemon Jefferson Dies in Chicago," that "Lemon Jefferson, 45, a blind Negro who was reared in Wortham and the community died of heart failure in Chicago and was shipped to Wortham for burial, arriving here on Christmas Eve."

When asked about the funeral, Quince Cox, then working as Wortham cemetery caretaker, was quick to reply. "Anyone over the age of sixty remembers that day well," he said in a hoarse voice. "They brought his body back to Texas by train. People said he died in the snow after a recording session in Chicago, that he was lost, couldn't find his way. Some thought it was foul play. Two or three hundred people came to the funeral, black and white, to watch his coffin lowered into the ground."[38]

Hobart Carter added that when the body arrived from Chicago, it was picked up at the station by somebody with a wagon and team. "Then they went straight to the funeral. The preacher was Uncle Warren Smith. Old Man Warren Smith. He was a Baptist. It was cold. Coldest weather we had.

R. T. X [Ashford] (right), San Francisco, California, ca. mid-1960s. Courtesy of Lurline Holland. Ashford left Dallas ca. 1938 and later became a miniser of Islam.

Zero." Carter recalled that Blind Lemon's parents did not attend their son's funeral and that there were only "three or four" Jeffersons in attendance. Many of the people were strangers, and because of the cold temperature, the funeral service was relatively brief. When asked about his understanding of the circumstances of Jefferson's death, Carter said, "He died in Chicago on the coldest night they had up there. He wanted to run around with some folks up there and got amongst the wrong bunch."[39]

Six months after Blind Lemon's death, Paramount attempted to capitalize on his tragic misfortune by issuing six posthumous records. The last was a sermon by the Rev. Emmet Dickenson, called "The Death of Blind Lemon," which compared the singer to Jesus Christ. The sermon did little to explain the reality of Blind Lemon's life and death.[40] But it was testimony to the magnitude of his career and its importance in African American culture.

Blind Lemon Jefferson's death marked the end of the riotous 1920s, a time when the commercial possibilities of African American popular music were first exploited. His art also looked forward. As an early recording artist, he was an influence on other performers and writers. He taught Lead Belly much about the blues and apparently introduced him to the slide

VISITING MOSLEM MINISTERS—Nine visiting ministers from established Temples of Islam represent eight large metropolitan areas of the East at the annual Moslem convention, held at Muhammad's Temple of Islam, Fifty-third and Greenwood Avenue, in Chicago. Ministers on the rostrum showing great concern of D. C. Minister Lucius X's talk at the Saturday session are, left to right: Asbury X of Cincinnati; George X. Philadelphia; Isaiah X, Baltimore; R. T. X, Chicago; Malcolm X, New York City; Ulysses X, Boston, and William X of Detroit.—Beatty Photo.

Newspaper clipping. From left to right: Lucius X, Asbury X, George X, Isaiah X, R. T. X [Ashford], Malcolm X, Ulysses X, and William X, ca. early 1960s.

guitar. The line "I walked all the way from Dallas to Wichita Falls," from Jefferson's "Long Lonesome Blues," has appeared in the repertoire of countless blues singers. A verse of "Black Horse Blues" turned up in slightly altered form in Mississippi singer Charley Patton's "Pony Blues": "Got to get on my black horse and saddle up my gray mare." His line "Well, the train I ride is eighteen coaches long" became the basis for Little Junior Parker's "Mystery Train," later recorded by Elvis Presley. There's also another Elvis connection, a line from Jefferson's "Teddy Bear Blues": "Say, fair brown, let me be your teddy bear / Tie a string on my neck, I'll follow you everywhere." Robert Johnson apparently borrowed from Jefferson's "Change My Luck Blues" in his "Walking Blues": "She got Elgin movements from her head down to her toes / And she can break in on a dollar anywhere she goes." In 1941 Joe Turner made a successful record of Jefferson's "Peach Orchard Mama." Jefferson's "Jack O' Diamond Blues" became a hit for Lonnie Donnegan during the 1950s skiffle craze in England. And, of course, "Matchbox Blues" was the basis of hits for both rockabilly pioneer Carl Perkins and the Beatles.

Relatively speaking, however, few of Jefferson's songs have been covered by other musicians. This may have been due in part to the poor fidelity of his records and the ensuing difficulties in transcription. Where Jefferson's influence is most profound is in the development of the modern electric guitar sound introduced by T-Bone Walker, who, in turn, had a powerful influence

Cover, *Jefferson* magazine, no. 100 (Summer 1993).

Blind Lemon Jefferson cartoon, *Jefferson* magazine, no. 100 (Summer 1993; see translation on p. 105).

on the jazz and blues musicians after him. Walker, Evans says, "was too much of an innovative artist himself to copy directly: but at a more general level, the influence of Jefferson on Walker is pervasive. Walker's guitar playing, always within an ensemble, and always within a twelve-bar blues setting or some other standard popular song structure, is shot through with string bending, long, dazzling, improvised staccato melody lines, and a flexible approach to rhythm. These are precisely the same characteristics that were so innovative in Jefferson's earlier solo playing, characteristics that were harnessed and then developed by Walker for use in more standardized song structures backed by an ensemble."[41]

Today, more than a century after his birth, Blind Lemon Jefferson lies buried in the black section of the sprawling Wortham cemetery. A state historical plaque erected in 1965 marks the burial place, which is flat and windswept, an eerie fulfillment of his plea, "See that my grave is kept clean." The town began a blues festival named for the singer in 1997 and erected a new headstone. Soon thereafter, what had once been referred to as "the Negro burying ground" was renamed the Blind Lemon Memorial Cemetery.

In his adopted city, Dallas, he is still relatively unknown, though he is the subject of a musical originally called *Blind Lemon: Prince of Country Blues,* which was presented in workshops and in a full production at the Addison WaterTower Theatre in 2001. This show became the basis of another musical, *Blind Lemon Blues,* which has been staged locally and in two off-Broadway productions at the York Theatre, in addition to touring extensively in Europe.[42]

For years, a caricature of Jefferson appeared each month on the inside back cover of a Swedish blues magazine called *Jefferson.* The singer is in the same characteristic pose as his publicity photo—but instead of wearing a suit and tie, he is depicted in a Hawaiian-style shirt. In each issue, the editor put new words in Swedish in the singer's mouth: "Can I change my shirt now? Is the world ready for me yet?"

The Contemporaries of
Blind Lemon

As a result of the success of Blind Lemon Jefferson, blues guitarists from around Texas and elsewhere in the South came
to Dallas in the late 1920s and early 1930s looking for work.
Undoubtedly, these musicians were influenced by Jefferson, but given the
transient nature of many blues singers of this generation, it is difficult to
assess the extent of any direct parallels in the music of those who recorded
after him. Clearly, Jefferson was most influential in the way he established
the commercial viability of downhome blues, and it was the potential for
financial success that attracted other musicians to Dallas.

Jesse Thomas and Willard "Ramblin'" Thomas, Alger "Texas" Alexander,
J. T. "Funny Papa" (or "Funny Paper") Smith, Gene Campbell, Carl Davis,
Bo Jones, Willie Reed, Coley Jones, and George "Little Hat" Jones all
played in the areas of Central Track, Deep Ellum, Freedmantown, and South
Dallas. Jesse Thomas came to Dallas in 1928, following his brother, Willard
"Ramblin' " Thomas, from Logansport, Louisiana (near where Lead Belly
was from), where they both were born (Jesse in 1911 and Willard in 1902).
In an interview with Bruce Nixon, Jesse recalled that when he was young
he didn't sing blues because he was "raised where the blues was all around.
People were singing in the fields, day and night. I thought it was something
lonesome and sad, not really something I liked. But when I came to Dallas, I
saw that people enjoyed them, and then I liked them better. I saw that there
was more to them than just a sad story."[1]

In Dallas, Jesse lived with his brother on Flora Street off Hall Street and
eked out a living playing on the street and at house parties. On summer eve-
nings he sometimes put together a small string band and went from house to
house in the Highland Park suburb of the city playing the popular songs of
the day (such as "Shine on, Harvest Moon" and "Meet Me in Dreamland")
to entertain the wealthy white families who sat on their front porches as the

sun went down. At house parties Jesse said, "We'd get paid a small salary to play. I carried that little wooden box [the guitar] everywhere I went. If you weren't hired, you'd just go visiting, take up a collection. People would tip you to play a certain tune. But the cost of living was so low, you could get by. A house was a dollar-and-a-half a week to rent, and if you were playing, you'd get meals and drinks practically for free everywhere you went."[2]

Willard Thomas was considered a more accomplished blues performer than his brother at that time. Willard had met Blind Lemon in Deep Ellum, and they reportedly played together. Evidence of this association, historian Bob Groom points out, can be heard in Thomas's "No Baby Blues," which incorporates a Jefferson-like guitar line.[3] Moreover, it was probably through Jefferson and R. T. Ashford that Thomas was able to get a recording contract from the Paramount label, which sent him to Chicago in February 1928 to record eight sides. Later that year, in November, Thomas was invited back to Chicago to record six more sides, including his song "Hard Dallas Blues," in which he warns his listeners:

Man, don't never make Dallas your home.
When you look for your friends, they will all be gone.

In February 1932 the Victor company recorded Willard Thomas in Dallas, and four songs were released, two of which were versions of his "Ground Hog Blues." After these sessions, Ramblin' Thomas moved on, and Jesse heard little of him until he died of tuberculosis in Memphis in 1935.

Through Ashford, Jesse Thomas was given an audition by Paramount around 1928, but he wasn't recorded until the following year, when Victor offered him a contract. On these four recordings he was identified as Jesse "Babyface" Thomas and was an accompanist on two Bessie Tucker titles, "Better Boot That Thing" and "Katy Blues."

Gene Campbell was a blues guitarist and singer who was a contemporary of the Thomas brothers, but the biographical details of his life are not as well documented as theirs.[4] In his song "Western Plain Blues," he says that he was "born in Texas, raised in Texas, too," although he never explains where. It is likely, however, that he lived in or near Dallas in 1929 and 1930 because he recorded in field sessions there. Possibly, however, he was an itinerant who happened to travel through Dallas during the time that the recording engineers had already set up their equipment.

In October 1929 an obscure group, Jake Jones and the Gold Front Boys (of unknown origins), recorded two "blues stomps" dance tunes for the

Brunswick label in a Dallas session: "Monkeyin' Around" and "Southern Sea Blues."[5] That same month Sam Price also recorded two sides for Brunswick, "Blue Rhythm Stomp" and "Nasty but Nice," with a band he called his Four Quarters, which featured "Kid Lips" on trumpet, Bert Johnson on trombone, Percy Darensbourg (from New Orleans) on banjo, and Price himself on piano.[6] A year earlier, in December 1928, Darensbourg had recorded on the Columbia label with Frenchy's String Band, which included Sam Harris on guitar and trumpet player Polite "Frenchy" Christian. Clarinetist Jesse Hooker is believed to have been the vocalist.

Discographies establish that the recording activity in Dallas during this period was intense and that the major companies came to the city on an annual basis, frequently during the fall months, when the weather was temperate. In November 1929 Gene Campbell made two sides for the Brunswick label (which had recorded Sam Price a month earlier), and in December Coley Jones, "Oak Cliff T-Bone" (Walker), and Willie Reed recorded for Columbia, and "Bo" Jones, for Vocalion.

Coley Jones lived in Dallas and performed as a solo guitarist and vocalist, as well as with his own string band. His repertoire consisted of blues, dance tunes, and popular songs but also included vaudeville and tent-show numbers such as "Army Mule in No Man's Land" (which is an ironic depiction of blacks in the armed forces) and "The Elder's He's My Man" (which parodies the relations between a minister and his church).[7] "Chasin' Rainbows" and "I Used to Call Her Baby" were turn-of-the-century popular songs, and "Dallas Rag," as its name suggests, was a ragtime tune.

Many talented musicians, such as Ailus Patterson, never recorded. Patterson was born just after the turn of the twentieth century near Brenham, in Central Texas. He showed musical talent early and had a mentor in Thomas Shaw, a friend of Blind Lemon Jefferson. Patterson performed at times at the Big House, a nightspot between Temple and Waco. He was a versatile musician who could play both four- and six-string guitars, mandolin, and bass. Around 1929 he met Coley Jones and his band on the streets of Deep Ellum and performed with them. He was scheduled to record with the band but became ill with smallpox and missed the session. Patterson remained active as a musician, playing around Central Texas with his band, the Five Black Aces, through the early 1960s.[8]

Blues recording activity in Texas tapered off in the early 1930s because of the Great Depression but picked up later in the decade. Gene Campbell recorded four sides for Brunswick in Dallas in November 1930, including "Don't Leave Me Blues," which includes references to Waco, Fort Worth,

Race record ad for "Little Hat" Jones, ca. 1920s. Courtesy Documentary Arts.

and San Antonio and seems to allude to his travels around the state. Kip Lornell has suggested that his "expressive, though easy drawl" was reminiscent of the singing of brothers Willard Thomas and Jesse Thomas, although his "vocal inflections are restricted in range, almost always less than an octave," and "his penchant for descending vocal phrases calls [George] 'Little Hat' Jones to mind."[9]

Like Campbell, Jones was known to perform around Dallas, but he never recorded in the city.[10] Jones was from the San Antonio area and recorded twelve songs there in 1929. He had an idiosyncratic approach to the guitar that is especially evident in his solos in "Cross the Water Blues" and "Hurry Blues." However, some of his repertoire was traditional; his song "Kentucky Blues," for example, is a version of W. C. Handy and Chris Smith's "Long Gone" (1920). Jones is also credited with backing the blues singer Alger "Texas" Alexander on eight songs in a San Antonio session in June 1929. Jesse Thomas remembered Alexander from his days in Dallas and told interviewer Bruce Nixon that Alexander was "always singing with some guitarist or piano player in the black joints around Deep Ellum and South Dallas."[11] Alexander, however, traveled often and recorded regularly mostly in New York, where he was backed by Lonnie Johnson or guitarist Eddie Lang or both.

Another blues guitarist who reportedly played in Dallas during the 1920s and thirties but did not record there was J. T. Smith. Smith called himself "Funny Papa" (though it was misspelled on his records as "Funny Paper") or "Howling Wolf" after the success of his "Howling Wolf Blues." Between September 1930 and April 1935 Smith recorded forty-one songs, only twenty of which were issued at the time.

Very little is known about Smith's birthplace or life, although bluesman Thomas Shaw (who was rediscovered in 1970 and died in 1977) said that Smith was an overseer "at the plantation where he worked" and that he allegedly killed a man in an argument over a woman.[12] Shaw met Smith in late 1930 in a small town in the southwest corner of Oklahoma, and thereafter they played regularly together for weekend dances until Smith was arrested for murder.

Musically, Shaw said that "Wolf wasn't too great of a guitar player"[13] because his guitar seemed to always be out of tune, even on his recordings. Yet, his stylistic approach was similar to that of many of the Texas guitarists of his generation, and in some ways he was more sophisticated. "While he often used the same steady, non-alternating thumb basic to Texas blues," record producers Stephen Calt, Woody Mann, and Nick Perls

Race record ad for Henry "Ragtime Texas" Thomas, ca. late 1920s. Courtesy Documentary Arts.

Alius Patterson, ca. 1940. Courtesy of Danny Williams.

Aaron "T-Bone" Walker, assistant to Dr. Breeding's Medicine Show, mid-1920s. Courtesy of Helen Oakley Dance.

indicate in their notes to one of Smith's reissue albums, "he also used alternating thumb picking. The various thumb rolls, rapid thumb runs (as on 'Hungry Wolf') and double-timed notes produced by the thumb gave his work much rhythmic variation. When using a regular thumb bass, he had the unusual tendency to accentuate the first beat of each measure rather than play the more standard four or five basically equal beats per measure."[14] Smith's lyrics were often unconventional and reflected upon his travel and personal experience. His song "Seven Sisters Blues," like "Howling Wolf Blues," is divided into two parts; the first recounts an anticipated visit to a conjurer in New Orleans, and the second looks at the visit in retrospect.

> *Part One*
> They tell me Seven Sisters in New Orleans,
> that can really fix a man up right.
> And I'm headed for New Orleans, Louisiana,
> I'm travelin' both day and night.
> *Part Two*
> I went to New Orleans, Louisiana,
> just on account of something I heard.
> The Seven Sisters told me everything I wanted to know
> and they wouldn't let me speak a word.

In "Fool's Blues" he begins by admitting his weakness ("You know, I'm a single-handed fool, and getting old, too"), but later he assumes a more bitter tone:

> This musta been the devil I'm serving,
> it can't be Jesus Christ
> 'Cause I asked him to save me
> and look like he tryin' to take my life.

Overall, Smith's life and career typified those of the blues guitarists of his generation who traveled in and around the Dallas area. Although these performers were influenced to varying degrees by the guitar style of Blind Lemon Jefferson, they nonetheless displayed their own idiosyncrasies, combined with other regional variations. Babe Kyro Lemon Turner, nicknamed the "Black Ace," and Oscar "Buddy" Woods, for example, liked to tune their guitars to an open chord (often a D major), placing the instruments in their laps and then using a bottleneck or slide to fret them.[15] This style

Race record ad for Texas Alexander, "Blue Devil Blues," OKeh Records 8640. Courtesy of Documentary Arts.

of playing was used as early as the late 1800s and early 1900s but gained widespread popularity due to the influence of Hawaiian music during the teens of the twentieth century.

Turner was born in 1907 in Hughes Springs, in East Texas; in the early 1930s he moved to Shreveport, where he met and later teamed up with Woods. By 1936 they both had moved to Fort Worth, where they worked as musicians in local nightspots and were featured in live broadcasts over KFJZ from 1936 to 1941 (when Turner appeared in the all-black film *The Blood of Jesus*).[16]

Woods and Turner, however, never recorded together. Woods had recorded first in Memphis in May and November 1930 in a band that featured him and Ed Schaffer on twin slide guitars, accompanied by kazoo and with Schaffer and the white singer Jimmie Davis on vocals. Two years later

Race record ad for Henry "Ragtime Texas" Thomas, "Texas Easy Street Blues," Vocalion Records 1197. Courtesy of Documentary Arts.

Texas Alexander, ca. late 1920s. Courtesy of Documentary Arts.

Davis arranged another session at the Jefferson Hotel in Dallas, and Schaffer and Woods accompanied him on four sides. Davis, at that time, was a struggling hillbilly singer who favored the yodeling of Jimmie Rodgers and the blues he had heard among blacks when he was growing up in Louisiana. Later in life, Davis claimed authorship of "You Are My Sunshine" and was twice elected governor of Louisiana.

Turner's early efforts at recording were not as successful as those of Woods. His first sides, made in an ARC field session in April 1936, were never issued, although he was invited to record six sides for the Decca label in Chicago in February 1937. On these recordings, including "Trifling Woman," "You Gonna Need My Help Some Day," and "Christmas Time Blues," Turner was accompanied by guitarist Andrew "Smokey" Hogg.

The recording scouts of the day searched for virtuosity in performance and attempted to record as many different styles of blues as possible in their search for commercial success in the "race" market.[17] Consequently, there is little homogeneity in the recordings made during this period. Some guitarists, like the obscure Sammy Hill, Otis Harris, and Bo Jones, were given an opportunity to record two sides each but were never invited back; others, such as Willie Reed and Carl Davis, were recorded as solo performers and then as accompanists for musicians as varied as "Texas" Alexander and with the Dallas Jamboree Jug Band, which featured a washtub bassist named Shorty and a washboard player named Charles "Chicken" Jackson.

With the exception of T-Bone Walker, the blues musicians who followed Blind Lemon Jefferson never achieved the success that he did. Still, they were afforded recording opportunities that might have been precluded had Jefferson not been discovered. Despite their limited audience, they brought a rich array of musical talent. It is evident that they represented a variety of musical styles, most of which were rooted in East Texas and elsewhere in the South but nonetheless became emblematic of the character of Deep Ellum during its heyday.

Blind Willie Johnson and Arizona Dranes

The "Holy Blues" of Deep Ellum

While blues singers and string bands vied for the attention of passersby on the sidewalks of Deep Ellum, street preachers and religious singers prayed to the Lord and proselytized anyone who might stop to listen. Recording scouts who came to Dallas may have looked hard for musical heirs to Blind Lemon, but they were attracted to African American religious music as well. Contrary to popular belief, there was considerable interaction between blues musicians and religious singers, who were often part of the same community and were sometimes friends or relatives. Moreover, the blues and religious songs drew from similar musical forms, especially evidenced in the use of twelve- and sixteen-bar structures, flatted or "blue" notes, slide guitar, and barrelhouse piano styles.

Deep Ellum's greatest exponent of what has been called "holy blues" was Blind Willie Johnson, who made thirty recordings for the Columbia label between 1927 and 1930. He was born on January 22, 1897, near Brenham, Texas, but as a baby moved with his family to Marlin, a small town about a hundred and twenty miles south of Dallas. Johnson's interest in music began at the age of five, when he told his father he wanted to be a preacher and made his first guitar out of a cigar box. Johnson's widow, Angeline, told music historian Samuel Charters that Willie was blinded at age seven by his stepmother, who threw lye in his face after his father found her with another man.[1] Bluesman Thomas Shaw, however, said that Johnson told him that he had gone blind from wearing a pair of discarded eyeglasses. Another unidentified source, folklorist David Evans wrote, stated that Johnson went blind by watching an eclipse through a piece of glass.[2] In any event, Johnson's father nurtured Willie's interest in being a performer and took him to Marlin, Hearne, and other nearby towns to play on the streets for tips.

Race records ad for Blind Willie Johnson,
ca. 1927. Courtesy of Documentary Arts.

Adam Booker, a minister living in Brenham, remembered that on Saturday afternoons in Marlin, the farm people came to town, and Johnson sang religious songs on one corner while Blind Lemon Jefferson sang blues on another. About Johnson, Booker said, "He was there, you know, he came to see his daddy, and while being there, that being good cotton country, people were all there picking cotton, and they would come on the street every Saturday, and he'd get on the street and sing and pick the guitar, and they would listen and would give him money . . . every Saturday, he wouldn't hardly miss."[3]

Johnson made his first recordings for Columbia on December 3, 1927, in a field session in Dallas, where he was already known as a street singer of religious songs with a tin cup on a wire loop around the neck of his guitar near the tuning pegs. During his first session in Dallas, he recorded six songs, including some of his greatest performances: "I Know His Blood Can Make Me Whole," "Jesus, Make Up My Dying Bed," "It's Nobody's Fault but Mine," "Mother's Children Have a Hard Time," "Dark Was the Night, Cold Was the Ground," and "If I Had My Way I'd Tear the Building Down."

Interestingly enough, Washington Phillips, another religious singer from East Texas, was recorded by Columbia in Dallas on December 2, 1927, and then invited back on December 5. Phillips apparently came from a little town called Simsboro in Freestone County, the county where Blind Lemon Jefferson also lived, and the two may have played together. Charlie Hurd, an elderly resident of Mexia, recalled that Jefferson sometimes played in a string band with three Phillips brothers, Wash, Tim, and Doc. This "Wash" Phillips may have been the same Washington Phillips who recorded in Dallas for Columbia in the late 1920s, accompanying himself on a boxlike instrument similar to a zither or an autoharp. Other older residents around Mexia, interviewed in the 1990s, recalled hearing a Washington Phillips singing religious songs and playing such an instrument, though they didn't know what it was called.

Frank Walker, who directed the field recording unit that recorded both Phillips and Johnson, remarked of Phillips's instrument: "He had no name for it; it was something he made himself. Nobody on earth could use it except him. Nobody would want to, I don't think."[4] Like almost everything else associated with Phillips, however, the origin and nature of the instrument are confusing.

From Phillips's promotional photograph, the instrument looks like a zither with a few dozen strings, which he may have gotten from German immigrants in Central Texas. He plucked and strummed it, accompanying himself much as guitarists did and achieving a similar sound. The instrument may not in fact have been Phillips's creation. Some music historians believe he was playing an obscure instrument that was marketed as a Dolceola. According to the liner notes of a compilation of his recordings, the Dolceola was invented around 1902 by an Ohio piano tuner named David Boyd. According to the notes, Boyd and his brother produced the instrument at a small factory called the Toledo Symphony Company, and Boyd and his wife sold them out of their car throughout the country. After his death, production ceased. The notes describe the Dolceola as consisting of a walnut and cherrywood zither frame and a keyboard that played the strings. Subsequent research has borne out this information.[5] A photograph shows Phillips with two instruments. These may have been Dolceolas that he had modified; the keyboards were easy to remove.

Recent research, however, has cast doubt on the idea that Phillips played the Dolceola, without definitively establishing what instrument he used. Memphis music producer Jim Dickinson, who played a Dolceola on roots-rock musician Ry Cooder's soundtrack to the 1986 movie *Crossroads,* said he was "one hundred percent sure" that this was the instrument Phillips used.[6] Researchers Gregg Miner and Kelly Williams, however, after examining the photos of Phillips holding two instruments, theorize that they were two variants of the fretless "chord group" zither.[7] The question may never be completely resolved.

What is certain is that Phillips recorded eighteen sides in three sessions in Dallas, in December of 1927, 1928, and 1929. About half of his recorded songs were traditional, half original. His most powerful recording, made in the 1927 sessions, was "Denomination Blues," which takes up both sides of a record. A holy blues, as the title suggests, the song lambastes dogmatic Christians and predatory preachers: "Lot of preachers is preaching and think they're doin' well / And all they want is your money, and you can go to hell." He is largely forgotten, though Ry Cooder recorded versions of this song and "You Can't Stop a Tattler" in the 1970s. Other bands, including Austin's Knife in the Water, have also covered Phillips's songs.

Earlier research indicated that Washington Phillips was born in 1891 in Freestone County and died in 1938 in the state mental hospital in Austin. However, Austin music writer Michael Corcoran, based on documents and interviews with surviving relatives and acquaintances, concluded that this was a different Washington Phillips. The musician, Corcoran found, was born in Freestone County on January 11, 1880, and died there on September 20, 1954. As for Charlie Hurd's assertion that Blind Lemon played with Wash, Tim, and Doc Phillips, it is interesting to note that the death certificate found by Corcoran lists the singer's father as Tim Phillips.[8]

Johnson was more extensively recorded than Phillips. With the success of his first records in the popular Columbia 14000 Race series, he was invited back for sessions in Dallas in 1928, in New Orleans in 1929, and in Atlanta in 1930. Despite conflicting accounts about Johnson's early life and the date he married Angeline, it is likely that his first marriage was to another woman named Willie B. Harris, who was found by researcher Dan Williams in Marlin. Harris had vivid memories of Johnson, whom she said she had married in 1926 or 1927. She recalled that Johnson wasn't a preacher but "just a songster" and that he was a member of the Church of God in Christ on Commerce Street in Marlin, where he played both piano and guitar for services and revival meetings.

While Angeline Johnson did not remember traveling with her husband to his recording sessions, Harris recalled that these trips often took longer than the actual days spent in the recording studio. "They come and got him and carried him," she told Williams, "and when they would come and get him it didn't cost nothing to ride. . . . He'd be gone sometime thirty days, something like that, but he wouldn't be over there doing all that much work. He would, you know, just go, and then after he'd go he'd just stay over there and then play on the streets. He loved to play on the streets."[9]

It is likely that Johnson was accompanied by Harris's vocals in his Dallas session of December 5, 1928, when he recorded four songs: "I'm Gonna Run to the City of Refuge," "Jesus Is Coming Soon," "Lord, I Can't Just Keep from Crying," and "Keep Your Lamp Trimmed and Burning."

Blind Willie Johnson Memorial, Beaumont, Texas. Courtesy of Shane Ford and Anna Obek

Johnson often used open tunings, especially open D, and played his guitar with a slide; according to bluesman Blind Willie McTell, Johnson used a steel ring as a slide. When playing slide, he often hammered at the bass strings with his thumb, yielding "an insistent, chugging bass sound" similar to that employed by Blind Lemon Jefferson, Lead Belly, and other blues musicians and songsters. He often sang in a rough bass voice with

Blind Willie Johnson, "I Know His
Blood Can Make Me Whole," Columbia
14276-D. Courtesy of Documentary Arts.

Washington Phillips, "Take Your Burden
to the Lord and Leave It There," Columbia
14277-D. Courtesy of Documentary Arts.

which Harris harmonized beautifully. Johnson's recordings sold well and
were released as late as 1935, though he made his last records at the April
1930 Atlanta session.

After the Depression ended his recording career, Johnson moved with his
wife to Beaumont, Texas, where he continued playing on the streets and in
churches, sometimes venturing about ninety miles west to Houston to play
for larger religious gatherings. He died in 1945 of malarial fever, with syphi-
lis and blindness as contributing factors, according to a death certificate
cited by Corcoran[10] (who rightly questions the accuracy of the document).
Though Johnson has never become a household name, his music has been
covered by contemporary musicians, including Bob Dylan, Eric Clapton, the
Grateful Dead, the Staple Singers, and Led Zeppelin. His own recording of
"Dark Was the Night, Cold Was the Ground" was included on *Sounds of
Earth,* an album that went into space aboard *Voyager* 1 in 1977. In December 2010, a Texas Historical Marker was dedicated at Pilgrim's Rest Baptist
Church in Beaumont, at the site of Johnson's last residence and his House
of Prayer, and a privately funded monument was placed at the nearby cemetery, where the musician is believed to have been buried. The Museum of
the Gulf Coast's Music Hall of Fame in Port Arthur has recognized him as a
music legend.

Religious music continued to be a presence on the streets of Deep Ellum after the recording stopped. Taxi driver and dispatcher Julius Walker, who came to Dallas from East Texas in the 1920s, remembered the music made by the followers of a Reverend Stevenson. The minister, Walker said, "stayed out there long enough and got enough money. He built him a church. He'd have six or seven singing (accompanied by a tambourine and a drum), and, boy, I'm telling you, they'd have themselves a time. They were out there every day and every night."[11]

Moreover, pawnbroker Label Feldman recalled, "Saturday, or sometimes in the middle of the week, some black preacher would come and get right in the middle of the Cenetral Track and start preaching. And you could hear them from pretty far away. Everybody would come running. All the blacks would come and listen to the preacher, you see. And on some days, those Holy Roller women would join in and start singing."[12]

Rocky Goldstein had a similar recollection: "There were fights on the corner of Central and Elm all the time, and they had these Holy Roller women trying to convert these guys."[13] The term "Holy Roller" is an essentially derogatory name for members of the Church of God in Christ or Holiness Church. Historian Tony Heilbut explained, "Because the holiness people jumped, shouted, danced, and fell out for Jesus, because in a word they acted 'crazy,' they became a national laughingstock, the 'Holy Rollers' of fable and cliché."[14]

The best known of these women was probably Arizona Dranes, who performed not only in the Dallas–Fort Worth area but also traveled to Oklahoma City and Chicago, where she ultimately built a reputation for herself through her recordings for the OKeh Phonograph Company. Arizona Juanita Dranes's birthdate has not been definitively established. According to Michael Corcoran, her death certificate gives her birthdate as April 4, 1894, in Sherman, Texas. Blind from birth, Dranes grew up in Greenville, Texas. She attended the Texas Institute for Deaf, Dumb, and Blind Colored Youth in Austin, where she studied music with Lizzie S. Wells. By the time she was a teenager, she was playing for religious services and singing on the street with the followers of the Church of God in Christ in the Dallas–Fort Worth area. The Church of God in Christ was one of many small storefront sanctified and Pentecostal churches that flourished in Texas and elsewhere across the South around the turn of the twentieth century. These small churches nurtured the personal and emotional involvement of their members and welcomed the use of musical instruments, such as piano, guitar, and tambourines, which were considered too worldly by other Christian denominations.

Arizona
Dranes
(right, at pia-
no). Courtesy
of Michael
Corcoran.

Based on record company correspondence, it appears that Rev. Samuel Crouch of Fort Worth recommended Dranes to OKeh, which sent talent scout Richard M. Jones to audition her. By then she was living at 3102 Thomas Avenue in North Dallas.[15] Dranes was then invited to Chicago for a recording session. Once there, Dranes signed a basic recording contract, which gave her twenty-five dollars per issued side and 25 percent of royalties collected on any of her compositions recorded by other artists.

Dranes's first session on June 17, 1926, led to the release of four songs, "In That Day," "It's All Right Now," "John Said He Saw a Number," and "My Soul Is a Witness for the Lord." This session was followed by another on November 15, 1926, which included Dranes as vocalist on piano with Rev. F. W. (Ford Washington) McGee and the Jubilee Singers.

McGee was raised near Honey Grove, in northeast Texas; he was born in 1890 while his mother was visiting Winchester, Tennessee. When he was five, his family moved to Hillsboro, Texas, between Dallas and Austin, where his "performing abilities were first noted during his involvement in school plays."[16] Around 1912 McGee moved to Oklahoma with his wife to accept a position teaching school, and in 1918 he converted to the Church of God in Christ. While pastoring in Oklahoma City, McGee met Dranes, who helped him to build his congregation.

Dranes, however, made only two recordings with McGee on the OKeh label and did not record again until 1928, when she was invited to a session in Dallas. In these recordings, she was accompanied by a choir and possibly

WASHINGTON PHILLIPS
Who Will Sing Gospel Records for
the Columbia Phonograph Co.

Race record ad for Washington Phillips,
December 1927.

also by Coley Jones. Later that year she was apparently again recorded by OKeh in Dallas, this time accompanied by the Texas Jubilee Singers; the songs released were "He's the Lily of the Valley" and "He's Coming Soon." Little is known about the Texas Jubilee Singers, though it is likely they were itinerant musicians who were members of the Church of God in Christ.

Dranes's recording career also ended with the onset of the Depression, after which she apparently left Texas. According to the notes for a Document collection of her work, "It would seem she returned to the network of sanctified churches where a number of later gospel celebrities recalled her impact. Alex Bradford remembered her performing in Bessemer, Alabama, at the 'America Back to God Day' presented at the local white ball park, Legion Field. 'And there was Arizona Dranes, the blind Sanctified lady. She'd sing "Thy Servant's Prayer," and crackers and niggers be shouting everywhere.'"[17] Rosetta Tharpe heard her sing 'The Storm Is Passing Over' in Saint Louis.[18] Ray Funk, in the liner notes to the Columbia compilation, mentions a last intriguing item: an August 1974 advertisement for a gospel concert with an "all star program, the greatest ever presented in Cleveland, including 'nat'l [sic] known Blind Pianist Arizona Dranes from Chicago, Ill."[19]

The record company seems to have had trouble marketing Dranes and her piano style. According to Michael Corcoran's research, Dranes apparently lived in Oklahoma City and Memphis after leaving Dallas and gave her last known public performance in 1947 in Cleveland before moving to Los Angeles, where she continued to play in churches and died on July 27, 1963. With some perspective, we can see that she was playing a sanctified version of the piano style variously known as "fast Western," "fast Texas," boogie-woogie, or barrelhouse. In its more secular incarnation, it had people shouting and dancing in places Arizona Dranes probably would never have entered.

Alex Moore

Dallas Piano Blues

The wide success and influence of Texas blues guitar styles has tended to obscure the importance of the piano. Yet blues historian Paul Oliver has written that Dallas produced a very distinctive style of piano blues, featuring lyrics full of allusions to the city and the trains that constantly passed through it:

> No other blues school, with the possible exception of Chicago, gives us such a picture of the urban life that inspired it. It could, of course, be coldly descriptive, sensational, or even sentimental, but the special quality of the Dallas tradition is its poetry. Here the piano is used as a complementary poetic instrument, setting off the words and the mood of the blues instead of challenging it with pyrotechnic displays.[1]

Oliver's thesis is backed up by anecdotal evidence and discographies of the 1920s and '30s, which suggest that there probably were as many blues pianists as guitarists in Dallas. Like their guitarist counterparts, blues pianists were usually solo performers, whose virtuosity and idiosyncratic styles made it difficult for other musicians to work with them. Blues piano, however, proved to be much less viable in the "race" marketplace than downhome guitar blues, and no pianist attained the fame of a Lemon Jefferson. Consequently, there is less documentation of blues pianists. Much of what is known preserved to the greatest extent in the performance style of Alex Moore, whose career in Dallas spanned nearly seven decades.

Moore was born in North Dallas in 1899 and lived in the city until his death in 1989. He may not have been the best of the local piano men, but he certainly had the greatest longevity and was the best documented. In his youth, he was one of many who played at Saturday-night suppers and house-rent parties and in chock houses and cafés. As Moore said, in

Alexander H. Moore, in Dallas, 1938. Courtesy of Documentary Arts.

the 1920s "there was a piano in every shack in Deep Ellum, Elm Thicket [a black neighborhood near Love Field airport], and Froggy Bottom [near downtown Dallas and the Trinity River]."[2]

The settings in which Moore played reflect the origins of the music he performed. In the sawmill and turpentine camps of the late nineteenth and early twentieth centuries, black laborers lived apart from women in crude quarters and had little in the way of recreation. But the companies did provide entertainment by setting up "barrelhouses," shacks where liquor was served over a bar that typically consisted of a plank set on barrels. Here the workers could listen to music played on battered upright pianos by traveling musicians, who developed a style sometimes called "fast Texas" or "fast Western" piano. However, within this general approach, which came to be known as "barrelhouse music," there were distinct regional variations even within the state of Texas. And as we have seen in the music of Arizona Dranes, it could be performed in both spiritual and secular settings.

Blues historians distinguish between the piano styles found in different areas of the state: the "Santa Fe group," who worked in Fort Bend County, the Thomas family from Houston (which included the legendary Sippie Wallace), the musicians centered around Galveston, and those in Dallas and North Texas. Within those areas, the blues pianists demonstrated certain similarities in style and approach that reflected the environments in which they worked, their friendships and associations with other pianists, and, in some instances, their isolation.[3]

Dallas pianists of the twenties included Neal Roberts, Willie Tyson, Lovey Bookman, and Frank Ridge. Some of these musicians never recorded, and their names were kept alive only in the memory of survivors such as Moore, who passed them along to interviewers. Those who did record often sang the blues or accompanied women blues singers of the "classic" variety, the slow or medium-tempo music interacting in call and response with the vocal. Other instruments were seldom involved in these recordings, though Coley Jones did play guitar on some of Bill Day's sessions.

In "Frisco Blues," Roberts uses gently rolling bass figures to evoke the distant train rhythms of the Saint Louis–San Francisco line without resorting to mimicry. Similarly, Tyson in "Sun Beam" re-created the sounds of the passenger train of that name that ran during the day between Houston and Dallas on the Texas & New Orleans line. On this and other train songs, such as "Interurban Blues," about the electric line that brought country people to the city, Billiken Johnson whistled and added other effects that help shape the mood of the song.

Johnson, who was considered a clown by his musician friends, frequently employed his vocalizing to accompany their piano playing and singing. On Day's "Wild Jack Blues," Johnson provided a braying noise, while on Day's "Elm Street Blues," he made vocal effects through what sounds like cupped hands, rather than using a kazoo or comb and paper, as a kind of bluesy response to the lyrics.

In "Elm Street Blues" Day compares Elm Street to Main and comments on the women of ill repute:

> Main Street's paved in gold (repeat).
> I've got a good girl lives on East Commerce
> I wouldn't mistreat her to save nobody's soul.

The verse was followed by Johnson's vocal effects, to which Day in turn replied:

> Oh, Billiken, Elm Street women
> don't mean you no good (repeat).
> When you turn your back
> they're with every man in the neighborhood.

Ida May Mack, in her version of "Elm Street Blues," which was released a year earlier, used Elm Street as a metaphor for her unrequited love. She began the song by pleading, "Lord, have mercy," and then sang:

> I woke up after midnight.
> I took to walking my floor (repeat).
> Trying to find my daddy
> and some place to go.
> I walked up Elm
> And then I went back up Main
> And the way that I cried,
> Lord, was a dirty shame.

In the song, Mack was accompanied by pianist K. D. Johnson, whom she called "Forty-Nine," a name that appears to imply where she may have met him, since "Forty-Nine" was a slang term that was sometimes used for tent shows. Johnson's style of performance bore similarities to those of Day and others from Dallas, but it was also somewhat idiosyncratic in its emphasis and was perhaps reflective of the music performed in tent shows.

In 1928 Johnson was an accompanist not only for Ida May Mack but also for Bessie Tucker on her recordings "Penitentiary" and "The Dummy."

Alexander H. Moore playing at the Southern House, a "White Patrons Only" club, 1947. Moore is still wearing his dishwasher's coat. The club's owner, Walter E. Wilden, is dancing with his wife in the background. Courtesy of Documentary Arts.

According to Alex Moore, Tucker in fact served time at a prison farm and sang about her personal experiences. In her songs she also made reference to the railroads, especially the Fort Worth and Denver, the Santa Fe, and the "Dummy," which was a traditional name for a logging-company train.

The origins of these piano players and their musical training are largely unknown. Here again, we have Alex Moore, who recalled that he first heard pianos played in the white homes along Ross Avenue, where he delivered groceries as a boy. "Every time I'd walk by, I'd pluck one note," he recalled, "and every day it would be a different note. That's the way I learned the piano."[4] During the 1920s Moore, nicknamed "Papa Chitlins," was much in demand, going from his day job to playing till all hours in joints around town. He said that, once, he didn't pull his clothes off for a week.[5]

Highly regarded among his contemporaries, Moore was one of the first to record. In 1929 he was recruited by Columbia and traveled to Chicago, where he recorded six sides, including "Blue Bloomer Blues," "Ice Pick Blues," and "West Texas Woman." However, these recordings did not sell well, and he was unable to get his music issued on record again until 1937, when he recorded four sides for Decca and was accompanied by guitarist Blind Norris McHenry on two others.

On these records, Moore sang original compositions and accompanied himself by whistling, somewhat like Billiken Johnson, and got the nickname "Whistling" Alex Moore. His distinctive piano style included elements of ragtime, barrelhouse, boogie, and blues and showed the influence of musicians he had heard on record, including Pete Johnson, Albert Ammons, Pine Top Smith, and Meade Lux Lewis, as well as local players.

In 1947 Moore was recorded at the KLIF studios in Dallas, but only two sides were issued, "Miss No Good Weed" and "Dishwasher's Blues." The latter selection may have been autobiographical, for Moore was never able to support himself through his music and worked at a variety of jobs, including dishwashing, driving mules to haul gravel, and serving as a custodian and hotel porter. A photo shows him playing for dancers while still clad in the coat he wore to wash dishes. In the background is his boss, Walter E. Wilden, dancing with his wife. On the photo Moore inscribed his name, followed by the address where he was performing: "3817 Lem[m]on Avenue, playing at the Southern House, White Patrons Only." When asked about this particular occasion, Moore laughed, "He liked my playing so much he took me down to KLIF on that very day to record eight songs."[6]

In 1951 Moore made four sides for RPM Records. In 1960 blues researchers Paul Oliver and Chris Strachwitz found him on the screened porch of a small North Dallas bar and recorded him for Strachwitz's Arhoolie label. About these recordings Oliver wrote the following:

> Alexander Moore had boundless ideas. Betraying hardly a hint of any influence from other singers, he played with great variety and sang in a throaty, husky voice. A man rich in worldly wisdom he was yet a man curiously limited in his knowledge of the world. Only once in his life had he left Texas; most of his life had been spent in a small section of Dallas. So, his blues reflected a very personal, singular view of life, and because he is an eccentric man his words are often unexpected and manifestly original. The immediate circumstances of his environment are reflected in "Going Back to Froggy Bottom" or "From North Dallas to the East Side," but his sharp eye and neat wit led to such highly unconventional blues lines as "Sack dress is all right but I'd rather see you in a pair of pants."
>
> Interspersed with his playing were reminiscences of playing at "Minnie's Tea Room" or of police raids in district chock-houses: memories that would lead him to new blues improvisations. He talked of the years he had driven his horse and cart through the streets of Dallas; years when life was wild and cheap and money scarce—and broke into "Black-Eyed Peas and Hog Jowls." Such blues as "Rubber Tired Hack" or "Miss No Good Weed" were spur-of-the-moment creations played and sung with feeling and pleasure in his own music. His bass figures were varied and intensely interesting and he took an off-beat pride in sudden flashes of inventiveness and flurries of right-hand creations. Then he doubled back his lip and shrieked a piercing whistled blues by which he had gained his name of Whistling Alex Moore but which had in the past, as now, presented problems in recording.[7]

In the mid-1960s, as a result of the Arhoolie recordings, Moore was invited to perform at festivals in the United States and abroad. In 1969, during a tour with the American Folk Blues Festival, he did a session in Stuttgart, Germany, that resulted in the Arhoolie album *Alex Moore in Europe*.

Moore kept working at his various trades by necessity until he retired in 1965. From the sixties until his death, he played for a predominantly white audience. In his later years Alex Moore's style changed. His performances became more autobiographical, his ramblings at the piano more freestyle. He interspersed details from his life with piano sounds that changed tempo with his mood. Short vocal passages were followed by long piano interludes in which the bass was soft and steady and the right hand wandered unpredictably on the keys. The tone was sometimes contemplative, sometimes

Alexander H. Moore, 1981. Photograph by Alan Govenar.

Alexander H. Moore, Dallas, Texas, 1988. Photograph by Alan Govenar

thunderous and fast. Heartfelt blues gave way to ragtime, barrelhouse, boogie, and stride. Moore's approach was intuitive and took shape in performance. He said he never knew exactly what he was going to play until he played it. Throughout his career of more than six decades, he never owned a piano and said he never practiced or rehearsed. An interesting perspective comes from Robin Sullivan, a Dallas blues musician who performs as "Texas Slim" and befriended Moore in the late 1970s. They often played and performed together. He called Moore "a warm-hearted, wonderful guy" and said:

> It was a complete joy because we had so much fun together. Alex would play all different numbers of bars. He seldom played a straight twelve-bar blues. Like a Lightnin' Hopkins, he would change chords when he felt like it. I would try to keep up with him. He would say, "No, I'm just messing with it. You play it right, and I'll meet you at the end." When we got to the V chord, we'd land together. And he'd kind of look up and raise his brow and laugh, like "you thought I was lost." He never got lost. He knew what he was doing.[8]

Like Lightnin' Hopkins, Moore was willing to perform with younger white musicians who admired him, but he always remained in control. Historically, barrelhouse blues pianists were solo artists who prided themselves on improvisation and, by choice, made it very difficult for others to accompany them.

In addition to piano, Moore had a passion for dominoes, which in his later years he played daily at the Martin Luther King Recreation Center in South Dallas. "I love to play dominoes," he said. "The music is always here when I get ready. I just go sit down at that piano and play it. That piano kind of plays itself. That's what I'm talking about. That's why nobody can play with me. They can write that stuff, blues, boogie, ragtime, that's me. I've always said that if I don't improve every night, then you don't owe me nothing, but they always paid me."[9]

Alex Moore's life spanned much of the history of blues and jazz, and his music represented a synthesis of a wide variety of styles. But Moore was also atypical in having a certain sensitivity. His lyrics could be bawdy, but as folklorist Mack McCormick said, "Unlike any other bluesman I've ever encountered, he had a romantic sense—that kind of gentleness, sense of romance. He was focused in the human condition—I think that's what made him unique."[10]

Alexander H. Moore's daughter, Pearl Mae Glynn, Los Angeles, California, 1947.
Photograph by Alexander H. Moore. Courtesy of Alexander H. Moore.

Della Totten and Lula Hayden, Alexander H. Moore's mother, Dallas, Texas, 1947. Courtesy of Documentary Arts.

Moore was also a visual artist whose letters became keepsakes. Even the envelopes were artworks, embellished with colorful curlicues and asides such as "Music, Maestro, Please."

His humanity is embodied in the lyrics of his "Heart Wrecked Blues":

> Hatred is self-punishing.
> Forgiveness is better than revenge.
> There's no heart in buying love
> Or to lose and not to win.

Oliver has described Moore as a "true original, a folk blues singer of the city who can sit at the piano and improvise endless piano themes and blues verses that are sometimes startling, sometimes comic, sometimes grim, and very often pure poetry."[11]

Near the end of his life, Moore received numerous accolades. In 1983 the mayor of Dallas declared June 17 "Alex 'Blues Artist' Moore Day." His fellow senior citizens at the Martin Luther King Center voted him Senior Citizen of the Month, noting that he was "very easy to get along with, always cooperative in every way and everybody loves him. He sings, plays a whole lot of piano and sometimes he whistles."[12] In 1987 Moore was awarded the prestigious National Heritage Fellowship from the National Endowment for the Arts, and in December 1988, one month before he died of a heart attack on a city bus, he received another mayoral proclamation in Dallas, recognizing his achievement in a concert honoring him at the Majestic Theatre, just across Harwood Street from historic Deep Ellum. At the concert, Moore talked about how his only previous experience at the Majestic was in the "crow's nest," the upper balcony reserved for blacks in an otherwise segregated theater.[13]

Throughout his career, Moore lived in poverty. Over the course of his life, he moved from one low-income housing apartment to another, first in North Dallas's Freedmantown, which came to be known as the State-Thomas area, and later the Uptown neighborhood, then in South Dallas and Oak Cliff. Shortly before his death, Moore, laughing, said that he couldn't afford apartments that cost more than $50 a month. When he died, he did not have enough resources to cover the cost of his own funeral and burial. Nevertheless, he was laid to rest in style, wearing a suit with lapel pins proclaiming him a blues artist.

An exemplar of his generation, Moore attributed his longevity to "clean living." In many ways he typified the music of Deep Ellum and Dallas's black community in the 1920s and 1930s. Although his piano playing was essentially traditional, his performance style was idiosyncratic. He was a solo performer who defied accompanists and whose enduring legacy is in the limited recordings he made. The extent to which Moore exemplified a Dallas piano style was defined mostly by his associations with other pianists in his youth and by his isolation as an adult, having outlived his contemporaries by two or three decades. Ironically, Deep Ellum was the place where Moore began and ended his career. In the last few years of his working life, like a few others of his generation, he was performing in newly renovated clubs in places he recalled from years before.

Buster Smith

Dallas Jazz Goes to Kansas City and New York

Dallas did not play as clear or dramatic a part in the development of jazz as in blues. There is no single towering figure who was the obvious Dallas jazz counterpart to Blind Lemon Jefferson. Yet in the mid- to late 1920s, in the words of jazz historian Ross Russell, Dallas was "the most important band town in Texas."[1] The city and the region produced a number of musicians who went on to play vital roles in swing and bebop: saxophonists Budd Johnson, Herschel Evans, Buddy Tate, and Henry "Buster" Smith; trombonist Jack Teagarden; and electric guitar pioneer Charlie Christian, who was born in Bonham, in northeast Texas, and grew up in Oklahoma but spent a great deal of time in Dallas.

Buster Smith, though he recorded little under his own name and never achieved national recognition, was the most significant of these: Russell called him "a Dallas man with roots in the urban blues, pioneer of the early barrelhouse bands in the city, self-taught musician unblooded in musical schools, master of an empirical method on alto saxophone, and major saxophone stylist."[2]

Smith was born in 1904 on a cotton farm in Ellis County, south of Dallas. This was Texas's blues country, the east-central area that produced Blind Lemon Jefferson and Blind Willie Johnson and, a bit later, Lightnin' Hopkins, Albert Collins, and Johnny Copeland. As Smith said later, "The blues was all around when I was growing up." As a child, Smith played an old organ at home, but his first serious musical experience came when he was about eighteen, after his family had moved to Collin County, north of Dallas. He saw a $3.50 clarinet in a store in town and got permission from his mother to buy it if he picked 400 pounds of cotton daily for several days. A few months later, when the family moved to Dallas, he had become fairly proficient on the instrument.[3]

In Dallas, Smith found a vital music scene. "On Central Track, you could

The Tip Top tailor shop and dance hall, ca. early 1920s. Courtesy of the *Dallas Morning News*.

at times hear four different interpretations of the blues," Booker Pittman wrote of his boyhood. "They would drift from some of these fellows from Memphis, Georgia, Alabama, with their banjos and guitars, each telling a different story."[4] A similar account came from Margaret Wright, a white woman, who recalled a childhood trip to Deep Ellum with her mother in 1924:

> I was born in Dallas, and as a small child, I can remember an occasion when my mother took me walking down Elm Street, across Central Tracks, and on to wherever an errand carried her. My mother was a tall, stately woman and was always treated with the utmost respect, no matter what the surroundings. On this day, I remember holding tightly to her hand. I was really frightened. There was certainly no need to be, but I was out of familiar surroundings. As we walked down the street near the Central Tracks, loud music could be heard up and down the streets. Black musicians seemed to be in every store and "joint." Blues and jazz players were everywhere. At that time, I had never seen so many black people. One thing I distinctly remember, every black man who was on the sidewalk, stepped back, took off his hat, and bowed slightly when my mother passed.[5]

In addition to street singers such as Jefferson, who performed alone, there were groups such as Coley Jones's Dallas String Band, which became well known around the city by playing at community picnics, dances, and shows for both white and black audiences and by serenading on the streets in front of Ella B. Moore's theaters. The band had varying personnel and configurations that sometimes inlcuded one or two violins, two guitars, mandolin, string bass, clarinet, and trumpet.

The bass player for Coley Jones was Marco Washington, who also led a string band that included his wife and stepson, Aaron "T-Bone" Walker, as a child musician and dancer. The family played on the streets for money on weekends, employing string bass, guitars, fiddles, mandolins, and homemade instruments. Sometimes Jesse Hooker joined in on sax and clarinet. Like other street bands, they played both blues and popular tunes to satisfy a diverse audience, white and black. "I couldn't play good then, but I had learned to dance," Walker said later. "I learned splits and spins. That's what put change in the kitty most times. When I got older, maybe twelve, I could play the ukulele, and I worked up an act. I would sing anything they asked. I entertained at church picnics and at Riverside Park."[6]

Jazz was being played in Dallas as well, indoors and out. Brass bands played in parks and in "colored carnivals." They were even used in funerals

Henry "Buster" Smith (left) and the Heat Waves of Swing, with T-Bone Walker (third from left), Louisiana, 1949. Courtesy of Sumter Bruton.

to some extent. A 1925 *Dallas Morning News* article recalled a black funeral procession with a brass band coming up South Lamar Street. In these and other ways the music reflected the influence of New Orleans, whose jazz was a marching music, collectively improvised into a dense tapestry of intertwining melodies—in musical terms, it used polyphony, or counterpoint.

A number of New Orleans musicians played in Dallas, too, as they fanned out across the country following the closing of the Storyville red-light district in 1917. Booker Pittman recalled being inspired to take up clarinet after hearing Kid Ory's New Orleans jazz band in Dallas. He bought his first instrument from a bearded Jew in a Deep Ellum pawnshop for $3.

Despite the New Orleans presence, Dallas had its own musical identity. Don Albert put it this way: "The rhythm was especially the thing that was different from New Orleans. The drums used a silent beat . . . and the sustained beat which was different with the big bands in Texas. The drummers would read in parts and consequently got off of the rhythm a little bit and came back to it, which the New Orleans drummers didn't do."[7]

As Smith said,

We didn't hear as much about New Orleans in those days as we did a little later on. We called that kind of music gutbucket or barrelhouse. The trumpet players and clarinet players concentrated on that. I'll tell you, a lot of it started around here on these medicine shows. We used to have them all over town, and that's where it started. A medicine show used to have four or five pieces: trombone, clarinet, trumpet and a drummer, and every man blowing for himself as loud as he could blow to attract a crowd for the "doctor." Then there would be a couple of comedians clowning a little bit, then the doc would have the boys blow again to attract another crowd after he'd sold the first crowd. He'd sell them this patent medicine—good for anything—at a dollar or a dollar-fifty a bottle, and the comedians would go through the crowd selling it. Then the boys would get up and blow again to attract another bunch of suckers. That's how all that jazz started down in these parts. They tried to get me on one of those things in 1922, but I didn't go.[8]

T-Bone Walker, did, though; he spent a summer during his youth working for Dr. Breeding's medicine show.

Smith found steady work in Dallas: "I got playing around with a little three-piece band—Voddie White. Voddie played piano. I played clarinet, and [there was] a drummer—I forget his name. We played around town at a few places and at Saturday night suppers and that sort of thing. That was

An Evening of Pleasure at the
Rose Room
1710 Hall St.   *Dallas, Texas*

Rose Room souvenir photo wallet, 1940s. Courtesy of the Texas African American Photography Archive.

around 1923 and 1924." Around this time, too, Smith became acquainted with the alto sax. That nameless drummer gave him an old horn he'd given up on playing. "It was so old it was turning green," Smith recalled. "Anyway, I cleaned it up and learned it in three days."[9]

Of the Dallas scene, Smith said:

> T-Bone Walker was around; he used to dance where I played down on the Central Track. He wasn't singing much then, just dancing. Sammy Price was down there, too. He was a dancer, too, at first. Of course there were a lot of bands around here, too. Alphonso Trent, Jap Allen, T. [Terrence] Holder, George E. Lee. They all made a circuit around here from Kansas City, Oklahoma City, Houston, Dallas, San Antonio, and a lot of the smaller towns, too. We had two bands here as good as you could find anywhere: Troy Floyd and Alphonso Trent. In 1928, Trent was playing at the Adolphus Hotel. Another band was Fred Cooper's. And then there was Carl Murphy's little seven-piece band. They called themselves the Satisfied Five or something like that when they first started out. They played at the Adolphus Hotel evenings, and Trent played there later in the night. Then there were any number of four- and five-

piece bands playing around the roadhouses and after-hours spots. Trent and Floyd were the big bands and did most of the traveling.[10]

Smith's words were echoed by Ross Russell, who wrote that Trent's band had "the greatest success ever achieved by any band, black or white, in the city."[11] And Budd Johnson said, "Let me tell you about Trent; that was the greatest band I'd ever heard! They used to thrill me. They were gods back in the '20s, just like Basie was later, only many years ahead of him. Nobody else had gold instruments in those days; his whole band had them! They made $150 a week a man. Imagine! They worked nothing but the biggest and finest hotels in the South."[12] Trent's band may not be better remembered because its only recording sessions were done while on the road in 1928 and apparently fell far short of what it played for live audiences.

Though some black musicians played for white audiences in the big hotels, many played exclusively for black audiences in areas such as Deep Ellum. "Man, Deep Ellum was wide open," Buster Smith said. "You could see everybody you knew in Deep Ellum; they'd hang out by the railroad

Henry "Buster" Smith and an unidentified black-faced comedian, the Rose Room, Dallas, 1940s. Photograph by Marion Butts. Courtesy of Marion Butts and the Texas African American Photography Archive.

Alphonso Trent and his Adolphus Hotel Orchestra, WFAA radio broadcast, Dallas, 1920s. Courtesy of the Texas African American Photography Archive.

tracks and listen at the medicine shows, and then go to the Tip Top. It was the most popular place down there. . . . There were other places, but the Tip Top was the most popular because they used the biggest bands."[13] That was where Smith heard Hooker, whom he called "an awful good clarinet player. . . . He couldn't read [music], either. I'd go down there and listen to him till he moved on. This was in 1922."[14]

In 1925, apparently while playing at the Tip Top, Buster Smith was hired by the Blue Devils, a highly regarded territory band headquartered in Oklahoma City. The leader was Walter "Big 'Un" Page, a versatile musician who played tuba, string bass, and baritone sax. The Blue Devils, formed in 1923, included at one time or another many of the top musicians of the time, including a number of Texans: Dallas trumpet player and vocalist Oran "Hot Lips" Page (no relation to Walter Page); trombonist Dan Minor of Dallas; singer Jimmy Rushing of Oklahoma City; trombonist, guitarist, and arranger Eddie Durham, originally from San Marcos, Texas, near San Antonio; pianist Bill (later Count) Basie; and, late in the Devils' career, alto sax player Don Byas and Mississippi-born tenor player Lester Young.

Basie opened his autobiography with a description of his first encounter with the Blue Devils, in Tulsa in 1927. The band, playing outside ("ballyhooing") to advertise a dance that night, awakened him after a rough night: "I forgot all about my hangover and about catching up on my sleep. I just wanted to hear those guys play some more. . . . Everything about them got to me, and as things worked out, hearing them that day was probably the most important turning point in my musical career so far as notions about

Herbert Cowens, the Kat and the Kittens, ca. 1930s. Courtesy of the Herbert and Rubye Cowens Collection, Texas African American Photography Archive.

Herbert Cowens on drums, *Buck and Bubbles Show*, New York, ca. 1930s. Courtesy of the Herbert and Rubye Cowens Collection, Texas African American Photography Archive.

what kind of music I really wanted to play was concerned." The Blue Devils was the first big band he had heard, Basie said, "and it was the greatest thing I had ever heard. I had never heard the blues played like that. . . . Not that the Blue Devils were just playing the blues. They were not really playing all that much blues that night. But they were still bluesy. But the main thing about that band was that they had their own special way of playing everything."[15] Basie was determined to join the band, and he did a bit later in Oklahoma City.

He didn't stay long; in fact, he had moved to Bennie Moten's band in Kansas City by the time the Devils made their only recording, in November 1929. One side of that record is "Blue Devil Blues," a fairly conventional blues with a Jimmy Rushing vocal. As Basie says, even in his early days the Oklahoma-born singer had a very distinctive style. The other side, the instrumental "Squabblin,' " is more interesting from a musical standpoint. It marks a transition between New Orleans jazz and swing. The piece is in 2/4 time, but it definitely swings, looking forward to the looser, more flexible Kansas City 4/4. Smith's alto work is light and flowing; as Budd Johnson said, Smith was already playing in his "lope-along style."[16] The banjo and tuba, hallmarks of New Orleans music, were gone; Walter Page had switched to string bass.

Herbert Cowens at a rehearsal for the 1986 Dallas Folk Festival. Photograph by Alan Govenar.

By the time they made their record, the Blue Devils were facing the end of their road. At the urging of Basie and Durham, Moten had begun raiding the band. Even Walter Page finally made the move, though he was nominally the Devils' leader. The group was a "commonwealth" band, in which all the money was split equally and everyone had an equal vote. This may have contributed to the camaraderie Basie found so appealing, but, as Smith noted, it also figured in bad decisions, such as turning down a radio date with Fats Waller because a slim majority of the musicians thought he wasn't offering enough money. When Walter Page left, Smith took over leadership of the Blue Devils, which continued to attract good musicians such as Lester Young, a revolutionary on the tenor sax, who was recruited on a foray into Minnesota.

However, the country was in the depths of the Great Depression, and times were tough for bands. The Blue Devils broke up in 1933 after being stiffed by a promoter and stranded in Binkley, West Virginia. The musicians could not pay their bills, so the sheriff impounded their instruments and locked them in the jail. Some of the band members "hoboed back home," as Smith said, but he and others joined Moten, who sent a car to pick them up. Moten was based in Kansas City, where the musicians found a scene that Smith characterized as "like Dallas had been, only more so."[17] Fueled by money from the corrupt Tom Pendergast regime, the city jumped twenty-four hours a day, with clubs that offered jazz and earthier pleasures, including live sex shows in some cases. Big Joe Turner held forth as a singing bartender in Piney Brown's Sunset Club on Vine, sometimes wandering into the street in full cry, often improvising lyrics on the spot. Moten's band came to an abrupt end with his death in 1935 following surgery. He was just thirty-four years old. His brother Ira "Buster" Moten tried to keep the band together but proved too hotheaded. Smith and Basie formed a band called the Barons of Rhythm, which included "Hot Lips" Page and Durham. By this time, Smith had taught himself to read music and had become a skillful arranger. Because of his scholarly appearance and total immersion in his music, he became known as "Prof" to his fellow musicians. "He'd be up there on the bandstand blowing for all he was worth," Kansas City pianist and band leader Jay McShann recalled. "He'd get into the number so much, you know, totally involved, and his eyeglasses would slip down to the end of his nose. The guys used to look at him and say, 'Hey, don't he look like some absent-minded professor standing up there?' And then somebody piped up and yelled 'Prof' at Buster. From that time on we called him Prof."[18]

Carden Cowens at Abe and Pappy's, ca. late 1940s. Courtesy of Rubye Cowens.

According to several accounts, Basie's theme song, "One O'Clock Jump," resulted from a session involving Smith, "Hot Lips" Page, Durham, and Basie. Smith set the riff, the recurring musical figure on which the tune is based, then wrote the arrangement that Basie made famous. Unfortunately for Smith, he failed to copyright it. The song was retitled after the original name, "Blue Ball," was deemed too racy for a radio broadcast. Basie's band, of course, went on to world fame, but without Buster Smith, who left just before the group was discovered. The band moved to New York and received national radio airplay, thanks to John Hammond of Columbia Records. The Basie band sound, which came to embody hot swing-band music, fused the influences of the Blue Devils and Moten. As Basie's longtime drummer Jo Jones said, "When Bennie Moten's two-beat, one-and-three rhythm [that is, the stress on the first and third beats] and the two-and-four of Walter Page's Blue Devils came together in the Basie band, there was an even flow, one, two, three, four."[19]

Smith started his own band, which included a teenage alto player named Charlie Parker. "Well, he used to tell me he wanted to play like me," Smith said. "He used to call me his dad, and I called him my boy. I couldn't get rid of him. He was always up under me. . . . He did play like me quite a bit, I guess. But after awhile, anything I could make on my horn, he could make, too, and make something better out of it. We used to do that double-time stuff all the time. I used to do a lot of that on clarinet. Then I started doing it on alto, and Charlie heard me doing it, and he started playing it."[20]

In the early forties Smith tired of life on the road and returned to Dallas, where he continued to lead bands that played in Texas and neighboring states. He made a living from music while enjoying a home life and finding time for his hobbies, fishing and working on cars. Though he disappeared from the national scene, he remained a vital musical force. He played the 1942 opening engagement at the Rose Room, a prime nightspot in North Dallas, and played there regularly for years. T-Bone Walker and other noted figures sometimes sat in with his bands. Smith made his only recording under his own name in 1959, when musicologist and composer Gunther Schuller came to Dallas and tracked down the leader and his musicians for an album on Atlantic. The album is long out of print but is now available on CD on the Koch Jazz label. Listeners hear what Ray Charles called "some of the filthiest alto around,"[21] a loping, fluid, imaginative style. It's not hard to see why Charlie Parker regarded Buster Smith as his musical father. In the words of writer Nathan W. Pearson, Smith "strongly influenced Charlie Parker by stretching the harmonic dimensions of the alto saxophone

Herbert Cowens and Sam Price at the Dallas Folk Festival, 1991. Photograph by Alan Govenar.

and using a lightning-fast 'dancing' style that anticipated and influenced Parker's."[22] An interesting perspective came from Jay McShann: "I don't think anybody ever knew just how much alto Buster could play. I don't think Buster ever found out, himself, how far he could go."[23]

Basie and other old friends visited Smith when they played Dallas, but he never saw Parker again. "Bird" died in 1955, thirty-four years old, ravaged by alcoholism, heroin addiction, and other personal demons. "Charlie came down, too, one time, but I missed him," Smith said. "He was here for a couple of days with Stan Kenton. . . . It was just a little while before Charlie died. I didn't even hear about them being here till they were already gone. They told me Charlie was looking for me up on Hall Street. I went on up there, but he was gone."[24]

Henry "Buster" Smith in South Dallas, ca. 1981. Photograph by Alan Govenar.

Smith's early influence, Jesse Hooker, recorded with several bands in Dallas in the late 1920s. He played clarinet on blues singer and harmonica player William McCoy's "Out of Doors Blues." He is also listed as vocalist on Frenchy's String Band's recording of "Sunshine Special," a blues about a fast daytime Texas and Pacific train:

> That mean TP Railroad sure have done me wrong.
> That mean TP Railway sure have done me wrong.
> It let that Sunshine Special carry my good gal from home.
> The blues come down like showers of rain.
> I can see nothing but smoke from that train.
> Every time I hear that Sunshine Special blow
> Every time I hear that Sunshine Special blow
> It makes me want to pack up all my clothes and go.

Hooker's life illustrated the overlapping of blues and jazz. He moved to Fort Worth about 1930 and lived there until he died, around 1950. He played for a time in a street band led by Jesse Thomas, brother of blues singer Willard "Ramblin'" Thomas. Apparently Hooker quit performing in his later years, perhaps influenced by his wife, Birdie, a churchgoer who did not want him playing the "devil's music." A former neighbor remembered him as a

Henry "Buster" Smith in South Dallas, ca. 1981. Photograph by Alan Govenar.

medium-sized, medium-complexioned, round-shouldered man who would sometimes sit on the back steps and play one of his horns or a tambourine. Perhaps he was thinking about his younger days on Central Track. Sammy Price, too, left Dallas in the twenties. Bert Goldberg, manager of Alphonso Trent's orchestra, accompanied Trent to a dance in the black community and saw Price dancing the Charleston, surrounded by an attentive crowd. He was asked to join the band as a dancer, and Price "jumped at the chance." He toured and recorded widely and lived the remainder of his life in New York. In his later years, he returned to Dallas several times, playing and reminiscing for local audiences. Herbie Cowens, who became known as "Kat," left town in 1927 with Cleo Mitchell's Shake Your Feet vaudeville company.

Booker Pittman made records with bands led by Lucky Millinder and Cab Calloway's sister Blanche Calloway. Pittman played alto sax and sang in a raspy voice somewhat similar to Louis Armstrong's.

Budd Johnson remained musically active almost until his death in 1984. His importance as a jazz figure is often overlooked, possibly because he seldom led his own bands. He was a common thread linking the large bands of the early and mid-1940s, which were involved in the transition from swing to bebop: those of Earl Hines, Boyd Raeburn, Billy Eckstine, Woody Herman, and Dizzy Gillespie. Johnson wrote music for all of these bands and played tenor sax in live performance or on records with all but Raeburn's. Johnson organized an early bebop record date, a 1944 Coleman Hawkins session featuring Gillespie. That same year, Johnson played in the first small bebop combo, with Gillespie and Oscar Pettiford, at the Onyx Club on 52nd Street. Jazz historian Dave Oliphant said Johnson played tenor like Lester Young and alto like Charlie Parker before he had met or heard either.

Eddie Durham, a trombonist and pioneering electric guitarist, became an important arranger for Basie and other bandleaders. According to one story, he received $5 from Glenn Miller for his arrangement of "In the Mood," which became a huge hit for Miller. Durham was also a mentor to Charlie Christian, who became one of the first black musicians with a major white band when Benny Goodman hired him at the urging of John Hammond, his brother-in-law. Christian took part in late-night jam sessions in the early 1940s that were the leading edge of bebop. Had he not died of pneumonia at age twenty-five in 1942, Christian would have taken part in the postwar jazz revolution with Johnson, Miles Davis, Dizzy Gillespie, Charlie Parker, and others.

Buster Smith quit playing sax after extensive dental work in 1959, not long after his Atlantic session. He taught himself electric bass, but by the early 1970s he had stopped playing professionally and was roofing houses with his brother, pianist Boston Smith. Buster Smith remained well known among Dallas musicians, however, and became a mentor to figures such as David "Fathead" Newman, who played tenor sax with Ray Charles for a

Henry "Buster" Smith and David "Fathead" Newman at a rehearsal for the 1986
Dallas Folk Festival. Photograph by Alan Govenar.

number of years. Rediscovered by Alan Govenar in the 1980s, Smith organized a band named after one of his earlier outfits, the Heat Waves of Swing.
It included Boston Smith on piano, trumpet player Benny "Chops" Arredondo, and Cowens, who had enjoyed a career that included working
in New York City in vaudeville, Broadway shows and musicals, and playing with notable bandleaders, including Eubie Blake, Fats Waller, "Stuff"
Smith, and Fletcher Henderson. In addition, Cowens led his own band,
The Kat and the Kittens, and made annual overseas USO tours. When
he returned to Dallas in 1980, he reconnected with Buster Smith, and
together they led the Heat Waves of Swing. They played Govenar's Dallas
Folk Festivals, and some of these performances were recorded and released
by Govenar's nonprofit organization, Documentary Arts.[25] Smith was also
featured, along with Basie and Budd Johnson, in the 1977 documentary film
The Last of the Blue Devils.

By the last phase of Smith's career, the Deep Ellum of his youth was long
gone. The building that had housed the Tip Top was torn down in 1968.
An article in the *Dallas Morning News* reviewed the building's days as a
railroad hotel but said nothing of its more recent history as a dance hall.

Marvin Montgomery

*The Cross-Fertilization of White and
Black Musical Styles*

W hile Blind Lemon Jefferson and Buster Smith are generally acknowledged as seminal figures, Marvin "Smokey"
Montgomery has not been, though some books and articles
written since his death in 2001 have begun to remedy this. The standard
works on the history of country music have failed to recognize Montgomery's importance as a musician and his contribution to the Dallas–Fort
Worth area.[1] This is due in part to the style of banjo that he performed.
Clearly, the five-string Appalachian banjo has been studied far more than
the four-string tenor that Montgomery and some of his contemporaries
played. As an instrument the tenor banjo has not been adequately credited
for its importance in the crossover of white and black musical styles. Tenor
banjo was used in the rhythm sections of early country, classic blues, and
New Orleans–style jazz.

Montgomery touched on all of the musical diversity that Deep Ellum,
Dallas–Fort Worth, and the Southwest have come to represent. He performed in touring vaudeville-inspired tent shows and Western swing
bands, as well as in country and jazz groups over the years. Stylistically,
Montgomery was completely eclectic, integrating elements of black and
white minstrelsy, popular songs, and show tunes with strains of traditional
country, jazz, and blues. He studied music at Texas Christian University in
Fort Worth and, late in his life, performed with classical orchestras and a
ballet company. Except for a hiatus during World War II, he played with
the Light Crust Doughboys from 1935 until weeks before he died. In 1948
he became the leader of the band and acquired his nickname "Smokey,"
bestowed by a TV announcer who commented that the speed of his hand as
it strummed his banjo made it look like smoke.[2] In addition, he served for
more than a decade as musical director of the *Big "D" Jamboree*, a weekly
live country-music radio broadcast that began in Dallas in 1947. On the

Jamboree, Montgomery led a house band, the Country Gentlemen, essentially a renamed version of the Doughboys, playing the popular country music of the day.

In retrospect, Montgomery's arrival in Dallas was fortuitous since it positioned him to play a major role in the transition of country music from relatively straightforward dance tunes to more complex forms that incorporated African American blues and jazz and other influences, such as Hawaiian steel guitar. Born in 1913 in Rinard, Iowa, he had started playing the banjo ukulele at age nine. His mother played the piano, and whenever she would

> go up to Fort Dodge, she'd bring back two or three new songs, and the sheet music would have ukulele chords. Then she bought a $10 banjo for my younger brother, and he didn't do anything with it. So, I picked it up and tuned it like a ukulele and played it in that style. Then one night outside a dance I saw this banjo player from St. Paul playing, and he was doing different fingering than what I knew. And when he came out to smoke a cigarette during his break, I asked him, and he said it was called tenor banjo style. Next day I ordered a chord book from Sears and Roebuck, and I learned that style and have been playing ever since.[3]

When he was a teenager, Montgomery and his mother played together in a small dance band called the Iowa Orioles. His parents had divorced when he was thirteen; his father, Charlie Wetter, was an alcoholic gambler, and Montgomery had to help support the family:

> My mother played piano, and I played banjo and sometimes drums and sometimes both. And we had a guy named Dick Danson who played drums and sang a lot with a megaphone. Farlow Matice was the sax player, and we'd play two round dances, then maybe a waltz, and then we'd have to have a square dance. For the square dance we'd need a fiddler, and that fiddler was Charlie Hogan, who was the foreman of a section gang on the railroad during the day. Charlie Hogan was a good fiddler. He was the head cat on the breakdowns and waltzes. We played all the popular songs of the twenties: "That's My Weakness Now," "The Waltz You Saved for Me," "Five Foot Two," "Ain't She Sweet," and others. That's the way we did it, round and round, all night long, no curfew. You played till 2 or 3 o'clock in the morning sometimes. I'd get back just in time to go to school.[4]

The Neale Helvey-J. Doug Morgan Tent Show, 1933, in Iowa. Courtesy of Marvin Montgomery.

Montgomery, whose given name was Marvin Dooley Wetter, joined the Neale Helvey-J. Doug Morgan tent show after finishing the spring semester of his sophomore year at Iowa State College, where he was majoring in industrial arts and planning to become a schoolteacher. His mother, Mabel Wetter, had wanted him to become a Methodist preacher, but he said he got sidetracked: "I entered a talent show at the tent show, and you only played one song, 'The World Is Waiting for the Sunrise.' I imitated two banjos at once. I played the lead on the A string and the rhythm part on the other three strings, and I won second prize. Three dollars. [First prize went to a five-year-old female tap dancer.] Well, they took down my name, and in about three weeks they wired me a telegram me and asked me to join them."[5]

Jobs were scarce during the Great Depression, and Montgomery seized the opportunity:

The tent show usually had a three-act play like *My Wild Irish Rose*—they had maybe seven people in the crew and about ten actors and actresses. And I'd play as part of the vaudeville orchestra twenty or thirty minutes before the show and during intermission. They had a five- to seven-piece band: saxophone, trumpet, piano, drums, and two banjos. Sometimes I'd play solos; other times I'd follow the midget, King Rector, who played the xylophone and tap-danced.

Marvin Montgomery (left) and his cousin Orville Dooley, 1932, as hoboes. Courtesy of Marvin Montgomery.

Neale Helvey, who was co-owner of the show, played piano in the vaudeville orchestra and was a real showman. And he didn't like my real name, Wetter. He'd say to me, "One day your name will be in lights, and we have to give you a better name than that." And I said, "Well, I like the name Robert Montgomery" (He was a famous movie star at the time), and he said, "Okay, we'll call you Marvin Montgomery," and that's the name I've kept ever since.[6]

The Helvey-Morgan tent show toured into the Midwest during the summer months, traveling through Iowa, Illinois, and Missouri before returning to its home base in Jacksonville, in East Texas. In the tent show Montgomery was able to both expand his repertoire and play a lot of the popular tunes he already knew.

In December 1934 he was passing through Dallas by train on his way home to Rinard, Iowa, for Christmas after spending more than a year and a half with the Helvey-Morgan tent show. Montgomery had been earning $11 a week and had managed to save $30, but when he got to Union Station in Dallas he realized he didn't have enough cash to make it all the way back home. As he recalled,

> It was three or four in the morning, and I stayed there at the station. I curled up on one of those benches until about six o'clock. And then I went looking for the Adolphus Hotel, where I knew that Blackie Simmons and his Blue Jackets had a radio show on KRLD. When I got there, the band was rehearsing, and I introduced myself as a musician. So, they let me listen, and then after a while, one of them handed me one of their guitars, and I strummed around on it. That's when Blackie said, "You lookin' for a job?" And I answered, "Yes," and he told me that Mrs. Davis, the manager of KRLD, was looking for a guitarist to play with the piano player that night. Well, I went and talked to Mrs. Davis, and she said the job paid $3, which I thought was great, but I needed it in advance to get my guitar, banjo, and suitcase out of the baggage check at Union Station and find a hotel room.[7]

Mrs. Davis was sympathetic, and Montgomery set off to get ready for his first job in Dallas. He found a hotel room on Elm Street near Dallas's theater row and on the western edge of Deep Ellum. Thinking back, Montgomery said, "The hotel must have been a house of ill repute—when I'd practice my banjo, I'd sit on the edge of the bed and these gals would stick their head in the door and listen, but they were wearing these fancy, black see-through type things, and I eventually caught on."[8]

The Light Crust Doughboys at Republic Studios, 1936, for the filming of the Gene Autry Western *Oh, Susanna!* Left to right: Muryel "Zeke" Campbell, Dick "Bashful" Reinhart, Marvin "Junior" Montgomery, Kenneth "Abner" Pitts, Clifford "Doctor" Gross, Bert "Buddy" Dodson. Courtesy of Marvin Montgomery.

But on that first night in Dallas, Montgomery didn't know exactly what to think. The piano player picked him up in front of the hotel and took him to the Dallas Country Club to play at a stag party, where a "gal took off everything," and he thought, "Boy, this is the wildest town I've ever seen."[9] As it turned out, the pianist—whose name Montgomery couldn't remember years later—told him that the Wanderers, a "hillbilly band" that performed on WFAA radio from the Baker Hotel across from the Adolphus, was looking for a banjo player. "Well," Montgomery said, "I went to talk to the

Wanderers and got the job. They tried me out on a dance they were doing in Kilgore, Texas, and paid me $12 for the night. And I had only made $11 a week on the tent show."[10]

Given this experience with his family dance band and the rigors of the tent show, Montgomery easily adapted to the busy schedule of dances and radio broadcasts that he played in Dallas and East Texas with the Wanderers. He and Dick Reinhart, the guitar player for the group, became close friends, and after a week in the hotel on Elm Street, Montgomery moved to South Dallas, which was still virtually all white. "Dick took me under his wing and got me a room out in South Dallas on Holmes Street, where he and his wife had an apartment. They had a three-room apartment, and I had a one-room bedroom."

In the spring of 1935 Montgomery returned to Iowa and moved his mother and sister to Dallas. "I got my old Model A and drove it to Texas. My grandfather had taken care of it when I was gone on the tent show. He jacked it up and stored it in an old corn crib." In Dallas, Montgomery rented an additional bedroom and kitchen in the house where he lived to accommodate his mother and sister. Later they moved to a duplex in Trinity Heights, south of Oak Cliff, and he rode the streetcar back and forth to the Baker Hotel for the daily broadcasts of the Wanderers.

During this period Montgomery made after-hours forays to Deep Ellum with Reinhart, who introduced him to African American blues:

> Dick would say, "Come on, let's go down Elm Street." He'd name a place. I don't remember what the names were. But he'd take his guitar, and I'd listen and watch them play. We'd be the only white people in there . . . on Elm Street on down past the Majestic Theatre . . . down east. It was on ground level, and you'd just walk in. These guys knew Dick, and when he'd come in they'd wave him over, and he'd take his guitar. Mostly it was a drinking place . . . I don't remember any food; they probably had it. Some of them would get out there and kinda dance. Seems like there always was a little square where they could do a little dancing. They didn't have a stage. They'd be sitting on the floor in a corner of the building or at one end of it. Usually there were just one or two [black] guys, a guitar player, maybe a mouth organ. One of them might pick up a bottle or something. They all do that now, but that's the thing that amazed me. I was seeing things I'd never seen before . . . it was a kind of slide. They'd lay the guitar down flat in their lap and take that slide up and down [the neck]. They'd have an old six-string guitar all beat up and scratched up. I never did see a real good instrument.[11]

Zeke - J.B. - Bashful - Parker Willson - Cecil - Dolores Jo - Abner - Ted - Junior

The LIGHT CRUST Doughboys

The Light Crust Doughboys, 1941, in Saginaw, Texas. Courtesy of Marvin Montgomery.

Montgomery remembered that some of the songs Reinhart played in Deep Ellum were among those that he brought back to the Wanderers:

Dick was the only one I knew who really picked up their songs and learned them. He'd write down the words to them songs, and the first thing you know, we'd be doing them on the air. I was hearing things on his guitar I'd never heard before . . . bending the strings. Dick picked up on that stuff all the time. If he had made a record by himself on guitar, you'd probably think he was a black guy. He'd do "Matchbox Blues" . . . "Gulf Coast Blues." Others, we'd play at dances—"Trouble in Mind," "Sitting on Top of the World," all those we played, and Dick sang them on the dance jobs.

Montgomery said the Wanderers was a hot fiddle band that featured jazzlike improvisations. "We'd turn it loose on the first chorus," Montgomery recalled. "That's the reason we played so many blues. The blues format, you know, the three-chord thing, it's easy to follow, and there's always a hot chorus or two."[12]

The improvisation was also known as "hokum." The early twentieth-century slang term, which may have derived from "hocus-pocus" and/or "bunkum," originally referred to a put-on or a stock theatrical device calcu-

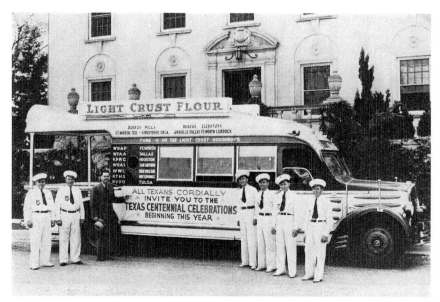

Light Crust Doughboys, 1936. Courtesy of Marvin Montgomery.

lated to elicit an audience response. "The hokum is when you play the hot chorus," Montgomery said.

> You're playing your own thing against the chords that are laid down by the tune. That's hokum. Uncle Art [Satherley, a Columbia record producer] used to call it "noodle"; he'd say, "Noodle on the bridge" or something. We'd improvise on the melody and the chords, follow the chord progression. You'd lose the melody a lot of times. A lot of these guys had about three or four licks, as they called them, and after they played one or two choruses, they'd play every lick that they knew, and they had to use them over on all the tunes. And on a lot of these tunes, if you didn't hear the first chorus, you didn't know what they were playing.[13]

In October 1935 Montgomery, Reinhart, and Bert Dodson left the Wanderers to join the Light Crust Doughboys About his beginnings with the Doughboys, Montgomery recalled, "The boss, Eddie Dunn, had just taken over for W. Lee 'Pappy' O'Daniel, who had been fired by Jack Burrus, the owner of Burrus Mills. One of the first things Eddie did was fire six out of the nine pieces in the band to improve its musicianship, and he hired the three of us to make a six-piece band. Milton Brown quit in 1932 and organized the Musical Brownies, and Bob Wills left in the early part of

1933. [Actually, Wills departed in August of that year.] Both Milton and Bob wanted to play for dances, and Pappy wouldn't let them. He started that, and it just kept on."

With the policy of not playing for dances, the repertoire of the Doughboys was considerably different from that of the Wanderers. "We had a strong dance beat with the Wanderers, but with the Doughboys, we played two or three hymns a week, cowboy songs, and the slow waltzes: 'Home on the Range,' 'Red River Valley,' and a lot of tunes written by the Sons of the Pioneers."[14]

When Montgomery joined the Doughboys, his banjo playing changed somewhat. With the Wanderers, he'd primarily played rhythm, whereas with the Doughboys, he started playing solos. In describing his approach to the banjo, Montgomery said, "I tuned my banjo like a viola and fingered it the same as a violin, only it was pitched a fifth lower. This came out so vaudeville musicians could switch from violin to banjo. When Dixieland jazz got popular in the 1920s and earlier, a lot of fiddle players began to lose their jobs, and they started playing the banjo."[15]

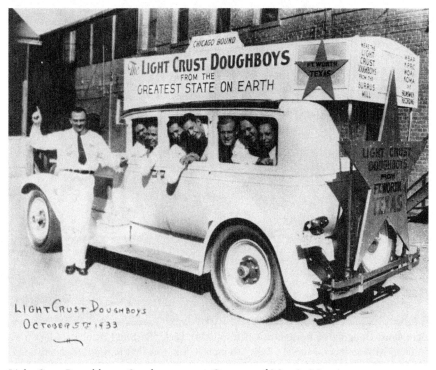

Light Crust Doughboys, October 5, 1933. Courtesy of Marvin Montgomery.

In assessing the differences between black and white tenor banjo players, Montgomery said that the black musicians

> played the rhythm the same way as I do. I probably copied them by listening to records I heard growing up; we had one of them hand-crank 78 players in Iowa; it was a portable that I took along on the tent show in my suitcase. As far as I can remember, the black banjo players didn't really solo for more than four bars, nothing like Eddie Peabody or Harry Reser, who played in the vaudeville show. Harry Reser was the guy I really tried to copy playing solo. "The World Is Waiting for the Sunrise" I learned from Eddie Peabody. Harry Reser had a radio show band called the Clicquot Club Eskimos. When I solo with the tenor banjo, I use a combination of single strings and chords: "Bells of St. Mary's," "Tiger Rag," "Sweet Georgia Brown." A lot of the songs the old Dixieland bands played adapted themselves well to banjo solos. I'm credited for introducing Dixieland banjo to Western swing.[16]

Light Crust Doughboys. Bottom row (left to right): Dick "Bashful" Reinhart, Marvin "Junior" Montgomery, Muryel "Zeke" Campbell. Top row (left to right): Kenneth "Abner" Pitts, Bert "Buddy" Dodson, Eddie Dunn, Clifford "Doctor" Gross. October 29, 1935. Courtesy of Marvin Montgomery.

Ramon "Snub" DeArman, Leon Huff, Clifford "Doctor" Gross, Herbert Barnum, Doc Eastwood, Kenneth "Abner" Pitts, Eddie Dunn. June 1935. Courtesy of Marvin Montgomery.

In addition to the Dixieland style evident in Montgomery's banjo playing, other Doughboys, most notably guitarist Reinhart and pianist John "Knocky" Parker, showed a strong African American influence. Montgomery recalled meeting Parker in 1934. "He played with Blackie Simmons, and I knew he was good. He was running across the street from the Adolphus Hotel to the Baker, where the Doughboys broadcast, and got struck by a car. Didn't hurt him very bad. I was there. That's where I got acquainted with him, and I'm responsible for him playing with the Doughboys."[17]

Parker started playing piano when he was four, while growing up near Palmer, Texas, south of Dallas, but never really learned to read music well. He said his first teachers were the black musicians he met when he accompanied his father to Dallas between 1925 and 1928:

Daddy would go there searching for musicians to come work in the cotton fields. . . . We'd go over there in Deep Ellum. . . . He'd go to all kinds of places. Sometimes the place he'd go to would have a piano, and I'd start playing. . . .

They'd call up all of the people around at these Negro . . . all kinds of, sometimes disreputable places, in degree at least, and people would come with their
homemade instruments. A lot of guitarists, especially—many, many guitarists,
I remember that would come there and we'd play together. The pianists, too,
would sit down, would play four hands on the piano, and shift your hand,
so there'd be my left hand, his left hand, my right hand, his right, and move
all over the piano, playing all kinds of ways and variations. I'd try to copy
everything they did, you see, and they liked this very much. They would laugh
and show me everything they played. This is how, then, I learned from them.
They were my first teachers. Terrific musicians, really. . . . They got to where
they would look forward to my coming up there. Blind Lemon [Jefferson] I
met one time up there. . . . They saw that I liked them, and there was never
any feeling of black and white at all. Never involved, which is kind of strange.
Sometimes I stayed behind the bar in the back room, or somewhere, and go to
sleep. Daddy would go off, doing some kind of business. . . . One time when
there was some kind of a fight, some of the people would hustle me out of
there. They sort of took care of me.[18]

Parker described the pianists' music as "very much like the later Chicago
barrelhouse idiom. Close to that sort of thing. Close to fundamental boogie
woogie. Not in the complicated forms of Pine Top [Smith]. But earlier, like
the Cow Cow [Davenport] school. Very much like that. A lot of times, they
would get on one note and repeat it for a long time, up high or low. Either
one. A whole lot of that." He described the music as "kind of stripped . . .
bare."[19]

Montgomery said that by the time they met, Parker

was a very good piano player. He liked the blues. When we were with the
Doughboys, he'd get those old Bob Crosby records and Dixieland things
and bring them in. I'd transcribe them, and we'd do them with the Doughboys. Two fiddles and guitar play the lead—songs like "South Rampart Street
Parade" and all those, "Bourbon Street Blues." Knocky played things like
"Honky Tonk Train," which is on the blues, and all those things the black
piano players were doing. Knocky could play them just as good as they could,
and we played them on the air. We recorded them. All the boogie-woogie and
blues things. Knocky could play stride and a variety of other styles. We did
"Dallas Blues," "Beale Street Mama," "Memphis Blues," of course, "St. Louis
Blues." All the fiddle bands played the "St. Louis Blues," and some of them
made up words kind of on the risqué side: "There was an old woman who

The Light Crust Doughboys in their own broadcasting studio (l. to r.): Muryel "Zeke" Campbell, Dick "Bashful" Reinhart, Kenneth "Abner" Pitts, Clifford "Doctor" Gross, Parker Willson, John "Knocky" Parker, Ramon "Snub" De Arman, Marvin "Junior" Montgomery. Saginaw, Texas, 1938. Courtesy of Marvin Montgomery.

lived in a shoe. She didn't have any children 'cause she knew what to do." Things like that. These came from the blacks. These were words that we'd hear those guys singing, and we'd pick up on them.[20]

The Doughboys' double-entendre songs included "Pussy, Pussy, Pussy," written by Montgomery, who opens the 1938 recorded version by asking in a falsetto voice: "Say, fellers, I've lost my little pussycat. Will you help me find it?" After they find a cat, he exclaims, "My pussy has no stripes, and it never smelled like that!" The record got a lot of jukebox play, and when Knocky Parker met the famous black musician Fats Waller, he introduced himself as a member of the Light Crust Doughboys from Fort Worth, Texas. "Oh, you were the boys who put out 'Pussy, Pussy, Pussy,' " Waller replied.[21] Decades later, Montgomery was startled to learn that the song had been used in the soundtrack of the 1996 movie *Striptease.* The Doughboys rerecorded the tune on their 2000 album *Doughboy Rock,* and it was covered by the Austin group the Hot Club of Cowtown on its 2003 live album *Continental Stomp.* Other bands used this sort of mildly risqué material as well. The

Brownies recorded "Garbage Man Blues," which was later covered by Roy Newman in a virtually identical treatment. Bob Wills and Tommy Duncan traded minstrel-show banter on the innuendo-laden "Oozlin' Daddy Blues."

Although Fort Worth is generally associated with the origins of Western swing, Montgomery said that during the 1930s he did not see a substantial difference in the music played in that city and Dallas, which are only thirty miles apart but have always been quite different in culture and atmosphere. Blues, in addition to the music of the hot fiddle bands of the period, may have also been as common in Fort Worth as it was in the Deep Ellum area of Dallas. In fact, Montgomery recalled seeing Lead Belly in Fort Worth in the 1930s, though he did not realize it until later, when he heard records of the singer with a twelve-string guitar. "I'd hear blues singers, maybe a blind guy with a cup out there with a guitar. I never saw any bands. And there was a black hotel [the Jim Hotel] right off downtown Fort Worth, where all the white musicians would go when they got off playing a dance around two o'clock in the morning. They'd go play with these black musicians in this hotel in a kind of jam session."[22] In October 1935, when the broadcasts of the Doughboys relocated from the third-floor studios of WFAA, at the Baker Hotel in Dallas, to WBAP, on the top floor of the Blackstone Hotel in Fort Worth, most of the musicians moved as well.

Essentially, Montgomery believed that stylistically, the fiddle bands of the mid-1930s were evolving in a manner parallel to that of the jazz groups of the period. "All the musicians listened to the swing bands—black and white—on radio and on record. Fred Calhoun, the piano player for Milton Brown, for example, tried to imitate Earl 'Fatha' Hines, a black musician who broadcast from Chicago. Instead of calling him 'Fatha,' though, they named him 'Papa.' Knocky Parker was the same way when we auditioned. He played that boogie-woogie piano. Cecil Brower would listen to a hot clarinet chorus by Benny Goodman, and he would copy it almost note for note on the fiddle."

Texas, of course, was segregated at that time, but the airwaves were not, and the white bands had black fans as well. "Papa" Calhoun recalled a Milton Brown gig at a feed store in Whitney, Texas, during which he heard clapping and cries of "Play it out, Papa!" from outside. During a break, he went outside to investigate. "I bet there was five hundred colored folks sittin' on there on a railroad dump," he said. "When they saw me, they yelled, 'Hey! There's old Papa now!' They couldn't come in but they had to listen."[23]

Knocky Parker said that the Doughboys had, in effect, three repertoires: "We had much more Dixieland, and more blues, in our radio programs."[24]

Marvin Montgomery, 1959. Courtesy of Marvin Montgomery.

Montgomery concurred: "Pappy O'Daniel never let us play dances in public ... he insisted upon at least one religious song or hymn ... but on the radio we incorporated more of that jazzy sound."[25]

Clearly, the influence of African American blues and jazz trumpet (Louis Armstrong), clarinet (Sidney Bechet), piano (Earl Hines), violin ("Stuff" Smith), and guitar (Charlie Christian) is apparent in the performance styles of an array of white musicians. "Even if they didn't show it all the time in their radio broadcasts and recordings," Montgomery maintained,

Ted Parrino, Dallas, ca. early 1940s. Courtesy of Ted Parrino.

This is what they played when they were jamming. We did it in the Wanderers and the Light Crust Doughboys, and I heard it in the playing of Milton Brown and the Brownies, Bob Wills and the Texas Playboys, as in the Shelton Brothers, Bill Boyd and the Cowboy Ramblers, Jim Boyd and the Men of the West, and Roy Newman and His Boys. Swing jazz was new, and that made us all want to try it. I wanted to play jazz on the side, and so did others. Cecil Brower went with Ted Parrino in the Ted Fio Rito band. Parrino was with

WRR and KRLD and was a Dallas-based jazz musician who had a number of different groups. Parrino and his contemporaries played at the country clubs and in hotels such as the Century Ballroom of the Adolphus Hotel."[26]

Montgomery continued to play jazz throughout his long career. After World War II, he started the Marvin Montgomery Orchestra, which played the swing and Dixieland standards of the day. "When the Doughboys reorganized after the war," Montgomery recalled,

they had Walker Kirkes [of Roy Newman's band] playing banjo with them for about three months. While this was going on, I was playing jazz. I was the drummer, and I had piano, bass fiddle, trumpet, and three saxophones. The trumpet also played sax. We played at a place called the Midway Inn, about halfway between Dallas and Fort Worth on Highway 80. It was an old gambling and bootleg place with a lot of secret rooms. We got to see most of them, but they were already closed down for that—dice tables, roulette wheels, the whole thing. When I played there, it was a dinner-and-dance kind of place. And we played a lot of Dixieland jazz—"When the Saints Go Marchin' In," "A Closer Walk with Thee," "Sweet Georgia Brown," "Rosetta," and Irving Berlin's "Blue Skies."[27]

Montgomery led a succession of jazz bands that changed their names to meet what he thought might have the most popular appeal—the Mississippi Ramblers and "anything that related to New Orleans: riverboats, ramblers, anything like that." In 1962 he started Smokey and the Bearkats ("Smokey the Bear was in back then"), which became his most successful group. "So I kept the name Bearkats . . . I think we must have opened every shopping center in Dallas in the 1960s."[28]

For Montgomery, transitioning between the music he performed with the Light Crust Doughboys and the Bearkats came easy. The role of the tenor banjo as a rhythm instrument, he liked to say, was essentially the same in Western swing and Dixieland jazz, and was in this way an embodiment of the cross-fertilization of white and black musical styles.

The Contemporaries of
Marvin Montgomery

Western Swing, Texas Fiddling, and
the Big "D" Jamboree

Smokey Montgomery's mainstay band, the Light Crust Dough-boys, from its earliest incarnation as the Wills Fiddle Band, was the incubator of the music that came to be called Western swing.[1] Many, notably including Wills biographer Charles R. Townsend, give Bob Wills virtually all of the credit for establishing the genre when he left the Doughboys and founded the Texas Playboys. Others, such as Milton Brown biographer Cary Ginell, say that Brown's post-Doughboys band, the Musical Brownies, was the first Western swing group and that Brown's contributions have been overlooked because of his early death as the result of a 1936 car crash. At any rate, when Brown died, the music that he and Wills played had not yet been labeled "Western swing." At the time, the term referred to the African American music of the Southwest that fueled the raucous nightlife of politically corrupt Kansas City. The Carolina Cotton Pickers' 1937 recording of "Moten Swing," popularized by the seminal Kansas City bandleader Benny Moten, was called "Western (Moten) Swing." Texas-born musician Henry "Buster" Smith, who began his career in Deep Ellum and went on to play with Count Basie and to mentor Charlie Parker, said years later while ruminating on his success as an arranger, "Several cats wanted me to do some arrangements for them. Out of all them great arrangers, they thought I had somethin' special—that Western swing."[2]

Within a few years, however, "Western swing" had come to mean the highly eclectic music of white bandleaders that incorporated elements of country, jazz, popular music, and what Wills called "the Spanish tinge." Brown had experimented briefly with horns, but others, such as Wills and Oklahoma-born California bandleader Spade Cooley, included large horn sections and, in Cooley's case, even a harp.

The transition in meaning of "Western swing" seems to have taken place in the early 1940s. In April 1942 a white Los Angeles–area publication, the

Roy Newman and His Boys, Dallas, ca. 1930s. Courtesy of Walker Kirkes.

Wilmington Press, ran a series of ads for local performances by an unnamed "Western swing orchestra" playing a "square dance." A few months later disc jockey Al Jarvis dubbed Cooley the "King of Western Swing,"[3] which was also the title of a short 1945 Warner Brothers film featuring Cooley and his band.

However complex and multilayered it became, Western swing had its roots in the fiddle music brought by settlers from the Appalachian region of the southeastern United States.[4] The early fiddlers who were part of this migration were exposed not only to African American music but also to the traditions of Mexicans and to those of Germans, Bohemians, and other Central Europeans who brought polkas, schottisches, and waltzes. Moreover, in southeast Texas, the influences of Cajun French and Creole cultures were prominent. It is known from oral accounts that the tradition of fiddling was fairly widespread among rural African Americans in Texas during the nineteenth century. A white fiddler who requested anonymity when interviewed at a fiddle contest in Hallettsville, Texas, in 1984 explained that "in the 1800s the fiddle was considered the devil's instrument, and only blacks could play the instrument because it was believed they didn't have any soul." The string and fiddle band traditions were, to some extent, carried on by African American musicians such as Coley Jones in Dallas and John T. Samples in Sweetwater, in West Texas. While Samples never recorded with his band, it is evident from Jones's recordings that black and white musicians drew from a shared repertoire. The origin of these tunes is unknown, but it is clear that the musicians were very much aware of each other, either through recordings or from simply hearing each other perform on the streets or on rare occasions playing together in sessions such as those in which Montgomery took part at the Jim Hotel in Fort Worth.

The improvisation that is a key element of Western swing evolved from the Texas style of fiddling, characterized by long bow strokes and intricately fingered and rhythmically varied interpretations of traditional tunes. In the 1920s, however, while this style was developing, some performers still clung to older modes of playing. Moses J. Bonner, for example, was a contemporary of well-known Amarillo, Texas, fiddler Alexander "Eck" Robertson. Bonner was recorded by Victor in 1925 as Captain M. J. Bonner (the "Texas Fiddler"), probably as a result of the renown he had achieved as the host of the initial broadcast of the WBAP "Barn Dance" on January 4, 1923. In this broadcast Bonner was backed by Fred Wagner's Hilo Five Orchestra and, over the course of an hour and a half, played an array of old-time fiddle tunes, interspersed with Hawaiian music. Like Robertson's, Bonner's repertoire was composed mainly of hoedowns; consequently, his recording career was relatively short lived.

In addition to Robertson and Bonner, Texas fiddlers from the Dallas–Fort Worth area were also recorded during the late 1920s. These included Ervin Solomon and Joe Hughes, as well as A. L. Steeley and J. W. Graham. Solomon on fiddle and Hughes on second fiddle were later accompanied by the guitar playing of Jim Solomon, Ervin's younger brother. Their only recording consisted of two traditional tunes, "Ragtime Annie" and "Sally Johnson." Steeley and Graham also had a traditional repertoire. In fact, Steeley and Graham recorded "Ragtime Annie" for Brunswick at the same time that Solomon and Hughes were recording it for Victor. However, Graham was somewhat atypical of the Texas tradition and played the five-string banjo.

James Robert "Bob" Wills came from several generations of fiddlers and started his performing career at an early age, playing for house dances in the Texas Panhandle with his father, "Uncle" John Wills, who also provided him with his signature "ah-haaa" holler. "Eck" Robertson once exclaimed, after losing a contest to John Wills, "Hell, no! He didn't outfiddle me. That

damned old man Wills outhollered me."[5] Western swing steel-guitar inno-
vator Bob Dunn, who played with Milton Brown, was the son of a fiddler.
Black musicians whose fathers were fiddlers included San Marcos, Texas,
native Eddie Durham, a pioneer of the electric guitar; Navasota, Texas, songster Mance Lipscomb; and Louisiana-born Clarence "Gatemouth" Brown,
who played the fiddle, as well as the guitar, throughout his long career.

Virtually all of the white country and Western swing musicians from
Texas and elsewhere in the Southwest were influenced by black music.
Wills once rode a horse fifty miles to hear Bessie Smith, the "Empress of the
Blues," and called her "the greatest thing I ever heard." White Texas fiddlers
often used "bent" or "blue" notes. Wills said, "I slurred my fiddle in order
to play the blues." Aside from hollering, he usually left the vocal duties to
others, such as longtime Playboy Tommy Duncan, but when he did sing,
Wills often performed a blues and said, "I have always been a blues singer."[6]

Perhaps a more overt example of this racial crossover was "Prince"
Albert Hunt, a white fiddler born in 1900 in Terrell, Texas, east of Dallas.
Hunt led a band called the Texas Ramblers and was a popular entertainer
at house dances and dance halls. He lived in the black section of Terrell
and, like Bob Wills, sometimes performed in blackface in medicine shows.
He even employed an "ah-haa" holler similar to Wills's. Guitarist Harmon
Clem recalled that Hunt would don a comic outfit, complete with top hat.
"He'd get that black on, wasn't a nigger that could imitate him at all, hardly.
He was, oh, he was terrific," Clem told filmmaker Ken Harrison. "I moved
to Dallas in 1928. . . . Well, we played them eating joints down on Deep
Ellum."[7] On March 21, 1931, a jealous husband gunned Hunt down outside
Confederate Hall on North Harwood Street after he had played a dance. A
newspaper account of the slaying said Hunt had performed on radio in
Dallas and had an address in the city, though he apparently regularly trav-
eled back and forth to Terrell, a distance of about forty miles. A cousin,
R. C. Hunt, said that the last time he saw the musician, a woman drove up
and ordered him into a car at gunpoint for a trip to Dallas.[8]

Hunt's 1928 OKeh recording of "Blues in a Bottle" is often cited by
music historians in the development of hot fiddle and Western swing music.
On the recording, Hunt was accompanied by another fiddler, Oscar Harper,
and his nephew, Doc. The Harpers also lived in Terrell and often performed
with Hunt. Those who knew them recalled that Hunt generally handled the
hot solos, while Oscar Harper played waltzes, at which Hunt was less pro-
ficient. Oscar Harper was well known in rural East Texas and was recorded
by John Lomax for the Library of Congress in 1942.

The Harpers were among several string bands in East Texas during this period but were not as commercially successful as the East Texas Serenaders, who recorded for Brunswick, Columbia, and Decca from 1927 to 1934. Led by a left-handed fiddler, D. H. Williams, whose parents had moved to Texas from Tennessee, the East Texas Serenaders included Claude Hammonds on guitar, John Munnerlyn on tenor banjo, and Henry Bogan on a string bass that was actually a three-string cello. Together they played traditional tunes such as "Sally Goodin" and "Old Joe Clark" but also performed rags, including "Mineola Rag" and "Combination Rag," which extended beyond the repertoire of most fiddle bands. Moreover, they introduced elements of swing jazz and in many respects were transitional figures in the development of Western swing.

Texas' population was shifting from rural to urban, and many players regarded music as a means of escape from the backbreaking labor of farmwork. When fiddler J. R. Chatwell approached bandleader Cliff Bruner for a job at a country dance, he exclaimed, "Man, get me out of this cotton patch!"[9] Similarly, fiddler Johnny Gimble, born in 1926 and reared on a farm east of Tyler, learned music from his brothers and performed with them from an early age. "I found out that picking cotton was a lot harder than playing the fiddle," he recalled:

> By the time I was twelve or thirteen years old, we were playing gigs for a flour company. You know, the Light Crust Doughboys were big on radio down there [Fort Worth]. So I guess a lot of the flour companies picked up the banner and did the same thing. We were playing for Peacemaker Flour from Morrison Milling Company in Sherman, Texas, and the old boy would pick us up at 5:30 in the morning on a Saturday and drive maybe a hundred miles down in East Texas, and we'd set up on a flatbed truck in front of a grocery store and play all day, and we'd get two dollars apiece. Which was about four times what I could make picking cotton.[10]

After graduating from high school in 1943, Gimble went to Shreveport, Louisiana, to play with the Shelton Brothers. Gimble recalled:

> A hillbilly band, as they were called then, could, if you could get a program on a radio station, whether you had a sponsor or not, you'd play for nothing if they'd let you advertise your dates. . . . So we were on the air early in the morning, and we'd say, "We're gonna be down in Navasota, Texas, at the high school auditorium playing the 4H Club," or whoever sponsored it. And

we'd go down and back every night; they would leave at two, three in the afternoon, drive down, play a show, come back and sleep a few hours and do an early-morning show and three times a week a noon show.[11]

Hailing from the northeast Texas community of Reilly Springs, the Shelton Brothers were also rural musicians. Their real names were Robert Attlesey and Joe Attlesey. Borrowing a family name, they performed as Bob and Joe Shelton. Bob was known as the "Hopkins County Firecracker" and frequently played the clown, complete with overalls and floppy hat. Together the brothers started singing in Longview, Texas, in 1929, playing for tips at root-beer and near-beer stands and at Clint Aycock's café. In late 1929 the brothers moved to Tyler, where they played with Leon Chappelear and changed the name of their group to the Lone Star Cowboys. In Tyler their performances were broadcast live on KGKB radio. The Sheltons and the Lone Star Cowboys reflected the development of country music, though they were more conservative than most groups. As a duet, they performed with mandolin and guitar and played songs similar to those of their duet contemporaries elsewhere in the South. However, their repertoire had a blues element that was uncommon in mandolin-guitar duets and was clearly influenced by the African American music of their day. In fact, the Shelton Brothers played Blind Lemon Jefferson's "Matchbox Blues," as well as hokum jazz tunes such as "Sittin' on Top of the World" and "Four or Five Times."

During the 1930s the Shelton Brothers played often in Louisiana, performing on KWKH in Shreveport and on WWL in New Orleans, where they teamed with Lew Childre and Curly Fox. In 1933, performing with Chappelear as the Lone Star Cowboys, they made the first recording of "Deep Elem Blues," for the Victor and Bluebird labels. In 1934, as the Shelton Brothers, they were among the first groups to sign with the new Decca label, and a year later they rerecorded "Deep Elem Blues."

With the success of "Deep Elem Blues," the Sheltons alternated between KWHK, where they were also billed as the Sunshine Boys, and WFAA in Dallas, where they became securely rooted in 1941. They also maintained close political and musical relations with singer Jimmie Davis. In fact, Joe Shelton fronted Davis's band from 1943 to 1949 and was involved in his successful race for governor of Louisiana in 1943.

Instrumentally, the Sheltons resisted the influence of the early Western swing bands and continued to maintain elements of their unique hillbilly style into the 1970s. They even forbade their youngest brother, Merle, who often played rhythm guitar with them after 1935, to play barre chords, which were identified with jazz. However, as folklorist Bill Malone notes, they gradually incorporated more swing elements in their music, and by the late forties they had become virtually indistinguishable from other swing-oriented country ensembles.[12]

Johnny Gimble joined the band that campaigned for Davis in 1943, a band that included fiddler Jimmy Thomasson, singer Curly Perrin, and East Texas pianist Aubrey "Moon" Mullican, whose honky-tonk style later made him a rock 'n' roll pioneer. "I was getting to play with the big boys then," said Gimble.[13] His career with the Sheltons was cut short in the spring of 1944, when he quit to prepare for military service.

The Shelton Brothers and Light Crust Doughboys were among a number of popular bands in Dallas in the 1930s and forties. Others, as Montgomery noted, included the bands of Roy Newman and Bill Boyd, brother of Jim Boyd. Neither Newman nor Bill Boyd worked much as a touring musician; instead, for many years both were associated with Dallas radio stations. Newman was a studio musician for both WRR and WFAA, while Boyd was an announcer and disc jockey on WRR. Both were part of a pool of musicians who played in varying combinations and remained popular in Dallas for more than twenty years. At various times, Jim Boyd played with the Light Crust Doughboys and the Hillbilly Boys.

Newman had been a radio staff pianist since the 1920s. He rarely played lead or solo passages in the bands he organized after 1931. Instead, he provided an unobtrusive, rhythmic background and tended to feature the musicians in his band, such as those in Roy Newman and His Boys, which performed on WRR's "Noontime Varieties" after 1933. In this group Newman produced what Malone has called "an infectious dance music which revealed little indebtedness to country music and much to blues and New Orleans jazz."[14]

Newman prided himself on enlisting hot fiddlers such as Art Davis, Thurman Neal, Jesse Ashlock, and Carroll Hubbard and sometimes used Jim Boyd on electric guitar. He emulated Milton Brown in his vocals and band arrangements, especially in his early recording sessions, but later, as Malone observed, moved in even jazzier directions. Bill Boyd's Cowboy Ramblers, on the other hand, remained essentially a country string band, though Boyd moved in more of a Western swing direction after 1937 by augmenting his band in recording sessions with Doughboys such as "Knocky" Parker on piano, fiddler Kenneth Pitts, banjoist Marvin "Smokey" Montgomery, and guitarist Muryel "Zeke" Campbell.

Jim Boyd, ca. 1930s. Courtesy of Walker Kirkes.

Bill Boyd and Jim Boyd were born in 1910 and 1914, respectively, on a cattle ranch and cotton farm in Fannin County, Texas, and began performing country music on radio in Greenville in 1926. In 1929 they moved to Dallas, where they stayed, aside from periodic touring. Bill was a talented musician who quickly became involved in the burgeoning Dallas scene. In 1932 he participated in Jimmie Rodgers's Dallas recording session and during that same year formed the Cowboy Ramblers. The band included

Bill Boyd and Jim Boyd (guitar and bass), Art Davis (fiddle), and Walker Kirkes (banjo); all were studio musicians at WRR. Together they made their first recordings for the Victor label in 1934.

The country music heard in taverns, dance halls, homes, and over the radio in Dallas reflected the widespread popularity of Western swing and other styles. The Sheltons' theme song was the popular tune "Let a Smile Be Your Umbrella." The music of Newman's and Boyd's bands ran the gamut. The Ramblers recorded, for instance, Western-themed songs such as "Ridin' Old Paint and Leadin' Old Ball" and "The Strawberry Roan"; sentimental songs of Mama, Daddy, and home, such as "By a Window" ("There's a little light always shining bright in a window at the end of the lane / There is someone there in her rocking chair by that window at the end of the lane"); and hot blues, hokum, and Western swing.

Newman's band played a similarly diverse repertoire. They recorded "(What Did I Do to Be So) Black and Blue," whose lyrics become ironic when performed by a white singer, as well as novelty songs such as "When There's Tears in the Eyes of a Potato." A September 1935 recording session produced "Shine on, Harvest Moon," "Corrine, Corrina," and "Hot Dog Stomp," featuring Jim Boyd in what some researchers believe is the first recorded use of standard electric guitar.

As Dallas continued to attract immigrants from rural Texas, interest in country music swelled. Live radio broadcasts on WFAA and KRLD attracted local, regional, and national performers. According to the late former disc jockey Johnny Hicks, he and "Pappy" Hal Horton "had the country music radio scene pretty well tied up from 1946 to 1949 on Dallas's KRLD. Pappy Horton had four nights with the *Hillbilly Hit Parade,* then he and I did the *Cornbread Matinee* daily stage show from the Arcadia Theater."[15] In 1947 Horton and Ole Top Rail nightclub owner Slim McDonald leased the Sportatorium, an octagonal wrestling arena on Industrial Boulevard south of downtown Dallas, for weekly country music broadcasts. The show was first called the *Texas State Barn Dance,* then the *Lone Star Barn Dance.* In 1948 wrestling entrepreneur Ed McLemore took control of the show and soon renamed it the *Big "D" Jamboree.* Hicks became a regular, first as a singer, then as emcee. *Big "D" Jamboree* became a showcase for some of the biggest names in country music. It attracted more than 4,000 people every Saturday. Among its early regular performers were Walter and Homer Callahan, North Carolina–born musicians who had been a popular duo for years and may have had a financial stake in the *Jamboree* as well. Apparently feeling that their given names were a little too uptown, they billed themselves as Bill and

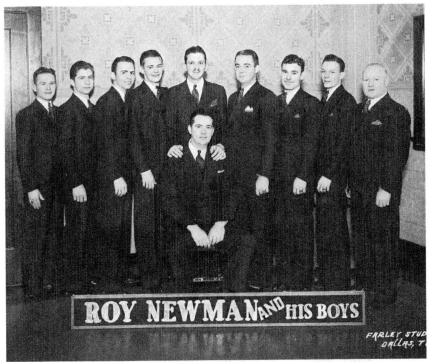

Roy Newman and His Boys, Dallas, ca. late 1930s. Courtesy of Walker Kirkes.

Joe Callahan. Homer (Bill) Callahan, who remained in Dallas until his death in 2002, said of the show, "It was strictly country; it was just like the *Grand Ole Opry*. We had different acts every week . . . even Elvis Presley before he got famous. He was always country until that little shake changed him."[16]

The Callahans combined guitar, mandolin, hillbilly singing, and comedy routines. Like the Sheltons, they incorporated blues into their repertoire. "Rattle Snake Daddy," originally recorded in 1934, was a solo by Bill (who for a brief period also worked as a soloist on several nationally broadcast radio shows) and was one of the Callahans' most popular records. "Rattle Snake Daddy" was a mainstay of their act and was rerecorded for eight different labels, staying in print as late as 1951, around the time the Callahan brothers became an opening act for Lefty Frizzell, whom Bill managed for a time.

The *Jamboree* featured an array of local, regional, and national acts, including Frizzell, Bill Monroe, Johnny Cash, June Carter, Rose Maddox, Patsy Cline, Hank Snow, George Jones, Willie Nelson, Roy Acuff, Ernest Tubb, Kitty Wells, Sonny James, teenage East Texan "Sunshine Ruby,"

Bill Boyd and His Cowboy Ramblers (left to right): Audrey "Art" Davis (fiddle), Bill Boyd (guitar/vocal), Jim Boyd (bass/vocal), and Walker Kirkes (tenor banjo).

Marty Robbins, Wanda Jackson, a young Doug Sahm, Bob Wills, and, separately, his former vocalist Tommy Duncan, Tex Ritter, Floyd Tillman, Hank Locklin, Roy Rogers, Merle Travis, Hank Thompson, and Webb Pierce. As rockabilly and rock 'n' roll grew in popularity, the *Jamboree* proved relatively open to the new music, though not without some backstage tensions. Elvis performed four times on the show and was backed in at least one East

Texas performance by the Country Gentlemen, the renamed Doughboys, under the direction of Smokey Montgomery. Carl Perkins appeared regularly for a time, and the show featured Jerry Lee Lewis and Gene Vincent. Local acts such as the Belew Twins, "Groovy" Joe Poovey, Sid King and the Five Strings, and Ronnie "the Blonde Bomber" Dawson had a strong following.

One of the most interesting *Big "D"* performers was Charline Arthur, an East Texas native who incorporated black rhythm and blues into her music. She was a flamboyant, crowd-pleasing performer and a rebel, a "Janis Joplin before her time," in the words of her friend Helen Hall, a Dallas singer who was also a *Jamboree* regular.[17] Elvis cited Arthur as an inspiration. Her outspokenness and possibly her lesbianism led to clashes with music-industry powers such as Chet Atkins, and, in the mid-1950s, she lost her marriage, her *Jamboree* job, and her RCA recording contract, and descended into a scuffling life of substance abuse and small-time gigs. Interest in her revived shortly before she died in 1985, and some now hail her as a feminist icon.

The *Jamboree*, beset by changing tastes, folded in 1966, a few years after Montgomery left the show. Among the many groups in which he was subsequently involved was the Levee Singers, which performed at the Levee Club, owned by Ed Bernet, a member of the group. The band also played Las Vegas, opening for comedian Joey Bishop, and appeared on national television programs such as *Hollywood Palace* and *Hootenanny* and on shows hosted by Jimmy Dean and Danny Kaye. The Levee Singers included former *Jamboree* star Ronnie Dawson. The versatile rocker also played rhythm guitar with the Doughboys, worked as a session musician, and recorded commercial jingles before being rediscovered by the British rockabilly crowd in the 1980s. He remained a popular recording and performing artist until his death from cancer in 2003.

Montgomery also co-owned a music-publishing company and became a successful record producer. He and Bernet owned the Sumet (later Sumet-Bernet) recording studio, and Montgomery produced and played on hits such as Bruce Channel's "Hey, Baby" (with Dawson on drums and a young Delbert McClinton on harmonica) and "Hey, Paula," by Paul and Paula. Bob Wills's last recording, *For the Last Time*, a two-album set overseen by Merle Haggard, was recorded at Sumet-Bernet in 1973.

In 1989 Montgomery formed the Dallas Banjo Band, which included more than thirty banjos and a tuba and included in its repertoire unlikely selections such as Beethoven's Fifth Symphony and George Gershwin's *Rhapsody in Blue*. The Doughboys added a much younger musician, Art Greenhaw, on bass. "We had to hire Art because we couldn't carry our

amplifiers anymore," Montgomery joked. The group performed regularly at
the Pocket Sandwich Theatre in Dallas and received several Grammy nomina-
tions, including one for a recording with James Blackwood of the famed Blackwood Brothers gospel quartet. Montgomery and the Doughboys received a
number of honors in his last years. They also collaborated with the Lone Star
Ballet in Amarillo. Montgomery played his last gig with the Doughboys and
the Abilene Philharmonic less than a month before his death from leukemia in
June 2001. His funeral was held in the Hall of State at Dallas's Fair Park. His
banjo sat in its stand onstage during the service, which featured the Bearkats,
the Dallas Banjo Band, and, of course, the Doughboys.

Montgomery's death marked the end of a career that spanned much of
the history of American popular entertainment. As a member of the Doughboys, he had even appeared in two Western movies, where he said he became
the target of good-natured ribbing as "a guy from Texas who couldn't ride
a horse." The first of these was *Oh, Susanna!*, starring Gene Autry, shot in
California in 1936. This film would have featured the Musical Brownies,
but after Milton Brown's death they were replaced by the Doughboys. That
same year the group made a second movie with Autry, *The Big Show,* part
of which was filmed at Dallas's Fair Park, where the Texas Centennial was
under way. Montgomery said that during the filming he became friends with
Len Slye, who later became famous as Roy Rogers. Contrary to his later
squeaky-clean image, Slye liked to party, and Republic Pictures locked him
in his room at the Adolphus Hotel. But he'd climb over the transom, Montgomery said, and the two would head for Deep Ellum.[18]

Other country performers, including the Callahans and Bob Wills and
the Playboys, also appeared in Western movies, capitalizing on the image of
the cowboy, which became a Hollywood staple starting in the 1930s. Some,
such as Wills, hailed from authentic Western backgrounds, but overall the
films had much more to do with the celluloid cowboy than the real thing.
Walker Kirkes recalled that when Roy Newman or Jim and Bill Boyd posed
for promotional photographs, they usually had their bands rent cowboy
costumes. In one instance, Jim Boyd even smeared cow manure on his boot
so it appeared that he had just come in from the pasture. Bill Callahan
recalled a show in which Tex Ritter's horse was brought onstage and pro-
ceeded to defecate, convulsing the audience and bringing the proceedings to
a halt for some time.[19]

Dallas has always been a moviegoing town, and before theaters moved
to the suburbs, they formed a glittery row, which African Americans sometimes sardonically referred to as "the great white way," on Elm Street just

BIG  D JAMBOREE

The Southwest's Biggest, Oldest, Boldest and Best Country Musical Attraction.

Official Program

10 cents

MARVIN MONTGOMERY

Starring Tonight

JOHNNY MATHIS
and
LES CHAMBERS
★ THE FIVE STRINGS
HANK LOCKLIN
DOUG BRAGG
JIMMIE COLLIE
CHARLINE ARTHUR
AND ALL OF THE
JAMBOREE GANG

BROADCAST ON KRLD EVERY SATURDAY NIGHT 8:30 TO MIDNIGHT
CBS SATURDAY NIGHT COUNTRY STYLE — COAST-TO-COAST

Look for Your Lucky Number!

Sportatorium

Ed McLemore
Producer

Big "D" Jamboree, program book cover, February 19, 1955. Courtesy of Marvin Montgomery.

west of Deep Ellum, near the hotel where Montgomery stayed in 1934. Westerns were also popular with black audiences, and African American theaters in Deep Ellum and North Dallas also screened "race" films such as *Brother Martin: Servant of Jesus* (1942), *Marching On* (1943), and *Juke Joint* (1947), directed by Spencer Williams and produced by the white entrepreneur Alfred N. Sack and his Sack Enterprises, then based in Dallas. Williams was an African American actor and filmmaker who worked in Dallas for ten years and is best known for directing the 1941 film *Blood of Jesus* and later playing Andy on the *Amos 'n' Andy* television show. Other films produced by Sack starred Herb Jeffries, who introduced the black movie cowboy in *Harlem on the Prairie* (1937), *Two-Gun Man from Harlem* (1938), *Harlem Rides the Range* (1939), and *The Bronze Buckaroo* (1939), which were all immensely popular with black audiences.

During the 1940s and 1950s, Western swing enjoyed a boom in California, where the bands of Bob Wills, Spade Cooley, and others packed huge dance halls. Wills lived in California for several years. In 1950 he returned to Texas and opened the Bob Wills Ranch House, on Corinth Street not far from the Sportatorium, in an enormous venue built by eccentric Dallas millionaire O. L. Nelms. The bar was inlaid with seventeen hundred silver dollars. Once each night Wills rode his horse, Punkin, onto the dance floor. The place drew large crowds, but Wills was a poor businessman and a binge alcoholic, and financial problems forced him to sell the Ranch House in 1952. The new owners included Jack Ruby, who a decade later became embroiled in the controversy surrounding the Kennedy assassination after he shot and killed Lee Harvey Oswald. The Ranch House was eventually renamed the Longhorn Ballroom and was owned and operated by bandleader Dewey Groom.

During the late forties and early fifties, Dallas became nationally known for its country-music recording activity, primarily as a result of the studio started by the legendary Jim Beck in his home off Mockingbird Lane near Southern Methodist University. In 1948 or 1949 he moved to 1101 Ross Avenue. Songwriter Jimmy Fields (born in 1924 in Sherman, Texas) said that at that time Beck was recording Lefty Frizzell, Ray Price, and Marty Robbins. "He recorded anybody and everybody. If he hadn't died in the mid-fifties, Dallas would have become Nashville, Tennessee. Paul Cohen from Decca brought his artists to Dallas. Don Law from Columbia brought his country artists, folks like Little Jimmie Dickens and others."[20]

Shortly before Beck's death, Fields started his own recording business. "I'd record both white and black musicians. I had three labels: Kick was for colored rhythm and blues, Felco was for contemporary-type white and black bands, and Jamaka, which was first intended for country and later for anything and everything." Fields used Beck's studio when it was available but was forced to take his black bands to Fort Worth because "no one would let me record them in Dallas."[21]

By the fifties, of course, Deep Ellum's image had faded from the wild and dangerous place of the Sheltons' "Deep Elem Blues." In 1940 they recorded "What's the Matter with Deep Elem" as a sort of musical postscript, posing a call-and-response question and answer:

> What's the matter with Deep Elem?
> Deep Elem's just too doggone slow.

Benny Binion

Gambling and the Policy Racket

Despite periodic reform efforts, prostitution and gambling had persisted in Dallas since its days as a frontier town. In 1876 Mayor Ben Long's attempts to enforce the law spurred the gambling-den proprietors to gather in the second story of a downtown building and defy Long and his deputies for three days and nights—until a truce was reached. In October 1883, when District Attorney Charles Clint mounted a campaign to drive gamblers out of town, a delegation of businessmen urged him to desist. They pointed out that Fort Worth was offering gamblers free rent and $3,500 cash to move. This attitude of unofficial tolerance persisted until after World War II.

In the 1920s gambling in Dallas was controlled by a man with the appropriate name of Warren Diamond. His headquarters was in the Southland Hotel on Commerce Street, where high-stakes card and dice games were played. "The biggest crap game in town was there," said Johnny Moss, who was born in 1906 and grew up in Dallas. "The biggest poker game in town was at the Southland." Moss became a childhood friend of Benny Binion, the city's future gambling boss, and learned to cheat at cards from a local gambler named Blackie Williams. "It was a bad town, Dallas," Moss said of the place when he was a young man. "That was Clyde Barrow days, you know."[1]

Binion, who got his start working for Diamond, was investigated in seven killings but was convicted of only one, the 1931 killing of a black liquor runner named Frank Bolding. Binion received a two-year suspended sentence. The killing earned him his nickname, "Cowboy," for the way he rolled off a box and came up shooting when Bolding pulled a knife. Binion went into business for himself in the late twenties. For a few years he had to deal with competition from Diamond and with occasional police raids. By the mid-1930s he had gained a virtual monopoly on gambling in Dallas.

After Diamond committed suicide in 1933, the city, anxious to boost revenues and to promote attendance at the State Fair of Texas, established a wide-open atmosphere—though the laws remained on the books.

The administration of Mayor Woodall Rodgers devised what amounted to a system of taxing and licensing gambling. Police vice officers counted heads in the casinos, and these places paid a weekly "fine" of $10 per patron. Will Wilson, who put an end to this practice as Dallas's district attorney in the late forties, recalled that these fines netted the city about $250,000 annually. In addition to the casinos, which numbered as many as twenty-seven in downtown Dallas, there were open bookie joints downtown. Many businesses and country clubs featured slot machines. People could gamble on horse races at Fair Park and at Arlington Downs in Arlington, halfway between Dallas and Fort Worth.

The flavor of the time is captured in an anecdote from Harmon Howze, who remembered a big win at the track as a young man in Dallas. After a day's work at Dallas Power and Light Company, he often went to the horse races at Fair Park. His brother-in-law manned the back gate, and Howze got to know the men who worked at the track.

One day one of the track employees told him, "Hey, I got us a deal today!" There was a horse in the seventh race, a little speckled filly named Thistle-Lucy, that was going to win. He asked Howze how much he could bet. Howze, who was making about $14 a week, said he could bet no more than $5; he had to keep some money to eat on till he got paid on Friday. His friend offered to lend him $5 if he lost.

"Anyway," Howze said,

this little old horse comes in and paid $42 on a $2 ticket! You could figure that one out. I had ninety-something dollars. I was really rich!

I went downtown that night—got on a streetcar and went downtown. The Palace Theater had a little shop called National Shirt Shop, [where] you could buy a shirt for a dollar. And then just across the street, there was a shoe outfit where you could buy a pair of shoes for $4.50. And I bought five shirts and I bought a new pair of shoes. I bought me a chamois jacket; that's when chamois jackets were really in. That was $14 I'd blown; that was a full week's work.

And this kid working in there, I gave him a $50 bill 'cause that was the way they'd paid me off at the window, you know. He looked at it, and he didn't know what to do. And he went back in the back and called his boss and told him that I was in there, and he probably thought that I stole that fifty. And his boss told him to "take that fifty over there to the Palace Theater and let that gal that sells tickets look at it, and she'll tell you whether it's a bad fifty or not."

So he came back and said, "Will you watch the store while I go over?" . . . I could have carried off the cash register! I said, "Sure, go ahead."

I was so rich I didn't know what to do with it. Room and board was $7 a week, and I was making $14 a week. That's the richest I've ever been.[2]

Many low-income Dallasites favored the numbers game, known as "policy," another of Binion's rackets. Essentially an illegal lottery, policy flourished in the black community, and bets were taken in virtually every café and in many other small, black-owned businesses on Central Track and in North Dallas. Betting slips reflected the names of the various "wheels" where winners were selected: White and Green, Texas and Louisiana, Harlem Queen, High Noon, Grand Prize, East West, and so forth. The White and Green wheel was located in a heavily guarded room over the White and Green Café in the 2400 block of Elm, in the heart of Deep Ellum.

Runners who stole from Binion were known to end up dead, and the police made little effort to find the killers. But Binion also provided employment for black men when times were tough. A Dallas physician, Dr. Emerson Emory, said his father, Cory Bates Emory, was a numbers salesman during the Depression and was glad to have the job:

That was a big employment thing for black men back in the late twenties and thirties. They had what the called the policy houses, where you would go and turn in the numbers. In North Dallas there was one behind the Powell Hotel, which was over on State Street, and there was one behind the State Theater. They had one in Deep Ellum, upstairs, over the White and Green Café, and that's what this policy was called, White and Green. The policy slip was much like one of those lotto slips. It was long, and it had twelve numbers down each side. You could play any amount. The most common play was for ten cents. And my father earned the nickname of "Tackem" because he would tell the people, "How about tackin' 'em down for a nickel?" So if you played, say, numbers 22, 13, 44, something like that, and they all came out on one side, you would win $10 for your ten cents. If you did what they called "flat-saddle," which meant they came out on either side in that combination, you would still win, but not as much: $5. Then later they had three numbers across the bottom that were called various things. And they picked the numbers the same way they do in the present lotto, with a big barrel with the numbers in it. And they would turn it, and the number would fall out. That was the wheel.[3]

Postcard showing Fair Park racetrack, 1930s. Courtesy of Documentary Arts.

Policy provided a measure of hope during rough times. Binion distributed "dream books," which assigned numbers to the subjects of dreams to guide people in making their bets. Other illegal businesses flourished, too. Brothels prospered in walk-up hotels and other places with little interference from the law. There seems to have been little in the way of hard drugs, but there was plenty of alcohol both during and after Prohibition. In cafés, soda-water stands, and social clubs, liquor and beer flowed, and homemade chock liquor was popular. One favored spot pictured in the *WPA Dallas Guide and History* bore the intriguing name Gypsy Tea Room, which in the late 1990s became the name of a club in the new Deep Ellum.

By the forties, marijuana was plentiful in Deep Ellum, too, sold by the stick. Writer Terry Southern recalled seeing the Clouds of Joy perform in a Central Track joint and assuming that they got their name became they were always wreathed in marijuana smoke. Retired police officer Gus Edwards, who patrolled the area from 1944 to 1953, said police knew the supply was plentiful when the price of a marijuana cigarette dropped from a dollar to seventy-five cents. Edwards's foot-patrol partner was an older cop named Harry Stewart. "We started there at Elm and Central and went through to Hall and Thomas," Edwards said. "Around Elm and Central was the hot spot. Boy, there on the weekend, we'd get [arrest] fifteen or twenty every eight-hour shift,"[4] mostly for public intoxication.

Officers Harry Stewart (left) and C. W. "Gus" Edwards pretend to arrest "Open the Door Richard," ca. late 1940s. Courtesy of C. W. Edwards.

Across the street, people would sit on railroad ties sunk in the ground, Edwards said, and "those farmers, back in the cotton-picking days, they'd come in their trucks, trying to hire them people, load 'em up just like stock and go to West Texas to pick that cotton. There was one of them [farmers] come to us mad as an old wet hen, says, 'Ain't there anything y'all call do about them people sitting out there on their butts and won't work?' " One of the loungers asked, "Say, ain't this ground around here kinda rolling?" Sure, said Edwards, playing along with the joke. "Well, roll that cotton down here and we'll pick it," the man replied.[5]

Edwards said he was sympathetic to blacks, though he'd hardly met any before coming to Dallas. He was raised in Sterling, Texas, west of San Angelo, and said,

There's no black people there. And see, they put me right in colored town. And in fact, I had officers to accuse me of being a nigger lover. You know, I didn't

Advertisement for businesses owned by C. S. McMillan, Quitman McMillan's son. 1947 *Negro City Directory. Courtesy of Documentary Arts.*

Raymond Hamilton, a member of
the Parker-Barrow gang, Dallas, ca.
early 1930s. Courtesy of the Texas/
Dallas History and Archives Division, Dallas Public Library.

have nothing against 'em. The ones that worked, and
old ignorant country boys come in here, somebody
mistreat 'em, I'd work to help 'em.

You know, when Harry Truman run for reelection,
they brought him in from Grand Prairie by road on
Jefferson, and they had every officer they had at that
intersection. And we was late getting up on the track
that evening. And when we got up there, there was
two dead ones in this one block. One of 'em was a gal,
but I don't remember who the other one was. One of
'em they drug out of McMillan's, just like you'd kill a
hog and drag it out. She'd rolled under a car and died.

We'd go in there when they were shooting those
dice, and there were knives and guns on the table.
They'd pitch them old East Dallas shankers on there,
and we'd go to the wall and stick 'em in there and
break them old long blades off. Pitch the knives back
on the table and walk out.[6]

Those who carried the long, thin knives, also
known as "Deep Ellum specials," sometimes
propped the blade open slightly with a matchstick
so they could be opened quickly in a pants pocket.
Edwards recalled at least one occasion when his
partner saved him from being stabbed in the back.
"Oh, hell, you had to watch each other."

Edwards said once, he was arresting a man for
attempting to assault "Black Ghost," who worked
at Open the Door Richard's shine parlor:

I was writing him up, and catty-corner across there
was Oatis drug store. He said, "Mr. Edwards, if
you're going to put me in jail, I'm going over to Mr.
Oatis and get me a box of snuff." And I said, "You'll
have to whip me before you go." And he took me serious and come into me
just like a panther. You know, you can slap anybody over the ear and knock
their equilibrium out. He just fell to the ground and grabbed that leg and just
went to chewin' on it like a dang tomcat. We carried those nightsticks on our
belt. I kicked him and hit him with it. Had him changed from paddy wagon

Bonnie Parker and Clyde Barrow, Dallas, ca. early 1930s. Courtesy of the Texas/Dallas History and Archives Division, Dallas Public Library.

to ambulance. When the ambulance come, he said, "Tell 'em to get them teeth out. I swallowed some of my teeth." I said, "You motherfucker, I don't care if you die."[7]

During World War II Dallas was a party town for servicemen on liberty in Texas and neighboring states. In fact, C. S. McMillan's wife told a friend that their café was so busy that they didn't have time to count the money; they'd throw it in big jars and count it later. But the end of the war brought a new mood. When Wilson ran for district attorney in 1946, he ran against "organized crime," which everybody knew meant Benny Binion. Incumbent Dean Gaulding chose not to run for reelection. Wilson's opponent in the general election was a tough lawyer named Priest, also a powerful revival preacher, who ran a scare campaign based on the fact that Wilson had black support. "My opponent is voting Negroes like running sheep through a dipping vat," he told the *Dallas Morning News*. Years later Wilson recalled, "I ran against Benny Binion, and my opponent ran against the blacks."[8]

Benny Binion knew when to fold. He shut his casinos on New Year's Day of 1947, the day Wilson took office. Binion packed suitcases with cash and headed for Las Vegas with his chauffeur, a large black man called "Gold Dollar." Borrowing the name of one of his Dallas bars, he started Binion's Golden Horseshoe casino. But Binion didn't give up the Dallas policy racket. He left it in the keeping of a confederate named Harry Urban.

Binion had competition from Herbert Noble, who earned the nickname "the Cat" because he survived numerous assassination attempts. Once when Noble was wounded, Will Wilson recalled, Binion's men rented an apartment across the street from the hospital and tried to shoot him through the window. In late 1949 a car bomb killed Noble's wife when she started the car he usually drove. The distraught Noble was arrested while loading his plane with bombs he planned to drop on Binion's home in Las Vegas. Two years later Noble's luck finally ran out. He was killed by a bomb planted near the mailbox of his ranch in Tarrant County.

Wilson was determined to bring Binion to justice. Working with police chief Carl Hansson, he had vice officers follow Binion's salesmen as they made their rounds and turned their money and betting slips over to "pickup men." These employees took the slips and cash to a counting house in a remodeled barn on a farm Urban owned in Irving, just west of the Trinity River, near the site where the Texas Stadium was built years later.

In late 1949 Wilson oversaw a series of police raids on the policy operation. At the stable, police seized $2,000, which Wilson said was a conser-

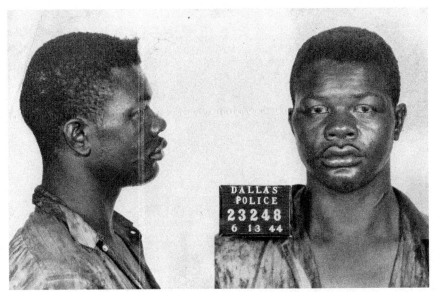

Mug shots of Travis Lee Morgan, June 13, 1944. He was shot to death by police officer
C. W. "Gus" Edwards in 1947. Courtesy of C. W. Edwards.

vative estimate of the daily net take. Police also raided Urban's vending-
machine business in the 2800 block of Main, near Deep Ellum, as well as
a room at the Southland Hotel, two black Deep Ellum cafés, and a shine
parlor on Central Track.

Sheriff Bill Decker was a friend of Binion's, and Wilson feared that a
police officer or deputy sheriff might warn the gambler's men that a raid
was coming. So the officers were not told until the last minute where they
were going. After reporting for duty, they were watched closely and were
not allowed to use the phone.

A safe-deposit box yielded Binion's income tax returns, and Henry Wade,
Wilson's successor, successfully prosecuted Binion for income-tax evasion
and gambling violations after he was extradited from Nevada. He served
four years in federal prison. After his release in 1957, he returned to Las
Vegas, where he lived out his life. Not long before Binion's death in 1989,
at age eighty-five, he received a visit from Dr. Emory and others from Dallas
who were in town for a medical convention. They reminisced about the old
days in Dallas.[9]

The breakup of Binion's empire hardly ended gambling in Deep Ellum.
Alto McGowan operated the Sportsman's Club in the 2400 block of Elm in
the early fifties and foiled police raids with a lookout who pushed an outside

Unidentified North Dallas pool hall, ca. 1920s. Courtesy of Nick Cammarata.

button to flash the lights. The place was upstairs from the club and liquor store run by C. S. McMillan, son of restaurant owner Quitman McMillan.

McGowan was a smart businessman who could be tough when he needed to be. Once, when Manuel T. "Lone Wolf" Gonzaullas, the famed Texas Ranger, raided his place and broke a radio, McGowan told him, "White man, you're going to buy me a new radio, or one of us is going to hell."[10] Gonzaullas went down a few doors and bought him a radio. McGowan said that at one time he was clearing $1,200 to $1,300 a week out of his gambling joint. In 1953 he joined a church, gave the club away, and opened a funeral home.

Even so, dice and card games continued in the cafés and beer joints from Deep Ellum to North Dallas. Eddie Goldstein, son of pawnbroker "Honest Joe" Goldstein, recalled crossing Central Track as a child in the 1940s and seeing men shooting dice on the sidewalk. Goldstein and others also remembered a huge man called "Open the Door Richard," who sold liquor after hours and on weekends out of his shine stand on Central, around the corner from the Harlem Theater.[11]

Nevertheless, when Will Wilson left office, Dallas was quite a different place from the wide-open town of the 1930s and early 1940s. Interestingly, the last case he prosecuted was that of Tommie Schwartz of Day and Night Pawn Shop. Schwartz went to prison for masterminding the robbery of a doctor's home, then turning in the men he'd hired for the job, Wilson said. Newspaper accounts of his trial called him "the pudgy pawnbroker." According to Wilson, Schwartz had been allowed to conduct illegal activities for years because he was a regular police informant. His prosecution was one more signal that things would no longer be done the old way.

Although gambling and vice were clearly spread throughout the city, their early association with Deep Ellum has persisted. In fact, Deep Ellum still has a reputation as a dangerous area of town. However, it was and is much more than that. Gambling and vice were ultimately only peripheral to the day-to-day lives of the people who frequented the Deep Ellum area.

Deep Ellum's Just Too Doggone Slow

Decline and Rebirth

In January 1940 Ernestine Claunch came to Dallas with a friend from Norman, Oklahoma, to work for the Frito Company. It was the end of the Depression; she had finished school, and there were still no jobs in Oklahoma. Her brother Marion was a Frito distributor, and he recommended that she go to Dallas to be interviewed by the company's founder and president, Elmer Doolin.

At that time, the Frito Company headquarters was located at 1405 North Haskell Avenue at the corner of Bryan Street and had about eighteen employees in the office and approximately thirty in the plant. "It was just like a big family," Ernestine said:

> They ran a very strict office during business hours, and then when we played, we played, because they would take us to lunch and have parties. We were part of a neighborhood.
>
> On the corner there was a City Service station. Next to the Frito office was Carolyn's Beauty Shop, then a Foster's Family Grocery, and at 1411 Haskell was the Frito plant. Directly across the street was Sun Drugstore, and on Bryan Street was the telephone exchange, in a three- or four-story building. There was a lot of activity at that building because all of the long distance was handled by operators, and people came to and from work on the street-car. Going to town on Bryan was residential for working people, and Ursu-line Academy was in that area. There were small businesses scattered around and some houses, some apartments, and what were called light-housekeeping rooms that might be converted in someone's home where, for example, a couple might live downstairs or in a different part of the house.[1]

Ernestine lived at first with her brother on Mary Street in East Dallas and then moved to the YWCA in the 1200 block of North Haskell. "It was

Juneteenth parade in North Dallas, 1946. Behind the float is the Pride of Dallas Café, owned by Quitman and Daisy McMillan. Courtesy of the Dallas Public Library.

called Proctor Hall," she said. "And it was filled with working women who worked all over town." Ernestine lived there for two years and then got an apartment on Swiss Avenue, which she shared with three friends. "We figured out how we could afford it," she remembered. "The rent was forty-five dollars a month, and at the 'Y' it was six dollars a week for room and board."

Ernestine kept that apartment until 1950, when she married Jack Putnam, who operated Dallas Office Machines in Deep Ellum, located in what had been the Pythian Temple. They met in 1947; Putnam had the Frito account, and Ernestine was responsible for ordering office supplies. While they were dating, they sometimes met in Deep Ellum. "Everyone rode the streetcar everywhere you went," Putnam said:

We didn't have a car. The streetcar went up Bryan and then crossed over to Main. On Elm they had electric buses. Deep Ellum was very active, lots of people and lots of pawnshops. Smith's Furniture and Model Tailors were there. That kind of activity. The part I remember the most was that the merchants had all of their wares out on the street. Not all of them, but a lot of them did. Families were down there with children. The merchants kind of

Segregated streetcar, Dallas, n.d. Courtesy of the Dallas Historical Society.

hawked their things. They had clothes on racks, and they tried to get you to come into their shops. And there was one café that was in the same block where my husband's shop was. I don't remember the address, but they had great food. For years and years we made chili from the recipe we got at this restaurant. Everybody went to lunch at this café. Maybe it would cost twenty-five cents. Jack had many friends there, all of the shopkeepers.

Everyone worked until Saturday noon and then went downtown for shopping. On payday you usually went someplace pretty nice for lunch, and you met other people. And then you did your shopping. At that time in the early forties, when you went to town, you always dressed. You wore white gloves in the summer whether you went to church or shopping or wherever. And the girls who worked with me wore gloves and hats to work because they worked downtown. I didn't have to because I was only walking over to Haskell.[2]

Ernestine remembered that the only problem her husband ever had in Deep Ellum was with the "winos" and homeless people who used the parking lot next to his building. "There were several small fires that were started and that type of thing. First of all, you don't want that kind of person near your place of business. Back then, people were more frightened than they are today."

By all accounts, Deep Ellum deteriorated in the 1950s, and slowly the small businesses began to close. Ernestine said that although her husband sold his business in the mid-1950s, the office supply company remained in Deep Ellum until the 1970s. Ernestine herself continued to work at the Frito Company, where she received numerous promotions, through all its transitions for forty-two years. In reflecting on the growth and demise of Deep Ellum, it is difficult to assess how and why the area declined. Ernestine speculated that the growth of strip shopping centers and then malls changed the shopping patterns of the people who patronized the small businesses. Moreover, integration and upward mobility for African Americans and Jews created new business and housing opportunities.

History itself conspired against Deep Ellum and Central Track. The 1911 Kessler master plan for Dallas called for replacing the tracks with a central boulevard, a goal that was accomplished decades later with the building of Central Expressway. The area acquired an unsavory reputation early on. In 1904 J. D. Smith established his furniture store in Deep Ellum because he thought the city's growth to the east would help the business prosper. After

NOTICE

IT IS REQUIRED BY LAW, UNDER PENALTY OF FINE OF $5.00 TO $25.00, THAT WHITE AND NEGRO PASSENGERS MUST OCCUPY THE RESPECTIVE SPACE OR SEATS INDICATED BY SIGNS IN THIS VEHICLE.

TEXAS PENAL CODE; ARTICLE 1659, SEC.4
DALLAS CITY ORDINANCE; NO. 2904

TEXLITE-DALLAS

Sign mandating segregated seating on Dallas streetcars, Dallas, n.d. Courtesy of the African American Museum, Dallas, Texas.

all, Union Station was nearby. When he tried to borrow money to construct his own building in 1912, however, the first bank he approached would not lend to him because he was building east of the station.[3] He got the money and built anyway, in the 2500 block of Elm. However, in 1916 Union Station was moved to the other end of downtown, to the corner of Young and Houston, where it still stands as the Amtrak station. The Central tracks remained, carrying freight trains that served the heavy industries north and south of Deep Ellum.

Even in its heyday during the 1920s, people were foreseeing the end of Deep Ellum. A 1925 *Dallas Morning News* article intoned, "The towers of industry, represented by the ever-extending sky line, are gradually crawling farther toward the vitals of 'Deep Ellum' and it won't be long until the picturesque highway will be history."[4] What happened, of course, was more complex than that. The Depression spelled the end of institutions like the Ella B. Moore Theater and made money for entertainment scarce. Starting in the late twenties, many black community institutions—stores, dance halls, professionals such as doctors and lawyers—moved north from Deep Ellum into the thriving community around Thomas and Hall, the old Freedmantown. The Green Parrot dance hall left Deep Ellum around 1927 and was reestablished under a different ownership on Hall. Few recall now that it was ever located in Deep Ellum. Also in 1927 the State Theater opened on Hall, giving African Americans a movie house outside Deep Ellum for the first time. In the thirties, Dr. Walter R. McMillan, a relative of restaurateur Quitman McMillan, established a clinic in North Dallas.

According to his daughter Lurline Holland, record merchant R. T. Ashford left Dallas sometime after 1936 and started a business in Tulsa before moving to Chicago and later to San Francisco, where he died in 1976. In Chicago, Ashford became a teacher and minister of Islam and called himself R. T. X. He was a colleague of Malcolm X and was associated with Temple No. 26.

Later in the 1930s the black population was moving again, this time into previously all-white areas of South Dallas. Some homes were bombed after African Americans moved in. Again, there was a movement of entertainment facilities and professionals. In 1937 the Queen Theater was opened in the Queen City neighborhood, near present-day Oakland Cemetery, bordering on Malcolm X Boulevard. The theater building later became a church.

The new North Dallas hot spots included the Hummingbird and Café Drugs, which opened in September 1938 at 3214 Thomas, so-called because it was next to Peoples Drug Store. The Rose Room opened at Ross and

"This is a picture of the Central Boulevard. It was completed as the children saw it in our neighborhood. The unit was developed after much questioning, discussion, and observation. The scene above is one of the activities children engaged in in developing this unit. It was developed by the high fifth grade at the B. F. Darrell School." Spring term, Dallas, 1947. Sadye Dupree Gee, teacher. Photograph by Wilson Studios. Courtesy of Sadye Gee.

Hall in 1942 with a performance by Buster Smith and his band. The Rose Room later closed and reopened as the Empire Room, where Ray Charles performed regularly early in his career, in the 1950s, raiding local bands for saxophonists David "Fathead" Newman and Leroy Cooper. Movie theaters moved, too. The Harlem remained in the 2400 block of Elm but acquired a reputation as a rowdy spot. A black physician, Dr. Emerson Emory, recalled his sole trip to the Harlem, in the forties. "The show started at two, and between noon and two, everything happened except murder," he said. "It was called the house of action, and it *was* the house of action."[5]

Deep Ellum was left with the lower-rent places and the Goodwill store. The *WPA Guide* said of Deep Ellum:

There are second-hand clothing stores, job-lot sales emporiums, gun and lock-smith shops, pawnshops, tattoo studios, barber shops, drug stores. Sales here are not the matter-of-fact transactions of other retail districts, but negotiations involving critical examination, head-shaking and loud argument by both seller and buyer. . . . Pitchmen hawk their wares. Street evangelists exhort, their frenzied appeals often but little noticed. An Indian herb store flourishes on the sale of a vermifuge made on the premises. This is not a place for the squeamish; the emporium's decorative motif is somewhat startling. A mangy bull-moose head towers amid stuffed, coiled rattlesnakes, armadillos, a boa-constrictor and snarling bobcats. On a wall among Indian relics are some beautiful prints of tribal life. But the main attraction here is a collection of ex-stomach worms, neatly preserved to posterity in jars of alcohol. . . . Clothing, like liquor and fighting equipment, is cheap in "Deep Ellum."

New clothing and foodstuffs, bought in job lots, from unclaimed freight sales and bankrupt stocks, find their way to consumers at amazingly low prices. But the second-hand store is the backbone of the clothing business. Suits may be bought for $3. Battered hats and caps start at 15 cents; good overcoats sell from $4 up; the badly worn for much less. Shoes are to be had for 25 cents and fifty cents; new footwear from $1.25. Three pairs of men's socks are offered for 10 cents. Women's dresses start at 50 cents and $1; hats for the feminine head at 15 cents.[6]

According to the *WPA Guide,* the most notorious nightspot had recently closed, the Cotton Club, a cabaret accessible by separate tunnels for male and female patrons.[7]

Some of the vivid street life remained. David Goldstein, son of pawn-broker Isaac "Rocky" Goldstein, said that when he went to his father's store in the forties, "Saturday was like the State Fair."[8] Eddie Goldstein recalled a man with a guitar who stood at the corner of Elm and Hawkins in the late forties and early fifties and a saxophonist who played on a nearby corner.[9] The streets still rang at times with the sounds of street preachers and gospel groups, and blues musicians such as Frankie Lee Sims still played outdoors around Central Track. Jack Richardson, better known as "Black Ghost," said a man called "Worm" played bucket with Sims, "and he got music out of that bucket, too."[10]

Clifford McMillan, known as "C. S.," operated several businesses in Deep Ellum into the late forties. Rudolph McMillan said his older brother had a soft spot in his heart for their father's old locations.[11] In fact, C. S. bought two of these locations and established businesses: a café in the 200 block of Central Track and the Mirror Bar and a liquor store at 2413 Elm, site of his father's old McMillan's Café.

In 1947 police officer Gus Edwards shot and killed Travis Lee Morgan, a large, powerful laborer, while trying to arrest him outside the Harlem

"Honest Joe" Goldstein (seated) and his son Eddie Goldstein (in doorway), at Honest Joe's Pawn Shop in Deep Ellum, ca. 1960s. Courtesy of Eddie Goldstein.

Theatre. The killing merited a two-paragraph story in the *Morning News* under the headline "Negro Shot Fatally in Resisting Arrest." The slaying of M. L. Patton, owner of the Patton Hotel on Central Track, by a holdup man was also covered in a couple of inside paragraphs. In an interview Edwards said he and his partner had to protect the killer from an angry crowd, but this was not reported in the *Morning News*. Generally, the *Morning News* tended to cover news of the African American community in a perfunctory way, if at all.

One of the more interesting latecomers to Central Tracks was known as "Open the Door Richard," mentioned earlier, a huge man who weighed at least three hundred and fifty pounds. His real name was Edward George Laffiton, though few knew that. Like a lot of others around Deep Ellum and Central Track, he was known by a nickname. In his Central Track days, Willard Watson was called "Pretty Boy." A con man who haunted the area was called "Walkie-Talkie." Everyone called Edward Laffiton "Open the Door" or just "Open." He employed Richardson, known to everyone as "Ghost" or "Black Ghost," a nickname he had earned for his speed at football when he was one of the first blacks to attend Lincoln High School in South Dallas. Deep Ellum stores regularly cashed checks for him made out to "Black Ghost."

Open the Door came from Springfield, Missouri, a racially troubled town in the Ozarks. In 1906, four years before he was born, the apparent calm of the place was shattered by the lynchings of three black men. Many African Americans left immediately, following the railroad tracks out of town to avoid being seen.[12] The Laffiton family left, too, but it is not certain when. Richardson recalled once driving with his boss to Honey Grove, in northeast Texas, to visit Open the Door's family, but there is apparently no one in town by that name now, and the name does not ring a bell with either black or white citizens.

Laffitons had been living in Dallas since at least 1878, when a Richard Laffiton, "colored barber," shows up in city directories with a shop on Main Street. Edward Laffiton, who was apparently related to the Dallas Laffitons, moved to the city in the late thirties. He worked at a succession of jobs, including a stint as a porter at the Lakewood Country Club. In 1947 he went into business for himself and established Open the Door Richard Shoe Shiners in the 100 block of Central, between Elm and Main.

The name he chose for his business is a history lesson in itself. It was the name of a routine performed by vaudeville comedian Clinton "Dusty" Fletcher. The performer would come onstage feigning intoxication and carrying a ladder. He'd repeatedly try to climb the ladder, only to fall to the floor, all the time inveighing his friend, "Open the door, Richard!" But Richard, apparently more pleasantly engaged, failed to heed the summons.[13] In 1947, the same year Laffiton's business first shows up in the Dallas city directory, a song called "Open the Door, Richard" became a huge hit for rhythm-and-blues artist Louis Jordan. The song was based on the old comedy routine,

King Edward Swap Shop on East Grand, late 1990s. Eddie Goldstein, son of "Honest Joe," made this store a replica of his father's old pawnshop. Photograph by Jay Brakefield.

and Dusty Fletcher was listed as one of the writers. It was so big a hit that some radio stations eventually banned DJs from using "Open the Door, Richard" gags on the air.

Dallas's Open the Door Richard lived on Pennsylvania Avenue, in the Queen City section of South Dallas, with his second wife, Brunetta, and her mother, Minnie Mae Clinton. Open's wife was big, too. They had no children, but there was a stepson, and they took in the troubled Black Ghost, who lived with them for several years as a teenager. But Laffiton had a rougher side, too, Gus Edwards remembered. Open the Door once hit his mistress with the butt of a gun and knocked her down the steps of the Patton Hotel.[14]

The shoeshine stand was the locus of several businesses, legal and otherwise. Open the Door and Ghost bought liquor from a store on Elm Street and sold it after hours and on Sundays. Sometimes, when the police were cracking down, the whiskey would be kept in a garbage can with a false lid on the sidewalk outside the stand. Laffiton shows up in court records for a string of liquor violations. Some of the customers were white, Ghost recalled, but the police made sure they got their booze and left immediately. "They didn't have no business down there," Richardson said.[15]

Ed Doran recalled tearing down Open the Door Richard's place after

Eddie Goldstein, King Edward Swap Shop, late 1990s. Photograph by Jay Brakefield.

Doran Chevrolet, located in the 2200 block of Main, bought the property for expansion. "The area out back was two feet deep in broken wine bottles," he said. Open the Door also operated a moving business. Doran recalled a truck with lettering that read, "If it's light, I'll move it right." Laffiton also operated a barbershop for a while, though he was not a barber.[16]

Ghost said his boss stayed clear of gambling, though some retired police officers and other veterans of the area said he was involved at least in steering people to dice games. Retired officer Edwards remembered that once during World War II, a prostitute stole a serviceman's money. Edwards told her that if she'd give the money back, he wouldn't put her in jail. She excused herself, ducked behind the curtain at Open the Door Richard's, and retrieved the money from her private parts.[17]

Open the Door survived the coming of Central Expressway and stayed in business on Central until 1963. A few years before his death in 1965, he accidentally shot himself while cleaning a pistol at the shine stand. His resulting long illness drained his funds, and he died broke. He and his wife lie in unmarked graves in South Dallas's Lincoln Memorial Cemetery, not far from the graves of C. S. McMillan and his wife, Grace, and Dr. P. M. Sunday, a physician who once had an office in the Pythian Temple.

In 1940 Dave and Dora Goldstein and their six children moved out of their store to a house in South Dallas. They prospered during World War II, in part because Dave had bought up a lot of radios and other merchandise that he knew would become scarce in wartime.[18]

The mood changed after the war. Reform District Attorney Will Wilson hired a bunch of young hotshots like himself, got the office moved to nicer, more spacious quarters, and cracked down on vice. Gus Edwards said that toward the end of his Central Track days, in the late forties or early fifties, Police Chief Carl Hansson told him and Harry Stewart to crack down on violent crime on their beat and not to worry about complaints. "We got to figuring that every murder we'd had either tied in with a pimp or a dice hustler or a whore," Edwards said. "We went to work on them whores. We didn't have no more murders up there for ages. I mean, that stopped it. Them whores and pimps, they was on the run. Some of 'em would beat the paddy wagon back up there; we'd grab 'em again and back they'd go, back they'd go. It didn't take long, I think, hittin' 'em $30 a lick, they didn't tarry long. I told them gals . . . as long as you sell them the meat and get on that bed and deliver it, long as you don't get 'em drunk and roll 'em, you're not gonna get no complaint from me."[19]

The new mood of reform coincided roughly with the building of the long-discussed Central Expressway, the first leg of which opened in 1949. Retired police officer Sam Tuck recalled chasing a suspect in the area during the expressway construction. The man disappeared, and officers were baffled until they shined a flashlight and realized that he had fallen into a hole dug for an expressway pillar.[20]

Deep Ellum may well have been on its last legs anyway, victim of a changing world. "I don't think Central Expressway killed Deep Ellum as much as two things: television and integration," said Eddie Goldstein.[21] But Central Expressway did begin sealing the area off from the rest of downtown Dallas and displacing many African American residents and businesses, many of whom relocated to South Dallas and to the Hamilton Park neighborhood, off Forest Lane in North Dallas. In the mid-fifties, the city installed parking meters in Deep Ellum and changed Elm to a one-way street, routing traffic to the west, back toward downtown. The merchants, led by Gene Smith of Smith Furniture, banded together in protest and staged a march up Elm carrying a coffin.

Also in the fifties, the Good-Latimer Expressway replaced Good Street, and the building that had housed the Indian Herb Store was demolished. In 1955 Dave and Dora Goldstein closed their pawn business and switched exclusively to selling guns. Dave died in 1964 after lapsing into a diabetic coma, and Dora and her sons moved the business to a site north of downtown, where they kept it going until the early nineties. Doran Chevrolet moved to North Dallas in 1960 after "thank God, they condemned the building," Ed Doran said.[22]

In addition, C. S. McMillan sold his liquor store to Label Feldman, whose pawnshop was across the street, and went into real estate and other businesses. McMillan bought the old Peoples Undertaking. He became, according to his brother, the first black Republican precinct chairman in Dallas. Ironically, C. S . McMillan profited from the white resistance to blacks' moving into South Dallas, where they worked for apartment developers and bought up white homes. Rudolph McMillan recalled accompanying his brother on his rounds. A white homeowner angrily told them, "You niggers get off my property." In response, C. S. McMillan calmly asked, "Don't you want to make some money?" and ended up getting the man to sign a contract.[23]

After Feldman bought the liquor store, an old carnival fighter named Ed "Cornbread" Smith ran a gym upstairs, where he trained Curtis Cokes, who later became world welterweight boxing champion. Cornbread went to the gym after his day's work at a nearby pawnshop and often stayed late, gambling there with his friends. "He stayed till his wife came and got him," Cokes recalled.[24]

The real killing blow was the elevation of Central Expressway in 1969. The city bought up the 2300 and 2400 blocks of Elm Street and razed the buildings. The elevated freeway passed so close to Honest Joe's, in the 2500 block, that part of the top floor had to be removed, exposing a part of the building that Eddie Goldstein had never seen before. Inside was an old speakeasy, complete with an antique pool table.[25]

Honest Joe and some of the other stalwarts hung on, though business became scarce. When Honest Joe died in 1972, his son insisted that the funeral procession pass the store. This, he said, would honor the Jewish tradition of carrying the body past the temple since the store was Honest Joe's temple. The Goldsteins also had their own tradition of checking the front of the store at the close of business to make sure all of the sidewalk merchandise had been brought inside. A *Dallas Morning News* story referred to Goldstein as "the Pascha of pawn" and quoted him as frankly describing much of his merchandise as junk.[26] A gallery owner hired by the family years later to clean the place out reported removing twenty-eight industrial dumpsters of scrap metal.[27] Eddie Goldstein said the first time he walked in and saw the place empty, he was shocked at how small it was. Full of junk, it had seemed cavernous.

C. A. Spain (left) with customers in his Deep Ellum shoe-repair shop, 1990. Photograph by Alan Govenar.

The last Deep Ellum pawnshop closed in 1983, just as the area was being reborn in a way the pawnbrokers and hustlers could hardly have imagined. The old buildings rang with music, loud rock that owed its existence to the blues and jazz that had been played there years before. Sometimes new and old crossed paths. In their final performing days, in the 1980s, Buster Smith and Herbie Cowens played in Deep Ellum clubs not far from where they had started, more than sixty years before. Again the sidewalks were crowded. These nighttime crowds consisted mostly of young whites in fashionable black clothing. Dave's Pawn Shop for a time became a coffeehouse called Dave's Art Pawnshop. The area also became home to art galleries, and some of the artists lived in lofts over the old stores. Wild artwork and graffiti decorated the walls of the brick buildings. Trendy restaurants and boutiques sprang up. Survivors like C. A. Spain, a second-generation shoe repairman, seemed like creatures from another world.

Spain finally closed his store in 1992. In early 1994 a dry-goods store owned by Holocaust survivors Henry and Frances Kirzner closed. The Polish immigrant couple had run the store in the 2200 block of Elm, once the western edge of Deep Ellum, for more than thirty-five years. Rocky Goldstein died in late 1995 and is best remembered today as the man who sold John Hinckley the gun that he used to shoot President Ronald Reagan and his press secretary, James Brady.

Today, in the 2500 block of Elm, the old Pythian Temple lies dying of neglect[28] and faces the buildings that once housed Dave's and Honest Joe's pawnshops, though the latter is plain now, stripped of its gaudy trappings. Today it is the home of Urban Paws, a pet-care business owned by Laurel F. Levin, daughter of Honest Joe's sister, Shirley, and her husband, Marvin L. Levin. Historic photos of the old Honest Joe's are on display. In the 2200 block of Elm Street, Rocky Goldstein's pawnshop has been replaced by a parking garage. In 1955 S&W Auto Parts, owned by Harry and Eli Wilonsky, moved to 2704 Second Avenue in South Dallas. Their son Herschel went into business with his father in 1966. He closed the store in 2008 and sold the building. In 2012 a street ministry was using it for storage and a thrift store.

Some of the old illicit excitement remains in Deep Ellum. In 1993 police broke up a call-girl racket operating out of a Deep Ellum lingerie store. Today some Dallasites are afraid to go to the area because of occasional incidents of violence, though it is probably safer than many other areas of Dallas. For a number of years, one could get some feel of historic Deep Ellum by going to Grand Avenue in East Dallas, where Eddie Goldstein made his King Edward Swap Shop a shrine to his father's place. Signs on the outside proclaimed "Little Honest Joe's on Deeep East Grand," and inside was an amazing collection of merchandise and junk, everything from tools to fishing poles. Many of the customers were African American, and the banter and haggling that went on were probably as close to old Deep Ellum as one could find. In 2012 the business had been closed for several years, and the colorful signage was gone, though Goldstein still owned the building.

By the middle of the first decade of the new millennium, Deep Ellum seemed to be fading again after the excitement that began in the 1980s with a lively music scene that launched the careers of bands such as New Bohemians and the Butthole Surfers. Nonetheless, the area rebounded once again with residential development, the coming of a new rail station, and the opening of new clubs and the rebirth of some that had closed. The area is the scene of film and art festivals, and its rich history and the efforts of organizations such as the Deep Ellum Community Association and Deep Ellum Foundation seem likely to keep it a vital part of Dallas.[29]

Nothing, however, is going to re-create the old Deep Ellum, because it was a different world, one that existed because of an odd confluence of racism and opportunity, sadness and hope, desperate poverty and good-time Saturday nights. It is a world that will not come again but one whose redevelopment attests to its enduring legacy.

Notes

Introduction. Deep Ellum: Fact and Fiction

1. Maxine Holmes and Gerald D. Saxon, eds., *The WPA Dallas Guide and History* (Denton: University of North Texas Press, 1992), 294. Hereinafter referred to as the *WPA Guide*.

2. A. C. Greene, *Dallas USA* (Austin: Texas Monthly Press, 1984), 63.

3. William L. McDonald, *Dallas Rediscovered: A Photographic Chronicle of Urban Expansion 1870–1925* (Dallas: Dallas Historical Society, 1978), 17.

4. Darwin Payne, *Dallas, an Illustrated History* (Woodland Hills, CA: Windsor, 1982), 185.

5. Larry Willoughby, *Texas Rhythm, Texas Rhyme: A Pictorial History of Texas Music* (Austin: Texas Monthly Press, 1984), 60–62.

6. Dave Oliphant, *Texan Jazz* (Austin: University of Texas Press, 1996), 43, 93.

7. As quoted in *WPA Guide*, 294.

8. "Hidden Nooks of Dallas: 'Deep Ellum' Has Its Renown But After All It Is Merely the Darkies' Parade Ground," *Dallas Morning News*, November 29, 1925.

9. *WPA Guide*, 294.

10. J. Mason Brewer, ed., *Heralding Dawn: An Anthology of Verse* (Dallas: June Thompson Printing, 1936), 4.

11. Louis Bedford, interview by Jay Brakefield, December 5, 1992.

12. Herschel Wilonsky, interview by Jay Brakefield, May 5, 1994.

13. Sammy Price, interview by Alan Govenar, September 27, 1984.

14. Isaac "Rocky" Goldstein, interview by Jay Brakefield, March 22, 1992.

15. Ibid.

16. Bill Neely, interview by Alan Govenar, August 29, 1984.

17. Isaac "Rocky" Goldstein, interview.

18. Willard Watson, interview by Jay Brakefield, July 16, 1992.

19. Robert Prince, interview by Jay Brakefield, January 1993.

20. Anna Mae Conley and Lucille Bosh McGauthey, interview by Jay Brakefield and Alan Govenar, October 3, 1992.

Chapter 1. "Deep Elem Blues": Song of the Street

1. Tony Russell, *Country Music Originals: The Legends and the Lost* (New York: Oxford University Press, 2010).

2. http://www.lizlyle.lofgrens.org/RmOlSngs/RTOS-BlackBottom.html.

3. Hank Wackwitz, letter to Alan Govenar, March 1992.

Chapter 2. The Railroads Create Deep Ellum

1. From a letter by John Milton McCoy to his brother Addie in Indiana, December 19, 1871, published in *When Dallas Became a City: Letters of John Milton McCoy, 1870–1881*, ed. Elizabeth York Entstam (Dallas: Dallas Historical Society, 1982), 46–47.

2. Quoted in John William Rogers, *The Lusty Texans of Dallas* (New York: Dutton, 1951), 117.

3. Barrot Steven Sanders, *Dallas, Her Golden Years* (Dallas: Sanders, 1989), 83.

4. Quoted in Rogers, *Lusty Texans*, 118–19.

5. Philip Lindsley, *History of Greater Dallas and Vicinity*, vol. 1 (Chicago: Lewis, 1909), 108.

Chapter 3. William Sidney Pittman: Architect of Deep Ellum

1. Most of the information in this chapter on William Sidney Pittman came from newspapers and from Louis R. Harlan's *Booker T. Washington: The Wizard of Tuskegee, 1910–1915* (New York: Oxford University Press, 1983), 118–20.

2. Sammy Price, interview by Jay Brakefield, June 7, 1991, Dallas, Texas.

3. The lodge, founded in Galveston, Texas, in 1883, was a fraternal organization and burial society.

4. *Negro Business Bulletin* (Dallas: Negro Business Bureau, February 1925).

5. October 2, 1920.

6. *Dallas Express*, March 14, 1919. Microfilm copies of the *Dallas Express* can be viewed at the J. Erik Jonsson Central Library (Dallas) in the Texas/Dallas Collection.

7. *Dallas Express*, October 18, 1919. Black troops were not unfamiliar to Dallas. They were deployed to the Texas-Mexico border in the years before World War I, and a photo shows a black regiment marching through downtown Dallas between 1911 and 1914.

8. *Dallas Express*, February 3, 1923.

9. *Negro Business Bulletin* (Dallas: Negro Business Bureau, February 1925).

10. Ophelia Pittman, *Por você, por mim, por nós* (Rio de Janeiro: Editora Record, 1984), 17–18.

11. Ruth Ann Stewart, *Portia: The Life of Portia Washington Pittman, the Daughter of Booker T. Washington* (Garden City, NY: Doubleday, 1977).

12. Eliana Pittman, interview by Jay Brakefield, August 8, 1996.

13. *Brotherhood Eyes*, July 28, 1934.

14. Rudolph McMillan, interview by Jay Brakefield, April 9, 1993.

15. Robert Wilonsky, "Knights' Tale: Another Historic Emblem of Black Dallas Stands on the Brink." *Dallas Observer*, December 20, 2007. http://www.dallasobserver.com/2007–12–20/news/knight-s-tale/full (accessed May 24, 2012).

16. Ibid.

Chapter 4. Black Dallas

1. J. H. Polk, "Brief Account of the Commercial Progress of the Negroes of Dallas," *Business and Professional Directory of Colored Persons in Dallas,* 1911, published under the auspices of the Dallas Negro Business League, no. 91.

2. *Dallas Times Herald*, July 19, 1890, 2. Copy on microfilm at the *Dallas Morning News;* also available at the J. Erik Jonsson Central Library, Dallas, Texas.

3. The first black film company was formed by William Foster of Chicago, who, between 1909 and 1913, produced the first black film shorts, including *The Pullman Porter* (1910) and *The Railroad Porter* (1912). After his company folded in 1913, blacks were played primarily by whites in blackface. Racist stereotypes perpetuated in such films as *Birth of a Nation* (1915) spurred a resurgence of African American filmmaking. For more information, see http://acinemaapart.com/.

4. *Dallas Express*, June 5, 1920.

5. *Freeman* (Indianapolis), September 11, 1920.

6. Paul Oliver, *Blues off the Record* (New York: Da Capo, 1988),162.

7. Neely quote is from Brakefield, interview, June 1989; Price quote from Brakefield, interview, June 7, 1991.

8. Herbert Cowens, interview by Alan Govenar, January 20, 1992

9. Don Albert, interview by Nathan Pearson and Howard Litwak, April 17, 1977. Official names of Tip Top are from Dallas city directories.

10. Cowens, interview, February 5, 1992.

11. Henry T. Sampson, *Blacks in Blackface: A Source Book on Early Black Musical Shows* (Metuchen, NJ: Scarecrow, 1980), 130.

Chapter 5. Jewish Pawnbrokers and Merchants of Deep Ellum

1. For more on the Galveston Plan and a bibliography, see the website of the Jewish Virtual Library, http://www.jewishvirtuallibrary.org (accessed September 6, 2012).

2. Dora Goldstein, interview by Jay Brakefield, February 28, 1992.

3. Isaac "Rocky" Goldstein, interview by Jay Brakefield, March 22, 1992.

4. Eddie Goldstein, interview by Jay Brakefield, April 3, 1992.

5. Joe Cody, interview by Jay Brakefield, June 18, 1992.

6. Max Wyll, interview by Jay Brakefield, March 25, 1992.

7. Herschel Wilonsky, interviews by Jay Brakefield, February 20 and 21, 2012.

8. Jim Boyd and Marvin Montgomery, interview by Alan Govenar and Jay Brakefield, January 29, 1992.

9. Dora Goldstein, interview.

10. Sam Luterman, interview by Jay Brakefield, August 19, 1992.

11. Max Wyll, interview by Jay Brakefield, March 25, 1992.

12. Sam Stillman, interview by Jay Brakefield, March 2, 1992.

13. Masha Porte, interview by Alan Govenar, March 4, 1992.

14. Willard Watson, interview by Jay Brakefield, July 16, 1992.

15. Joe Freed, interview by Jay Brakefield, May 6, 1992.

16. Dora Goldstein, interview.

17. Ibid.

18. Label Feldman, interview by Jay Brakefield, May 20, 1992.

19. Eddie Goldstein, interview.

20. Bill Minutaglio, "The Buried Past," *Dallas Life Magazine, Dallas Morning News,* September 5, 1993.

Chapter 6. Blind Lemon Jefferson: Downhome Blues

1. Isaac "Rocky" Goldstein, interview by Jay Brakefield, March 22, 1992.

2. Mack McCormick, "Biography of Henry Thomas: Our Deepest Look at Roots," liner notes to the album *Henry Thomas: Ragtime Texas,* Herwin 209.

3. Alan Govenar, "Blind Lemon Jefferson: The Myth and the Man," *Black Music Research Journal* 20(1) (Spring 2000): 7–21.

4. Quince Cox, interview by Alan Govenar, March 18, 1987. For more information, see Richard U. Steinberg, "See That My Grave Is Kept Clean," *Living Blues* 83 (1982): 24–25.

5. Samuel Charters, *The Country Blues* (New York: Rinehart, 1959), 60; Hobart Carter, interview by Alan Govenar, June 7, 1999.

6. Quince Cox, interview by Alan Govenar, June 7, 1999.

7. Charters, *The Country Blues,* 60.

8. Laura Lippman, "Blind Lemon Sang the Blues: Wortham Man Recalls His Memories of Musician," *Waco Tribune-Herald* (June 2, 1983), 11A. For more information, see Robert L. Uzzel, "Music Rooted in Texas Soil," *Living Blues* 83 (1982): 24–25.

9. Carter, interview.

10. Theaul Howard, interviews by Jay Brakefield, October and November 1993.

11. Charlie Hurd, interview by Jay Brakefield, November 1993.

12. Charters, *Country Blues,* 60.

13. Kip Lornell and Charles Wolfe, *The Life and Legend of Leadbelly* (New York: HarperCollins, 1992), 42–43.

14. Paul Oliver, *Blues off the Record* (New York: Da Capo, 1988), 64–65.

15. Giles Oakley, *The Devil's Music* New York: Harcourt, Brace, Jovanovich, 1976), 67. For more information on Blind Lemon Jefferson and Huddie "Lead Belly" Ledbetter, see William Barlow, *Looking up at Down: The Emergence of Blues Culture* (Philadelphia: Temple

University Press, 1989), and Kip Lornell, "Blind Lemon Meets Leadbelly," *Black Music Research Journal* 20(1) (Spring 2000), 23–33.

16. Lornell and Wolfe, *Life and Legend,* 45.

17. Alan Govenar, *Meeting the Blues* (Dallas: Taylor, 1988), 16.

18. Willard Watson, interview by Jay Brakefield, July 16, 1992, and Sam Stillman, interview by Jay Brakefield, March 2, 1992.

19. Samuel Charters, *The Bluesmen* (New York: Oak, 1968), 178.

20. Mance Lipscomb, 1970s interview by Glen Myers, Center for American History Collection, Austin.

21. Victoria Spivey, "Blind Lemon Jefferson and I Had a Ball," *Record Research* 78 (May 1966): 9.

22. Roger S. Brown, "Recording Pioneer Polk Brockman," *Living Blues* 23 (1975): 31.

23. "Reminiscences of Blind Lemon," a 1959 interview with Lightnin' Hopkins by Samuel Charters for a Folkways album that was re-released in 1990 as a Smithsonian/Folkways CD, *Lightnin' Hopkins,* CD SF 40019.

24. Mack McCormick, interview by Jay Brakefield, July 29, 1989.

25. "T-Bone Blues: T-Bone Walker's Story in His Own Words," *Record Changer* (October 1947), 5, 6, 12.

26. Oliver, *Blues off the Record,* 65.

27. Lurline Holland, interview by Alan Govenar, May 15, 1999.

28. Oakley, *Devil's Music,* 120.

29. Houston Stackhouse, "*Living Blues* Interview: Houston Stackhouse." Interview by Jim O'Neal. *Living Blues* 17 (1974), 20–21.

30. Carter, interview.

31. Stephen Calt, liner notes to *Blind Lemon Jefferson: King of the Country Blues,* Yazoo 1069.

32. Ibid.

33. David Evans, "Ramblin,'" *Blues Revue Quarterly* 9 (Summer 1993): 16–18.

34. David Evans, "Musical Innovation in the Blues of Blind Lemon Jefferson," *Black Music Research Journal* 20(1) (Spring 2000): 88.

35. Tom Wheeler and Jas Obrecht, "B. B. King," in *Blues Guitar: The Men Who Made the Music,* ed. Jas Obrecht (San Francisco: Miller Freeman, 1993), 141.

36. Evans, "Musical Innovation," 96.

37. Luigi Monge and David Evans, "New Songs of Blind Lemon Jefferson," *Journal of Texas Music History* 3(2) (Fall 2003): 8–28. For more information, see Luigi Monge, "The Language of Blind Lemon Jefferson: The Covert Theme of Blindness," *Black Music Research Journal* 20(1) (Spring 2000): 35–81.

38. Cox, interview.

39. Carter, interview.

40. Oliver, *Blues off the Record,* 69–70, and Paramount 12945-B.

41. Evans, "Musical Innovation," 98.

42. *Blind Lemon Blues* by Alan Govenar and Akin Babatunde builds on the success of their earlier work *Blind Lemon: Prince of Country Blues* (2001 Leon Rabin Award for Best New Musical or Play). The world premiere of *Blind Lemon Blues* was at Forum Meyrin in Geneva, Switzerland (February 27–28, 2004). It was also performed at the opening of the annual "Festival l'Imaginaire" at the Maison des Cultures du Monde in Paris, France (March 3–7, 2004). The World Music Theatre Festival toured *Blind Lemon Blues* to nine cities in the Netherlands and Belgium (March 10–25, 2007). In New York City, *Blind Lemon Blues* was featured as part of Central Park SummerStage (July 16, 2004) and the Works & Process series at the Guggenheim Museum (February 11–12, 2007) and was staged in two full productions off Broadway at the York Theatre (February 15–25, 2007) and (September 8–October 4, 2009). *Blind Lemon Blues* was published by Dramatic Publishing (Woodstock, IL) in 2012.

Chapter 7. The Contemporaries of Blind Lemon

1. Bruce Nixon, "The Sounds of Deep Ellum," *Dallas Times Herald* (September 23, 1983), C2.

2. Ibid., C3. Also see Keith Briggs, liner notes to *Jesse Thomas, 1948–1958* (1993), Document BDCD-6044.

3. Bob Groom, liner notes to *Ramblin' Thomas & the Dallas Blues Singers: Complete Recorded Works 1928–1932 in Chronological Order* (1992), Document DOCD-5107.

4. Kip Lornell, liner notes to *Gene Campbell: Complete Recorded Works 1929–1931* (1993), Document DOCD-5151.

5. Kip Lornell, liner notes to *Texas Black Country Dance Music, 1927–1935* (1993), Document DOCD-5162.

6. Sammy Price, *What Do They Want? A Jazz Autobiography* (Urbana: University of Illinois Press, 1990), 25, 28, 86.

7. Paul Garon, liner notes to *Texas Blues: The Complete Recorded Works of Coley Jones, "Bo" Jones, Little Hat Jones, Willie Reed, Oak Cliff T-Bone (Walker) 1927–1935* (1993), Document DOCD-5161, and Lornell, *Texas Black Country Dance Music*, Document DOCD-5162.

8. Danny Williams, letter to Alan Govenar, September 30, 1996.

9. Lornell, *Texas Black Country Dance Music*, Document DOCD5162.

10. Garon, *Texas Blues*, Document DOCD5161.

11. Nixon, "Sounds of Deep Ellum," C3.

12. Stephen Calt, Woody Mann, and Nick Perls, liner notes to *Funny Papa Smith: The Original Howling Wolf*, Yazoo L1031. Also see Teddy Doering, liner notes to *J. T. "Funny Paper" Smith, 1930–1931* (1991), Document BDCD6016.

13. Calt, Mann, and Perls, *Funny Papa Smith*.

14. Ibid.

15. Kip Lornell, liner notes to *"Texas Slide Guitars": Complete Recorded Works 1930–1938 in Chronological Order, Oscar Woods & Black Ace*. Document DOCD-5143.

16. For more information on the film *Blood of Jesus*, see George William Jones, *Black Cinema Treasures: Lost and Found* (Denton: University of North Texas, 1991).

17. For additional information, see Paul Oliver, *Blues off the Record* (New York: Da Capo, 1988), and Robert Dixon and John Godrich, *Recording the Blues, 1902–1940* (New York: Stein and Day, 1970).

Chapter 8. Blind Willie Johnson and Arizona Dranes: The "Holy Blues" of Deep Ellum

1. Samuel Charters, liner notes to *The Complete Blind Willie Johnson*, Columbia 52835.

2. David Evans, liner notes to Blind Willie Johnson, *Sweeter as the Years Go By*, Yazoo 1078.

3. Charters, *Complete Blind Willie Johnson*.

4. Ronald Clifford Foreman, "Jazz and Race Records, 1920–32: Their Origins and Their Significance for the Record Industry and Society," PhD diss., University of Illinois, 1968, 58.

5. For more information, see www.fretlesszithers.net.

6. Michael Corcoran, *All over the Map: True Heroes of Texas Music* (Austin: University of Texas Press, 2005), 67–73.

7. For more information, see www.minermusic.com/dolceola/phillips_instruments.htm.

8. Corcoran, *All over the Map*, 13.

9. Charters, *Complete Blind Willie Johnson*.

10. Corcoran, *All over the Map*, 68.

11. Julius Walker, interview by Jay Brakefield, August 1, 1992.

12. Label Feldman, interview by Jay Brakefield, May 20, 1992.

13. Isaac "Rocky" Goldstein, interview by Jay Brakefield, May 21, 1992.

14. Tony Heilbut, *The Gospel Sound: Good News and Bad Times* (New York: Simon and Schuster, 1971), 202.

15. Arizona Dranes Collection, Archives of African American Music and Culture, Bloomington, IN. Copies of correspondence and contracts provided by Michael Corcoran.

16. Ken Romanowski, liner notes to *The Complete Recorded Works of Reverend F. W. McGee in Chronological Order, 1927–1929*, Document BDCD-6031.

17. Malcolm Shaw, liner notes to *Arizona Dranes, 1926–1928*, Herwin Records, 210.

18. Heilbut, *Gospel Sound*, 202.

19. Ray Funk, liner notes to *Preachin' the Gospel: Holy Blues*, Columbia Legacy, CK 46779.

Chapter 9. Alex Moore: Dallas Piano Blues

1. Paul Oliver, *Blues off the Record* (New York: Da Capo, 1988), 107, 162.

2. Alex Moore, interview by Alan Govenar, April 9, 1982.

3. Oliver, *Blues off the Record*, 162.

4. Alan Govenar, *Meeting the Blues: The Rise of the Texas Sound* (Dallas: Taylor, 1988), 31.

5. Alex Moore, interview by Alan Govenar, November 5, 1988.

6. Ibid., November 8, 1988.

7. Paul Oliver, liner notes to *Whistling Alex Moore: From North Dallas to the East Side*, Arhoolie CD 408, 1994.

8. Robin Sullivan, interview by Jay Brakefield, April 22, 2012.

9. Govenar, *Meeting the Blues*, 32.

10. Mack McCormick, interview by Jay Brakefield, July 1989.

11. Oliver, *Blues off the Record*, 217: Alex Moore, interview by Alan Govenar, November 5, 1988.

12. Govenar, *Meeting the Blues*, 32.

13. Footage from this tribute became part of the documentary film *Black on White/White and Black*, Dallas: Documentary Arts, 1989. Documentary Arts also released the audiocassette *Alex Moore: Then and Now*, DA 105. This cassette includes Alex Moore's 1947 KLIF recordings and those made by Alan Govenar in 1988 at El Centro College in Dallas. The KLIF recordings were remastered by Chris Strachwitz and released on the CD *Whistling Alex Moore: From North Dallas to the East Side* with the 1960 recordings made by Strachwitz and Paul Oliver.

Chapter 10. Buster Smith: Dallas Jazz Goes to Kansas City and New York

1. Ross Russell, *Jazz Style in Kansas City and the Southwest* (Berkeley: University of California Press, 1971), 59.

2. Ibid., 74. For more information on Buster Smith, see Douglas Henry Daniels, *One o'Clock Jump: The Unforgettable History of the Oklahoma City Blue Devils* (Boston: Beacon, 2006), 36–48.

3. Alan Govenar, "Buster Smith: Dallas Jazz Patriarch," *Parkway* (April 1983), 34–35, and Alan Govenar, *Meeting the Blues* (Dallas: Taylor, 1988), 38–41.

4. Ophelia Pittman, *Por você, por mim, tor nós* (Rio de Janeiro: Editora Record, 1984).

5. Margaret Wright of Greenville, Texas, letter to Alan Govenar, March 20, 1992.

6. Helen Oakley Dance, *Stormy Monday: The T-Bone Walker Story* (New York: Da Capo, 1990), 12.

7. Nathan W. Pearson Jr., *Goin' to Kansas City* (Urbana: University of Illinois Press, 1987), 29.

8. Don Gazzaway, "Conversations with Buster Smith," *Jazz Review* (December 1959), 20.

9. Ibid.

10. Ibid.

11. Russell, *Jazz Style*, 61.

12. Frank Driggs, "Budd Johnson, Ageless Jazzman," *Jazz Review* 3(9) (November 1960), 4.

13. Tim Schuller, "The Buster Smith Story," *CODA* (December–January 1987–1988), 4–5.

14. Gazzaway, "Conversations," December 1959, 20.

15. Count Basie, as told to Albert Murray, *Good Morning Blues: The Autobiography of Count Basie* (New York: Random House, 1985), 3–8.

16. Driggs, "Budd Johnson," 4.

17. Gazzaway, "Conversations," Part 2, *Jazz Review* (January 1960), 11.

18. Mary Lee Hester, "Texas Jazz Heritage," *Texas Jazz* (June 1979), 3.

19. Albert Murray, *Stomping the Blues* (New York: Random House, 1982), 170.

20. Gazzaway, "Conversations," Part 2, 14.

21. Ray Charles and David Ritz, *Brother Ray: Ray Charles' Own Story* (New York: Dial, 1978), 147.

22. Pearson, *Goin' to Kansas City*, 197.

23. Hester, "Texas Jazz Heritage," 4.

24. Gazzaway, "Conversations," Part 3, *Jazz Review* (February 1960), 16.

25. For more information on Documentary Arts, see www.documentaryarts.org.

Chapter 11. Marvin Montgomery: The Cross-Fertilization of White and Black Musical Styles

1. In Bill C. Malone, *Country Music U.S.A.* (Austin: University of Texas, 1985); Charles R. Townsend, *San Antonio Rose: The Life and Music of Bob Wills* (Urbana: University of Illinois Press, 1986); and Cary Ginell, *Milton Brown and the Founding of Western Swing* (Urbana: University of Illinois Press, 1994). Marvin Montgomery is discussed in a cursory manner. Malone focuses his attention primarily on the five-string banjo but fails to adequately explore the role of the tenor banjo in early hillbilly and Western swing bands.

2. Early in his career in the Light Crust Doughboys, Montgomery was nicknamed "Junior," a moniker bestowed by the band's manager, W. Lee "Pappy" O'Daniel.

3. Marvin Montgomery, interview by Alan Govenar, July 31, 1996.

4. Montgomery, interview, August 2, 1996.

5. Montgomery, interview, August 8, 1996.

6. Montgomery, interview, July 31, 1996.

6. Montgomery interview, August 8, 1996.

7. Montgomery, interview, July 31, 1996.

8. Montgomery, interview, August 1, 1996.

9. Montgomery, interview, August 2, 1996.

10. Montgomery, interview, July 31, 1996.

11. Interview with Marvin Montgomery by Alan Govenar and Jay Brakefield, July 15, 1996.

12. Ibid.

13. Ibid.

14. Montgomery, interview, March 18, 1998.

15. Ibid.

16. Ibid.

17. Ibid.

18. John "Knocky" Parker, interview, August 28, 1963, Hogan Jazz Archive, Tulane University. In a 1973 interview by John Solmon Otto and Augustus M. Burns published on Pages 23–26 in the Spring 1974 issue of *JEMF Quarterly*, Montgomery changed a few details of this account, but the essence remained the same.

19. Ibid.

20. Montgomery interview, March 12, 1998.

21. John Mark Dempsey, *The Light Crust Doughboys Are on the Air* (Denton: University of North Texas Press, 2002),132.

22. Montgomery, interview, July 15, 1996.

23. Cary Ginell, *Milton Brown and the Founding of Western Swing* (Urbana: University of Illinois Press, 1994), 158.

Samples recorded late in life. He appears on a 1993 Documentary Arts CD, *Hallelujah Jubilee: East Texas Black Harmonica Players and their Songs*. For more information, see http://www.docarts.com/hallelujah_jubilee.html. He is also the subject of an artist book and an enclosed 45-rpm record, *Daddy Double Do Love You*, 1993 and 2002 by Govenar, Amos Kennedy, Daniel Dunnam, and Kelli Anderson. For more information, see http://www.docarts.com/daddy_double_do_love_you.html.

24. Parker, interview.

25. Montgomery, interview, March 18, 1998.

26. Ibid.

27. Ibid.

28. Ibid.

Chapter 12. The Contemporaries of Marvin Montgomery: Western Swing, Texas Fiddling, and the *Big "D" Jamboree*

1. The band traced its beginnings to 1929, when Bob Wills moved from his family's home-stead near the Texas Panhandle town of Turkey to Fort Worth, where he found work as a musician and blackface entertainer in a medicine show. He and guitarist Herman Arnspiger formed the Wills Fiddle Band, which soon doubled in size with the addition of vocalist Milton Brown and his teenage guitar-playing brother, Derwood Brown. On local gigs they were joined by other musicians such as Clifton "Sleepy" Johnson, who played six-string and tenor guitars, fiddle, and tenor banjo.

The Wills Fiddle Band performed briefly on KFJZ and at dances in and around Fort Worth. The group, augmented by Johnson and fiddler John Dunnam, appeared on radio station WBAP as the Aladdin Laddies, sponsored by the Aladdin Mantle Lamp Company. Their program lasted only three months, but they continued performing, primarily at Crystal Springs, a resort about four miles northwest of downtown Fort Worth. Wills, Arnspiger, and Milton Brown then auditioned for a show on KFJZ. Wills seemed to have known he was taking his music in a new direction. When house pianist Alton Stricklin, filling in as program manager, asked what kind of music they played, Wills replied, "Different. The Wills Fiddle Band plays different." Stricklin, who had been studying jazz, was astounded and amused by the band's rip-roaring style and, knowing nothing of Wills's background, surmised that it sounded like something from a medi-cine show. Ironically, he later became a mainstay of Wills's band, the Texas Playboys.

Early the following year, the group, renamed the Light Crust Doughboys, began a 6 a.m. show on KFJZ, advertising Light Crust Flour for the Burrus Mill and Elevator Company. Derwood Brown, who was still in school, played with the group at times but was not officially a member and was not paid by Burrus Mill. Arnspiger was replaced by Johnson. In late 1931 or early 1932 the Doughboys moved to the more powerful WBAP, owned by the *Fort Worth Star-Telegram,* appearing daily at 12:30 p.m., and soon gained widespread popularity. Through a network, they were also heard on stations in Houston, Dallas, and San Antonio. They made transcriptions, recordings on large discs that could be shipped to other stations or played on WBAP when the band was on the road, promoting flour. It was said that in warm weather, when people kept their windows open, one could walk down the street and not a miss a note of the Doughboys' show because it was playing in every Texas household. Eventually the Dough-boys were broadcast on 170 stations; in 1946, they had 3.2 million listeners. They remained on the air until 1952.

The band's growing popularity led to its first recording session in 1932, for Victor. But there was considerable friction between the Doughboys and their boss, Burrus Mill general manager W. Lee "Pass the Biscuits, Pappy" O'Daniel, who initially also forced the musicians to perform nonmusical duties for the mill. He apparently pocketed some of their money as well. These tensions led to the departures of both Wills and Brown before Montgomery joined the group and eventually to the sacking of O'Daniel, who later became governor of Texas and handed Lyndon Johnson his only political defeat, in the race for US senator from the Lone Star State in 1941. O'Daniel formed another band, the Hillbilly Boys, to use in his campaigns. Reports that he used the Doughboys for this purpose are false, though several musicians played in both bands at various times.

2. Tim Schuller, "The Buster Smith Story," *CODA* (December 1987–January 1988), 4.

3. Peter La Chapelle, *Proud to Be an Okie: Cultural Politics, Country Music, and Migration to Southern California* (Berkeley: University of California Press, 2007), 81, 262n11.

4. The presence of fiddlers in Texas has been traced to the period before the Civil War. These included Major L. Burns, who was born in Lexington, Tennessee, in 1835 and moved to

Montgomery County, Texas, when he was ten; Reverend A. McCary, born in Huntsville, Texas, in 1846; Arch Bozzell of Parker County, Texas, a veteran of the Civil War; Jim Heffington, born on South Bear Creek in 1852; and Joe Robertson. Robertson's birthdate is unknown, but he was one of the earliest known Texas fiddlers and the grandfather of the legendary A. C. "Eck" Robertson, who was born in 1883. From the mid-nineteenth century through the 1920s, the fiddle was played primarily at dances held on ranches and in homes and city venues such as dance halls. Generally, it was accompanied by one or two guitars. As a dance music, traditional fiddling in Texas was highly rhythmic and was clearly derivative of its Appalachian roots. However, as fiddling became a contest music, a distinctive Texas sound began to develop. The origins of the fiddle contest are obscure. The first documented event of this kind was the annual Atlanta, Georgia, Old Fiddlers Convention, which apparently began in the 1880s. In Texas, the earliest recorded fiddle contest was in Fort Worth in 1901. A photograph of the event by C. L. Swartz shows one woman and fifteen men, one of whom is black.

5. Townsend, *San Antonio Rose*, 30.

6. Townsend, 40.

7. Ken Harrison, *Prince Albert Hunt* (originally *Memories of Prince Albert Hunt*), documentary film, 1974. Dallas: Moonlight Productions, 1974. http://www.youtube.com/watch?v=QnWKK8NPA6M. http://www.folkstreams.net/film,180.
Transcription at http://www.folkstreams.net/context, 314, accessed April 4, 2012.

8. Ibid.

9. Cliff Bruner, interview by Jay Brakefield and Allan Turner, June 7, 1981.

10. Johnny Gimble, interview by Alan Govenar, September 22, 1994.

11. Ibid.

12. Malone, *Country Music U.S.A.*, 168–70.

13. Gimble interview.

14. Malone, *Country Music U.S.A.*, 168.

15. A. C. Greene, *Dallas Morning News* (January 16, 1994), 44A.

16. Homer "Bill" Callahan, interview by Jay Brakefield, December 6, 1993.

17. Helen Hall, interview by Jay Brakefield, October 1992.

18. Dempsey, *Light Crust Doughboys*, 108.

19. Callahan, interview.

18. Jimmy Fields, interview by Alan Govenar, January 23, 1994.

19. Ibid.

20. Ibid.

21. Ibid.

Chapter 13. Benny Binion: Gambling and the Policy Racket

1. John H. Moss, interview by Alan Govenar, August 12, 1993.

2. Harmon Howze, interview by William Howze, October 10, 1984.

3. Emerson Emory, interview by Jay Brakefield, December 5, 1992.

4. C. W. "Gus" Edwards, interview by Jay Brakefield, May 1, 1992.

5. Ibid.

6. Ibid.

7. Ibid.

8. Will Wilson, interview by Jay Brakefield, May 15, 1993.

9. Emory, interview.

10. Alto McGowan, interview by Jay Brakefield, April 15, 1992.

11. Eddie Goldstein, interview by Jay Brakefield, April 3, 1992.

Chapter 14. Deep Ellum's Just Too Doggone Slow: Decline and Rebirth

1. Ernestine Putnam, interview by Alan Govenar, September 10, 1993. All subsequent quotes by Putman are from this interview. For more information on the Frito Company, see Kaleta Doolin, *Fritos Pie: Stories, Recipes, and More* (College Station: Texas A&M University Press, 2011).

2. Putnam, interview.

3. Junious Smith and Jay Smith, interview by Jay Brakefield, July 11, 1992.

4. "Hidden Nooks of Dallas: 'Deep Ellum' Has Its Renown But After All It Is Merely The Darkies' Parade Ground," *Dallas Morning News*, November 29, 1925.

5. Emerson Emory, interview by Jay Brakefield, December 5, 1992.

6. *WPA Dallas Guide*, 295.

7. Ibid., 296.

8. David Goldstein and Isaac "Rocky" Goldstein, interview by Jay Brakefield, March 22, 1992.

9. Eddie Goldstein, interview by Jay Brakefield, April 3, 1992.

10. Jack Richardson, interview by Jay Brakefield, May 23, 1992.

11. Rudolph McMillan, interview by Jay Brakefield, April 9, 1993.

12. Katherine Lederer, "And Then They Sang a Sabbath Song," *Springfield* (April–June, 1981), 24–28, 33–36, 24–26, 24–29, 33–36.

13. Ted Fox, *Showtime at the Apollo* (New York: Holt, Rinehart and Winston, 1983), 96.

14. C. W. "Gus" Edwards, interview by Jay Brakefield, May 1, 1992.

15. Richardson, interview.

16. Ed Doran, interview by Jay Brakefield, April 24, 1992.

17. Edwards, interview.

18. Dora Goldstein, interview by Jay Brakefield, May 1, 1992.

19. Edwards, interview.

20. Sam Tuck, interview by Brakefield, June 15, 1992.

21. Eddie Goldstein, interview.

22. Doran, interview.

23. McMillan, interview.

24. Curtis Cokes, interview by Jay Brakefield, August 7, 1992.

25. Eddie Goldstein, interview.

26. "'Honest Joe' Goldstein, Pawn Shop Owner, Dies," *Dallas Morning News*, September 4, 1972.

27. Bret Stout, interview by Jay Brakefield, June 12, 1993.

28. For more information on the controversy surrounding the Pythian Temple, see Robert Wilonsky, "Knights' Tale: Another Historic Emblem of Black Dallas Stands on the Brink," *Dallas Observer*, December 20, 2007. http://www.dallasobserver.com/content/print Version/833827/

29. For more information, see http://deepellumtexas.com/community/community-groups/ deep-ellum-community-association/.

Selected Discography

The following discography includes artists who recorded in Dallas and/or had strong ties to the city. The information was gathered from existing recordings and standard discographies, including Robert M. W. Dixon, John Godrich, and Howard Rye, *Blues and Gospel Records 1890–1943* (Oxford: Clarendon, 1997); Brian Rust, *Jazz Records 1897–1942* (London: Storyville, 1982), and *The American Dance Band Discography, 1917–1942* (New Rochelle, NY: Arlington House, 1975); Ross Laird, *Brunswick Records: A Discography of Recordings, 1916–1931* (Westport, CT: Greenwood, 2004); Ross Laird and Brian Rust, *Discography of OKeh Records, 1918–1934* (Westport, CT: Praeger, 2004); and Tony Russell, *Country Music Records: A Discography, 1921–1942* (New York: Oxford University Press, 2004). Additional discographical information was provided by Marvin Montgomery, Cary Ginell, and Kevin Coffey. We have indicated where information is uncertain or discrepancies exist among sources.

Elton Britt

Britt, Guitar, vocal, yodeling

New York, May 12, 1939

036942	Just Because You're in Deep Elem	Bluebird B-8166, Montgomery Ward M-8426, Regal-Zonophone (Australian) G24015

Hattie Burleson

Burleson, vocal; Don Albert, trumpet, 1; Siki Collins, soprano saxophone, 2; Allen Van, piano; John Henry Bragg, banjo; Charlie Dixon, brass bass

Dallas, c. Oct. 1928

DAL-706-A	Jim Nappy	Brunswick 7054
DAL-707-A	Bye Bye Baby-1	Brunswick 7054
DAL-744-A	Superstitious Blues-1, -2	Brunswick 7042
DAL-745-A	Sadie's Servant Room Blues-1, -2	Brunswick 7042

Burleson, vocal; possibly Bob Call, piano

Grafton, WI, c. Nov. 1930

L-614-1	Clearin' House Blues	Paramount 13050
L-615-1	High Five Blues	Paramount 13050
L-616-1	Dead Lover Blues	Paramount 13138

Note: This singer may also have recorded as Hattie Hudson.

Busse's Buzzards

Henry Busse, trumpet; Roy Maxon, trombone; Chester Hazlett, Hal McLean, clarinet, alto saxophone; Charles Strickfaden, alto and baritone saxophones; E. Lyle Sharpe, clarinet, tenor saxophone; Willard Robison, piano; Mike Pingitore, banjo; John Sperzel, brass bass; George Marsh, drums

Camden, NJ, July 9, 1925

32762-2	Deep Elm (You Tell 'Em I'm Blue)	Victor 19727, His Master's Voice B-5037

Bobby (Bobbi or Bobbie) Cadillac

Cadillac, vocal accompanied by unknown cornet, piano, and guitar; effects by Billiken Johnson

Dallas, Dec. 6, 1928

147576-2	Tom Cat Blues	Columbia unissued

Cadillac, vocal; unknown piano

Dallas, Dec. 8, 1928

147599-2	Carbolic Acid Blues	Columbia 14413-D

Bobbie Cadillac and Coley Jones

Vocal duets accompanied by Coley Jones, guitar; possibly Alex Moore, piano

Dallas, Dec. 5, 1929

149536-2	I Can't Stand That	Columbia 14604-D
149537-1	He Throws That Thing	Columbia 14604-D

Dallas, Dec. 6, 1929

149566-1	Listen, Everybody	Columbia 14505-D
149567-1	Easin' In	Columbia 14505-D

Gene Campbell

Campbell, vocal/guitar

Dallas, c. Nov. 1929

DAL-515	Mama, You Don't Mean Me No Good No How	Brunswick 7139, Supertone S2215
DAL-516	Bended Knee Blues	Brunswick 7139, Supertone S2215

Chicago, c. May 1930

C-5701-A	Wandering Blues	Brunswick 7170
C-5702	Somebody's Been Playin' Papa	Brunswick 7177
C-5703	Wash and Iron Woman Blues	Brunswick 7177
C-5704-B	Robbin' and Stealin' Blues	Brunswick 7170
C-5705	I Wish I Could Die	Brunswick 7184
C-5706	Lazy Woman Blues	Brunswick 7184
C-5707-A	Levee Camp Man Blues	Brunswick 7154
C-5708	Western Plain Blues	Brunswick 7154
C-5709	Freight Train Yodeling Blues, Part 1	Brunswick 7161
C-5710	Freight Train Yodeling Blues, Part 2	Brunswick 7161

Dallas, c. Nov. 1930

DAL-6789-A	Don't Leave Me Blue Blues	Brunswick 7214
DAL-6790-A	Doggone Mean Blues	Brunswick 7214
DAL-6791-A	Married Life Blues	Brunswick 7227
DAL-6792-A	Fair Weather Woman Blues	Brunswick 7227

Chicago, Jan. 22, 1931

C-7250	Lonesome Nights Blues	Brunswick 7197
C-7251	Wedding Day Blues	Brunswick 7197
C-7252-A	Main Papa's Blues	Brunswick 7206
C-7253-A	Face to Face Blues	Brunswick 7206

Chicago, Jan. 23, 1931

C-7255-A	"Toby" Woman Blues	Brunswick 7226
C-7256-A	Turned Out Blues	Brunswick 7226
C-7257-A	Crooked Woman Blues	Brunswick 7225
C-7258-A	Overalls Papa Blues	Brunswick 7225

Dallas Jamboree Jug Band

Carl Davis, vocal, swanee whistle, kazoo, guitar; unknown, second guitar; "Shorty," string bass; unknown, brass bass; Charles "Chicken" Jackson, washboard

Dallas, Sept. 20, 1935

| DAL-103-2 | Elm Street Woman Blues | Vocalion 03092 |
| DAL-104-2 | Tyler Texas Stomp | ARC unissued |

Note: Tyler Texas Stomp apparently was an instrumental.

Dallas, Sept. 25, 1935

DAL- 152-1	It May Be My Last Night	Vocalion 03132
DAL-153-2	Dusting the Frets	Vocalion 03092
DAL-157-2	Flying Crow Blues	Vocalion 03132
DAL-158-2	Tuxedo Stomp	ARC unissued

Note: Vocalion 03132 issued as by the Dallas Jug Band

Dallas String Band

Coley Jones, mandolin, vocal-1; probably Sam Harris, guitar; probably Marco Washington, string bass; vocal chorus, presumably by members of group-1

Dallas, Dec. 6, 1927

| 145343-2 | Dallas Rag | Columbia 14290 D |
| 145344-3 | Sweet Mama Blues-1 | Columbia 14290-D |

Dallas, Dec. 8, 1928

| 147612-1 | So Tired-1, -2 | Columbia 14389-D |
| 147613-1 | Hokum Blues-2 | Columbia 14389-D |

Dallas, Dec. 9, 1928

| 147622-2 | Chasin' Rainbows-1, -2 | Columbia 14410-D |
| 147623-2 | I Used to Call Her Baby-1, -2 | Columbia 14410-D |

Same as above, except Harris or Washington, second vocal

Dallas, Dec. 6, 1929

| 149568-2 | Shine | Columbia 14574-D |
| 149569-1 | Sugar Blues | Columbia 14574-D |

Texas Bill Day

Texas Bill Day, vocal; Day or Alex Moore, piano; Coley Jones, guitar

Dallas, Dec. 4, 1929

149512-1	Goin' Back to My Baby	Columbia 14494-D
149513-2	Don't Get Love in Your Mind	Columbia 14494-D
149514-2	Good Mornin' Blues	Columbia 14587-D
149515-2	Burn the Trestle Down	Columbia 14587-D

Texas Bill Day and Billiken Johnson

Texas Bill Day, vocal; Day or Alex Moore, piano; Billiken Johnson, kazoo, vocal, vocal effects; Coley Jones, guitar

Dallas, Dec. 5, 1929

| 149538-2 | Elm Street Blues | Columbia 14514-D |
| 149539-2 | Billiken's Weary Blues | Columbia 14514-D |

Note: Texas Bill Day may be the same man as Will Day, but, lacking definitive confirmation, we list them separately.

Will Day

Will Day, vocal; unknown clarinet and guitar; Willis Harris, vocal-1; Alberta
Brown, vocal-2

New Orleans, Apr. 25, 1928

146185-2	West Texas Blues-1	Columbia unissued
146186-2	Central Avenue Blues	Columbia 14318-D
146187-2	Unnamed Title-2	Columbia unissued
146191-2	Sunrise Blues	Columbia 14318-D

Deep Ellum Blues (Documentary Arts, DA1101)

Dallas, 1981–1985

| Hal Baker and the Gloom-chasers | Hal Baker, clarinet; unknown accompaniment | At the Jazz Band Ball |
| Heat Waves of Swing | Buster Smith, electric guitar; Herbert Cowens, drums; Benny "Chops" Arredondo, trumpet; Boston Smith, piano; James Clay, tenor sax | Kansas City, Monkey Jump, Walkin' to New Orleans |

Austin, 1984

| Lavada Durst | vocal, piano | How Long, Pinetop Boogie |

Dallas, 1981–1985

| Alex Moore | vocal, piano | Central Tracks Blues |

Austin, 1983–1984

| Bill Neely | vocal, guitar | Deep Ellum Blues, Graveyard Blues, Matchbox Blues (Blind Lemon Jefferson), Blues on Ellum |

Austin, 1984

| Robert Shaw | vocal, piano | Hurry Down, Santa Fe |

Rev. Emmett Dickenson

Sermon without congregation (despite contrary labeling)

Grafton, WI, c. Mar. 1930

| L-277-4 | Death of Blind Lemon | Paramount 12945 |

Arizona Dranes

Juanita Arizona Dranes, vocal, piano

Chicago, June 17, 1926

9737-A	In That Day	OKeh 8380
9738-A	It's All Right Now	OKeh 8353

Dranes, vocal, piano; with Richard M. Jones and Sara Martin, vocal

Chicago, June 17, 1926

9739-A	John Said He Saw a Number	OKeh 8352
9740-A	My Soul Is a Witness for the Lord	OKeh 8352

Dranes, piano solo

Chicago, June 17, 1926

9741-A	Crucifixion	OKeh 8380
9742-A	Sweet Heaven Is My Home	OKeh 8353

Dranes, vocal and piano; with Rev. F. W. McGee and the Jubilee Singers

Chicago, Nov. 15, 1926

9877-A	Bye and Bye We're Going to See the King	OKeh 8438
9878-A	I'm Going Home on the Morning Train	OKeh 8419
9879-A	Lamb's Blood Has Washed Me Clean	OKeh 8419
9880-B	I'm Glad My Lord Saved Me	OKeh 8438

Dranes, vocal, piano; vocals by female choir; possibly Coley Jones, mandolin on first four selections

Chicago, July 3, 1928

400980-A	I Shall Wear a Crown	OKeh 8600
400981-A	God's Got a Crown	OKeh unissued; Herwin H210; Library of Congress Folk Music in America series 1 (LPs); Roots 'n' Blues CK46779; Roots 'n' Blues (European) 467890-2; Roots 'n' Blues (Japanese) SRC5511; Document DOCD5186 (CDs)

400982-B	He Is My Story	OKeh unissued; Historical HLP34; Herwin H210; Columbia KG31695; CBS (European) 67280 (LPs); Roots 'n' Blues CK46779; Roots 'n' Blues (European) 467890-2; Roots 'n' Blues (Japanese) SRCS5511; Document DOCD5186 (CDs)
400983-B	Just Look	OKeh 8646
400984-A, -B	I'll Go Where You Want Me to Go	OKeh 8600
400985-B	Don't You Want to Go?	OKeh 8646

Louis Forbstein's Royal Syncopators

Louis Forbstein, clarinet, alto saxophone, violin; Willard Robison, piano; Rex Newman, vocal; other musicians unknown

Kansas City, c. May 15, 1925

| 9115-A | Deep Elm (You Tell 'Em I'm Blue) | OKeh 40379 |

Frenchy's String Band

"Frenchy" Polite Christian, cornet; unknown, guitar (possibly Sam Harris); Percy Darensbourg, banjo; probably Octave Gaspard, string bass (bowed); unknown vocal, probably Jesse Hooker, on Sunshine Special

Dallas, Dec. 5, 1928

| 147566-1 | Texas and Pacific Blues | Columbia 14387-D |
| 147567-1 | Sunshine Special | Columbia 14387-D |

Charlie Fry and His Million-Dollar Pier Orchestra

Charlie Fry, alto saxophone, violin; Julian Kurtzman, Theo Wohleben, trumpet; Ben Morgan, trombone; Ray Thwaite, Oscar Moldaur, clarinet, soprano and alto saxophones; John Baviton, clarinet, tenor saxophone; Ray Allen, piano; Frank Kriell, banjo, vocal; Herman Schmidt, brass bass; Fred Niehardt, drums

New York, July 23, 1925

| 10514 | Deep Elm (You Tell 'Em I'm Blue) | Edison Diamond Disc 51574 |

Georgia Crackers

Paul Cofer, fiddle and vocal; Leon Cofer, banjo and vocal; Ben Evans, guitar

Atlanta, Mar. 21, 1927

| 80596-B | The Georgia Black Bottom | OKeh 45111 |

Note: This recording is included because it appears to be the basis for "Deep Elem Blues."

Lillian Glinn

Lillian Glinn, vocals; Willie Tyson, piano; Octave Gaspard, brass bass, first three songs; unknown, guitar, "Brownskin Blues"

Dallas, Dec. 2, 1927

145312-1	All Alone and Blue	Columbia 14300-D
145313-2	Come Home Daddy	Columbia 14300-D
145314-1	Doggin' Me Blues	Columbia 14275-D
145315-1, -2	Brownskin Blues	Columbia 14275-D

Glinn, vocals; Willie Tyson, piano; unknown, cornet and brass bass, "Shake It Down"

New Orleans, Apr. 24, 1928

146176-3	The Man I Love Is Worth Talking About	Columbia 14330-D
146177-2	Best Friend Blues	Columbia 14330-D
146178-2	Lost Letter Blues	Columbia 14360-D
146179-2	Packing House Blues	Columbia 14360-D
146180	Shake It Down	Columbia 14315-D

Glinn, vocals; unknown piano, cornet, clarinet, brass bass

New Orleans, Apr. 25, 1928

| 146190-2 | Where Have All the Black Men Gone | Columbia 14315-D |

Glinn, vocals; possibly Pete Underwood or Henry Mason, trumpet; Taylor Flanagan or J. Neal Montgomery, piano; probably Perry Bechtel, guitar

Atlanta, Apr. 9, 1929

148212-1	I'm a Front Door Woman with a Back Door Man	Columbia 14433-D
148213-2	Atlanta Blues	Columbia 14421-D
148214-1	All the Week Blues	Columbia 14421-D
148215-2	Cannon Ball Blues	Columbia 14617-D

Note: Underwood, Flanagan, and Bechtel were white hillbilly musicians.

Atlanta, Apr. 10, 1929

| 148225-2 | Wobble It a Little, Daddy | Columbia 14617-D |
| 148226-2 | Black Man Blues | Columbia 14433-D |

Glinn, vocals; unknown, piano and banjo; possibly Octave Gaspard, brass bass.

Dallas, Dec. 6, 1929

149550-2	I'm Through (Shedding Tears over You)	Columbia 14559-D
149551-2	I Love That Thing	Columbia 14559-D
149552-1	Don't Leave Me Daddy	Columbia 14493-D
149553-2	Shreveport Blues	Columbia 14519-D
149556-2	Moanin' Blues	Columbia 14493-D
149557-2	Cravin' a Man Blues	Columbia 14519-D

Otis Harris

Harris, vocal, guitar

Dallas, Dec. 8, 1928

| 147608-1 | Walking Blues | Columbia 14428-D |
| 147609-1 | You'll Like My Loving | Columbia 14428-D |

Sammy Hill

Hill, vocal, guitar; Keno Pipes, second guitar, spoken part on "Cryin' for You Blues"

Dallas, Aug. 9, 1929

| 55319-1 | Cryin' for You Blues | Victor V38588 |
| 55320-2 | Needin' My Woman Blues | Victor V38588 |

Andrew Hogg

Hogg, vocal, guitar

Dallas, Feb. 18, 1937

| 612856-A | Family Trouble Blues | Decca 7303 |
| 61857-A | Kind-Hearted Blues | Decca 7303 |

Note: On his later recordings, this artist was generally identified as "Smokey" Hogg.

Hattie Hudson

Hudson, vocal; Willie Tyson, piano

Dallas, Dec. 6, 1927

| 145338-2 | Doggone My Good Luck Soul | Columbia 14279-D |
| 145339-2 | Black Hand Blues | Columbia 14279-D |

Note: This singer may also have recorded as Hattie Burleson.

Prince Albert Hunt

Prince Albert Hunt's Texas Ramblers: Archie "Prince Albert" Hunt, fiddle, vo-cal-1; unknown guitar

San Antonio, Mar. 8, 1928

400434-B	Katy on Time	OKeh 45230
400435-A	Blues in a Bottle-1	OKeh 45230
400436-A	Traveling Man-1	OKeh 45446

Harmon Clem and Prince Albert Hunt: Harmon Clem, fiddle; Prince Albert Hunt, guitar

Dallas, June 26, 1929

| 402726-A | Canada Waltz | OKeh 45360 |
| 402727-A | Oklahoma Rag | OKeh 45360 |

Prince Albert Hunt's Texas Ramblers: Prince Albert Hunt, fiddle, spoken part-1; Harmon Clem, guitar, possibly spoken part-1; possible unknown second guitar

Dallas, June 26, 1929

402728-A	Wake Up, Jacob	OKeh 45375
402729	Ragtime Annie	OKeh unissued
402730-B	Waltz of Roses	OKeh 45375
402731-A	Houston Slide-1	OKeh 45446

Blind Lemon Jefferson

Recording as Deacon L. J. Bates, vocal, probably own guitar

Chicago, c. Dec. 1925–Jan. 1926

| 11040-1 | I Want to Be like Jesus in My Heart | Paramount 12386, Herwin 93031 |
| 11041-1 | All I Want Is That Pure Religion | Paramount 12386, Herwin 93031 |

Note: Herwin 93031 was released by Deacon Jackson.

Recording as Blind Lemon Jefferson: vocal, own guitar

Chicago, c. Mar. 1926

2471-1, -2	Got the Blues	Paramount 12354
2472-1, -2	Long Lonesome Blues	Paramount 12354
2474-1	Booster Blues	Paramount 12347
2475-1	Dry Southern Blues	Paramount 12347

Chicago, c. Apr. 1926

| 2543-1 | Black Horse Blues | Paramount 12367 |
| 2544-1, -2 | Corinna Blues | Paramount 12367 |

Chicago, c. May 1926

2557-1	Jack O' Diamond Blues	Paramount 12373
2557-2	Jack O' Diamond Blues	Paramount 12373, 14022, Jazz Collector (British) L103
2558-2	Chock House Blues	Paramount 12373, 14022, Jazz Collector L 103

Chicago, c. Aug. 1926

| 2016-4 | Beggin Back | Paramount 12394 |
| 2018-1 | Old Rounders Blues | Paramount 12394 |

Chicago, c. Nov. 1926

3066-1, -2	Stocking Feet Blues	Paramount 12407
3067-1, -2	That Black Snake Moan	Paramount 12407
3070-1	Wartime Blues	Paramount 12425
3076-1, -2	Broke and Hungry	Paramount 12443
3077-1, -2	Shuckin' Sugar Blues	Paramount 12454, Tempo (British) R46, Jazz Collector L91

Chicago, c. Dec. 1926

3088-2	Booger Rooger Blues	Paramount 12425
3089-1	Rabbit Foot Blues	Paramount 12454, Tempo R46, Jazz Collector L 91
3090-2	Bad Luck Blues	Paramount 12443

Vocal, guitar; guitar solo and spoken part on "English Stop Time"

Atlanta, Mar. 14, 1927

80523-B	Black Snake Moan	OKeh 8455, Jazz Classic 511, Jazz Society (French) AA 513
80524-B	Match Box Blues	OKeh 8455, Jazz Classic 511, Jazz Society AA513
80525-B	'Stillery Blues	OKeh unissued
80526-B	Woman Labor Man	OKeh unissued
80527-B	My Easy Rider	OKeh unissued
80528-B	Elder Green's in Town	OKeh unissued
80529-B	English Stop Time	OKeh unissued

Vocal, guitar

Atlanta, Mar. 15, 1927

| 80536-B | Laboring Man Away From Home | OKeh unissued |

Note: David Evans and Luigi Monge, based on copyright deposits of the Chicago Music Publishing Company at the Library of Congress, have identified this song as "I Labor So Far from Home." They also identified other songs that were never recorded or were recorded and lost, including "Light House Blues" and "Pineapple Blues.

Chicago, c. Apr. 1927

4423-2	Easy Rider Blues	Paramount 12474
4424-2	Match Box Blues	Paramount 12474
4446-4	Match Box Blues	Paramount 12474

Jefferson, vocal; George Perkins, piano

Chicago, c. May 1927

| 4491-5 | Rising High Water Blues | Paramount 12487 |

Jefferson, vocal, guitar

Chicago, c. May 1927

| 4514-4 | Weary Dogs Blues | Paramount 12493, Tempo R38 |
| 4515-2 | Right of Way Blues | Paramount 12510 |

Jefferson, vocal; George Perkins, piano

Chicago, c. June 1927

| 4567-1, -2 | Teddy Bear Blues | Paramount 12487 |

Blind Lemon Jefferson and George Perkins, piano-1; Blind Lemon Jefferson
and his feet-2; as Deacon L. J. Bates-3; Blind Lemon Jefferson, vocal-4;
Jefferson, tap dancing and vocal comments-2; Jefferson accompanied by own
guitar-5

Chicago, c. June 1927

4577-2	Black Snake Dream Blues -1, -4	Paramount 12510
4578-3	Hot Dogs -2, -5	Paramount 12493
4579-1	He Arose from the Dead -3, -4, -5	Paramount 12585, Herwin 93004

Note: Herwin 93004 as by Elder J. C. Brown.

Jefferson, vocal, guitar

Chicago, c. Sep. 1927

| 20039-2 | Struck Sorrow Blues | Paramount 12541 |
| 20040-2 | Rambler Blues | Paramount 12541 |

Chicago, c. Oct. 1927

20064-1	Chinch Bug Blues	Paramount 12551
20065-2	Deceitful Brownskin Blues	Paramount 12551
20066-1	Sunshine Special	Paramount 12593
20070-2	Gone Dead on You Blues	Paramount 12578, Tempo R54, Jazz Collector L126
20073-2	Where Shall I Be?	Paramount 12585, Herwin 93004
20074-2	See That My Grave's Kept Clean	Paramount 12585
20075-2	One Dime Blues	Paramount 12578, Tempo R54, Jazz Collector L 126
20076-2	Lonesome House Blues	Paramount 12593

Note: Paramount 12585 as by Deacon L. J. Bates; Herwin 93004 as by Elder
J. C. Brown.

Chicago, c. Feb. 1928

20363-2	Blind Lemon's Penitentiary Blues	Paramount 12666
20364-2	'Lectric Chair Blues	Paramount 12608, Broadway 5059
20374-1	See That My Grave Is Kept Clean	Paramount 12608, Broadway 5059
20375-3	Lemon's Worried Blues	Paramount 12622
20380-2	Mean Jumper Blues	Paramount 12631
20381-3	Balky Mule Blues	Paramount 12631
20387-2	Change My Luck Blues	Paramount 12639, Tempo R38
20388-2	Prison Cell Blues	Paramount 12622

Chicago, c. Mar. 1928

20401-1	Lemon's Cannon Ball Blues	Paramount 12639
20402	Low Down Mojo Blues	Paramount unissued
20407-2	Long Lastin' Lovin'	Paramount 12666
20408-2	Piney Woods Money Mama	Paramount 12650

Chicago, c. June 1928

20636-1	Low Down Mojo Blues	Paramount 12650

Chicago, c. July 1928

20479-2	Competition Bed Blues	Paramount 12728
20750-2	Lock Step Blues	Paramount 12679
20751-1, -2	Hangman's Blues	Paramount 12679
20772-2	Sad News Blues	Paramount 12728

Jefferson vocal, guitar; unknown piano

Chicago, c. July 1928

20788-1	How Long, How Long	Paramount 12685

Jefferson vocal, guitar

Chicago, c. Aug. 1928

20815-2	Lockstep Blues	Paramount 12679, Tempo R39, E-Disc R2
20816-2	Hangman's Blues	Paramount 12679, Tempo R39, E-Disc R2
20818-2	Christmas Eve Blues	Paramount 12692
20819-2	Happy New Year Blues	Paramount 12692
20820-1	Maltese Cat Blues	Paramount 12712
20821-1	D B Blues	Paramount 12712

Chicago, c. Jan. 1929

21095-3	Eagle Eyed Mama	Paramount 12739
21096-1	Dynamite Blues	Paramount 12739
21110-2	Disgusted Blues	Paramount 12933
21132-1	Competition Bed Blues	Paramount 12728
21133-1	Sad News Blues	Paramount 12728

Chicago, c. Mar. 1929

21196-1	Peach Orchard Mama	Paramount 12801
21197-1	Oil Well Blues	Paramount 12771
21198-1	Tin Cup Blues	Paramount 12756
21199-1	Big Night Blues	Paramount 12801
21200-1	Empty House Blues	Paramount 12946
21201-2	Saturday Night Spender Blues	Paramount 12771
21202-1	That Black Snake Moan No. 2	Paramount 12756

Chicago, c. Aug. 1929

21400-2	Peach Orchard Mama	Paramount 12801
21402-2	Big Night Blues	Paramount 12801

Richmond, IN, Sept. 24, 1929

15664	Bed Springs Blues	Paramount 12872, Broadway 5056
15665	Yo Yo Blues	Paramount 12872, Broadway 5056
15666	Mosquito Moan	Paramount 12899
15667	Southern Woman Blues	Paramount 12899
15668	Bakershop Blues	Paramount 12582
15669	Pneumonia Blues	Paramount 12880
15670-A	Long Distance Moan	Paramount 12852
15671	That Crawlin' Baby Blues	Paramount 12880
15672	Fence Breakin' Yellin' Blues	Paramount 12921
15673	Cat Man Blues	Paramount 12921
15674	The Cheaters Spell	Paramount 12933
15675	Bootin' Me 'Bout	Paramount 12946

Billiken Johnson

Johnson, vocal effects, whistling; Fred Adams, vocal; Willie Tyson, piano; Octave Gaspard, brass bass

Dallas, Dec. 3, 1927

145322-1	Sun Beam Blues	Columbia 14293-D
145323-2	Interurban Blues	Columbia 14293-D

Johnson, vocal effects, kazoo; Neal Roberts, piano, vocal.

Dallas, Dec. 8, 1928

147606-2	Frisco Blues	Columbia 14405-D
14/607 1, -2	Wild Jack Blues	Columbia 14405-D

Blind Willie Johnson

Johnson vocal, own guitar; humming and moaning without vocal-1

Dallas, Dec. 3, 1927

145316-1, -2	I Know His Blood Can Make Me Whole	Columbia 14276-D
145317-2	Jesus Make Up My Dying Bed	Columbia 14276-D
145318-2	It's Nobody's Fault but Mine	Columbia 14303-D, Vocalion 03095, Jazz Classic 512
145319-2	Mother's Children Have a Hard Time	Columbia 14343-D, Vocalion 03021, Anchor 380
145320-1	Dark Was the Night, Cold Was the Ground-1	Columbia 14303-D, Vocalion 03095, Jazz Classic 512, Square M1
145321-3	If I Had My Way, I'd Tear the Building Down	Columbia 14343-D, Vocalion 03021, Anchor 380

Note: Anchor 380 as by the Blind Pilgrim; 145319 was titled "Motherless Children"; 145321 was titled "Oh Lord, If I Had My Way."

Johnson, vocals; Willie B. Richardson vocals

Dallas, Dec. 5, 1928

147568-1	I'm Gonna Run to the City of Refuge	Columbia 14391-D, Jazz Classic 527
147569-2	Jesus Is Coming Soon	Columbia 14391-D, Jazz Classic 527
147570-2	Lord I Just Can't Keep from Crying	Columbia 14425-D, Vocalion 03022, Square M1
147571-1, -2	Keep Your Lamp Trimmed and Burning	Columbia 14425-D, Vocalion 03022

Johnson, vocal, guitar

New Orleans, Dec. 10, 1929

149578-2	Let Your Light Shine On Me	Columbia 14490-D
149579-1	God Don't Never Change	Columbia 14490-D
149580-2	Bye and Bye I'm Goin' to See the King	Columbia 14504-D
149581-2	Sweeter as the Years Roll By	Columbia 14624-D

Johnson, guitar; Willie B. Richardson vocal, except on "God Moves on the Water"

New Orleans, Dec. 11, 1929

149594-1	You'll Need Somebody on Your Bond	Columbia 14504-D
149595-2	When the War Was On	Columbia 14545-D
149596-2	Praise God I'm Satisfied	Columbia 14545-D
149597-1	Take Your Burden to the Lord and Leave It There	Columbia 14520-D, Vocalion 03051, Hot Jazz Clubs of America HC113
149598-2	Take Your Stand	Columbia 14624-D
145599-1	God Moves on the Water	Columbia 14520-D, Vocalion 03051, Hot Jazz Clubs of America HC113

Atlanta, Apr. 20, 1930

150307; 194926-2	Can't Nobody Hide from God	Columbia 14556-D
150308; 194927-1	If It Had Not Been for Jesus	Columbia 14556-D
150309; 194928-2	Go with Me to That Land	Columbia 14597-D
150310-2; 194929-2	The Rain Don't Fall on Me	Columbia 14537-D, British Rhythm Society 24
150311-2; 194930-2	Trouble Will Soon Be Over	Columbia 14537-D, BRS 24
150312; 194931-2	The Soul of a Man	Columbia 14582-D
150313; 194897-2	Everybody Ought To Treat A Stranger Right	Columbia 14597-D
150314; 194890-3	Church, I'm Fully Saved To-Day	Columbia 14582-D
150315-2	John the Revelator	Columbia 14530-D
150316-2	You're Gonna Need Somebody on Your Bond	Columbia 14530-D

Note: The second title on this session is virtually a solo by Willie B. Richardson, with Blind Willie Johnson joining in the choruses. Columbia 14530-D was withdrawn shortly after issue. According to *Blues and Gospel Records, 1890–1943*, "Willie B. Richardson, later Willie B. Harris, was Blind Willie Johnson's first wife, and the balance of available evidence suggests that it is she rather than his second wife, Angeline, who is featured on his recordings."

Coley Jones

Jones vocal, accompanied by own guitar

Dallas, Dec. 3, 1927

145324-1	Army Mule in No Man's Land	Columbia 14288-D
145325-2	That's My Man	Columbia unissued
145326-2	Papa Coley's Past Life Blues	Columbia unissued
145327-2	You Go Ahead, I'll Stay Right Here	Columbia unissued
145328-3	O Death, Where Is Thy Sting	Columbia unissued

Note: Session originally credited to Coalie Jones in the Columbia files.

Dallas, Dec. 4, 1927

145329-1, -2	Traveling Man	Columbia 14288-D

Dallas, Dec. 6, 1927

145342-2	Frankie and Albert	Columbia unissued

Dallas, Dec. 6, 1929

149558-2	Drunkard's Special	Columbia 14489-D
149559-2	The Elder's He's My Man [*sic*]	Columbia 14489-D

George "Little Hat" Jones

Jones vocal, accompanied by own guitar

San Antonio, June 15, 1929

402647-A	New Two Sixteen Blues	OKeh 8712
402648-A	Two String Blues	OKeh 8712

San Antonio, June 21, 1929

402698-A	Rolled from Side to Side Blues	OKeh 8794
402699-A	Hurry Blues	OKeh 8735
402700-A	Little Hat Blues	OKeh 8794
402701-B	Corpus Blues	OKeh 8735

Note: "Hurry Blues" probably should have been labeled "Worry" or "Worried Blues"; vocal interjections by unknown female on "Corpus Blues."

San Antonio, June 14, 1930

404197-A	Kentucky Blues	OKeh 8815
404198-B	Bye-Bye Baby Blues	OKeh 8815
404199-B	Cross the Water Blues	OKeh 8829
404300-A	Cherry St. Blues	OKeh 8829

Jake Jones and the Gold Front Boys

Jake Jones, vocal; unknown clarinet, banjo, and guitar

Dallas, Oct. 27, 1929

DAL-473	Monkeyin' Around	Brunswick 7130
DAL-474	Southern Sea Blues	Brunswick 7130

Rev. Joe Lenley

Sermons with singing, possibly accompanied by Arizona Dranes, piano

Dallas, Dec. 5, 1929

149546-2	Let Us Therefore Come	Columbia 14521-D
149547-2	Lord Who Shall Abide in Thy Tabernacle	Columbia 14521-D

The Light Crust Doughboys

(Identified on this initial recording as the Fort Worth Doughboys)

Bob Wills, fiddle/ vocal, 1; Derwood Brown, guitar/vocal, 2; "Sleepy" Johnson, tenor guitar; Milton Brown, vocal.

Dallas, Feb. 9, 1932

70670-1	Nancy Jane, -1,2	Victor 23653, Bluebird B-5257, Electradisk 2137, Sunrise S-3340, Montgomery Ward M-4416, M-4757, Aurora 415
70671-1	Sunbonnet Sue	Victor 23653, Bluebird B-5257, Electradisk 2137, Sunrise S-3340, Montgomery Ward M-4416, M-4757, Aurora 415

Note: Montgomery Ward M-4757 was issued under the name Milton Brown & His Musical Brownies, the band that Milton Brown started after he left the Doughboys

(On the following sessions, the band was identified as W. Lee O'Daniel & His Light Crust Doughboys)

Clifford Gross, fiddle-1; Sleepy Johnson, fiddle, 2, tenor banjo, 3; Leon McAuliffe, steel guitar, 4; Leon Huff, guitar/vocal, 5; Herman Arnspiger, lead guitar; Ramon DeArman, string bass; W. Lee O'Daniel, leader; vocal quartet (Huff, DeArman, Johnson, Gross), 6; unidentified vocal, 7.

Chicago, Oct. 10, 1933

C-621-1,-2	Beautiful Texas, -1,2,4,5,6	Vocalion 02621
C-622-1	Blue Bonnet Waltz, -1,3,4	Vocalion 02621, Regal-Zonophone (Australian), G22095
C-623-2	Your Own Sweet Darling Wife, -1,2,4,5,6	Vocalion 02695, Panachord 25634, Regal-Zonophone (Australian) G22217
C-624-2	On To Victory Mr. Roosevelt, -1,3,4,5,6	Vocalion 02604
C-625-1	I Want Somebody To Cry Over Me, -3,5,7	Vocalion 02605, Panachord 25622
C626-2	Put Me In Your Pocket, -1,2,4,5,6	Vocalion 02731
C-627-1	Texas Breakdown, -1,3	Vocalion 02633

Clifford Gross, harmonica; Sleepy Johnson, tenor banjo; Herman Arnspiger, guitar; Leon Huff, vocal; W. Lee O'Daniel, leader, speech; band, vocal

Chicago, Oct. 11, 1933

C-628-1	In The Fall Of '29	Vocalion 02604

Clifford Gross, fiddle, 1; Sleepy Johnson, fiddle, 2/tenor banjo, 3; Leon McAuliffe, steel guitar, 4; Leon Huff, guitar/vocal, 5; yodeling, 6; Herman Arnspiger, lead guitar; Ramon DeArman, string bass; W. Lee O'Daniel, leader; vocal quartet (Huff, probably DeArman, Johnson, McAuliffe), 7

Chicago, Oct. 11, 1933

C-629-2	Please Come Back To Me, -1,3,5	Vocalion 02695, Panachord 25634, Regal-Zonophone (Australian) G22217
C-630-1	Memories Of Jimmy [sic] Rodgers, -3,4,5,6	Vocalion 02605, Panachord 25622, Regal-Zonophone (Australian) G22177
C-631-1	Roll Up The Carpet, -1,3,5	Vocalion 02842
C-632-1	One More River To Cross	Vocalion unissued
C-633-1	That City For Shut-Ins, -1,2,5,7	Vocalion 02929
C-634-1	Doughboy Rag, -1,3	Vocalion 02633

Clifford Gross, fiddle; Sleepy Johnson, fiddle, 1/tenor banjo, 2; Leon Huff, guitar/vocal, 3/yodeling, 4; Herman Arnspiger, lead guitar; Ramon DeArman, guitar; Leon McAuliffe, string bass; W. Lee O'Daniel, leader

San Antonio, Apr. 7, 1934

SA-2140-B	The Gangster's Moll, -1,3,4	Vocalion 02731
SA-2141-B	My Brown Eyed Texas Rose, -1,3,4	Vocalion 02726, Panachord 25640, Regal-Zonophone (Australian) G22311
SA-2142-B	Alamo Waltz, -2	Vocalion 02769, Regal-Zonophone (Australian) G22255
SA-2143-A, -B	Texas Centennial Waltz, -2	Vocalion unissued

Clifford Gross, fiddle; Sleepy Johnson, tenor banjo; Leon Huff, guitar/vocal; Herman Arnspiger, lead guitar; Ramon DeArman, guitar; Leon McAuliffe, string bass; W. Lee O'Daniel, leader; band, vocal

San Antonio, Apr. 7 or 8, 1934

Doughboys Theme Song #1	ARC unissued; Columbia C4K47911 (CD)
Doughboys Theme Song #2	ARC unissued; Columbia C4K47911 (CD)

Clifford Gross, fiddle; Sleepy Johnson, fiddle, 1/ tenor banjo, 2; Leon Huff, guitar/vocal, 3; Herman Arnspiger, lead guitar; Ramon DeArman, guitar; Leon McAuliffe, string bass; W. Lee O'Daniel, leader; vocal trio (Huff, DeArman, Johnson), 4

San Antonio, Apr. 8, 1934

SA-2144-A	Saturday Night Rag, -2	Vocalion 02842
SA-2145-A	Kelly Waltz, -2	Vocalion/OKeh 02727
SA-2145-B	Kelly Waltz, -2	Vocalion 02727, Regal-Zonophone (Australian) G22249
SA-2146-A	Killem, -2	Vocalion 02892
SA-2147-B	Bill Cheatum, -2	Vocalion 02892
SA-2148-A	Rochester Schottische, -2	Vocalion/OKeh 02727
SA-2148-B	Rochester Schottische, -2	Vocalion/OKeh 02727, Regal-Zonophone (Australian) G22249
SA-2149-A	Heel And Toe – Polka, -2	Vocalion 02769, Regal-Zonophone (Australian) G22255
SA-2150-B	How Beautiful Heaven Must Be, -1,4	Vocalion 02929
SA-2151-B	She's Still That Old Sweetheart Of Mine, -2,3	Vocalion 02726, Panachord 25640, Regal-Zonophone (Australian) G22311

Clifford Gross, fiddle; Sleepy Johnson, fiddle, 1/tenor banjo, 2; Leon Huff, guitar/vocal, 3; Ramon DeArman, guitar/vocal, 4; Leon McAuliffe, string bass/vocal, 5; W. Lee O'Daniel, leader

Fort Worth, Oct. 1, 1934

FW-1150-1	When We Reach Our Happy Home, -1,3,4	Vocalion 02832
FW-1151-1	When It's Round-Up Time In Heaven, -1,3,4	Vocalion 02832
FW-1152-	That Silver Haired Mother	Vocalion unissued
FW-1153-1	Ridin' Ole Paint And Leadin' Old Bald, -2,3,4	Vocalion 02851
FW-1154-	The Morro Castle Disaster	Vocalion unissued
FW-1155-1	My Mary, -1,3	Vocalion 02872
FW-1156-1	When They Baptized Sister Lucy Lee, -2,5	Vocalion 02916

Clifford Gross, fiddle; Sleepy Johnson, fiddle, 1/tenor banjo, 2/ guitar, 3; Leon Huff, guitar/vocal, 4, yodeling, 5; Ramon DeArman, guitar/yodeling, 6; Leon McAuliffe, string bass; W. Lee O'Daniel, leader; vocal quartet (Huff, DeArman, Johnson, Gross), 7; unidentified vocal, 8; unidentified speech, 9

Fort Worth, Oct. 6, 1934

FW-1157-1	Texas Plains, -1, 4, 5	Vocalion 02851
FW-1158-2	There's A Little Gray Mother Dreaming, -3, 4, 7	Vocalion 02872
FW-1159-1	Thirty First Street Blues, -2, 6, 7?, 8, 9	Vocalion 02916
FW-1160-1	Texas Centennial March, -2,4	Vocalion 02863
FW-1161-1	The Governor's Ball, -1, 4	Vocalion 02863

Starting with the next session, the band is identified simply as the Light Crust Doughboys except where otherwise noted

Clifford Gross, fiddle; Kenneth Pitts, fiddle; Leon Huff, guitar/vocal, 1, yodeling, 2; Doc Eastwood, tenor banjo, 3; Ramon DeArman, guitar; Herbert Barnum, string bass; W. Lee O'Daniel, leader; vocal trio (Huff, Pitts, Gross), 4

Fort Worth, Apr. 22, 1935

FW-1182-3	Milenberg Joys, -3	Vocalion 03032
FW-1183-	West Texas Stomp	Vocalion unissued
FW-1184-	Business in "F"	Vocalion unissued
FW-1185-3	Prairie Lullaby, -1,2,3	Vocalion/OKeh 03017
FW-1186-1	Carry Me Back To The Lone Prairie, -1,4	Vocalion 03044
FW-1187-	When You Hear Me Call	Vocalion unissued
FW-1188-	Some Of These Days	Vocalion unissued

Note: Only one fiddle is present on some sides. Marvin "Smokey" Montgomery noted that Gross didn't read music well and was a slow learner, so the other band members sometimes recorded without him.

Clifford Gross, fiddle; Kenneth Pitts, fiddle; Leon Huff, guitar/vocal, 1, yodeling, 2; Doc Eastwood, tenor banjo, 3; Ramon DeArman, guitar/vocal, 4; Herbert Barnum, string bass; W. Lee O'Daniel, leader

Fort Worth, Apr. 23, 1935

FW-1196-	Copenhagen	Vocalion unissued
FW-1197-	Oh By Jingo	Vocalion unissued
FW-1198-2	There's An Empty Cot In The Bunkhouse Tonight, -1,2	Vocalion/OKeh 02992
FW-1199-1	My Million Dollar Smile, -1,3	Vocalion 02975
FW-1200-	I Don't Wanna Go To School	Vocalion unissued
FW-1201-2	Old Joe Clark, -1,3,4	Vocalion 02975

Note: Vocalion 02975 was issued under the name W. Lee O'Daniel & His Light Crust Doughboys

Clifford Gross, fiddle; Kenneth Pitts, fiddle, 1; Leon Huff, guitar/vocal, 2; Doc Eastwood, tenor banjo; Ramon DeArman, guitar/vocal, 3; Herbert Barnum, string bass; W. Lee O'Daniel, leader

Fort Worth, Apr. 24, 1935

FW-1207-3	Ragtime Annie	Vocalion 03032, Conqueror 9756
FW-1208-	Tug Boat	Vocalion unissued
FW-1209-	Rocky Mountain Goat	Vocalion unissued
FW-1210-	Waggoner	Vocalion unissued
FW-1211-3	El Rancho Grande, -1,2,3	Vocalion/OKeh 03017
FW-1212-	My Old Dog Tray	Vocalion unissued
FW-1213-	Bury Me 'Neath The Weeping Willow	Vocalion unissued
FW-1214-1	My Pretty Quadroon, -1,2,3	Vocalion/OKeh 02992

Clifford Gross, fiddle; Kenneth Pitts, fiddle; Leon Huff, guitar/ vocal, 1; Doc Eastwood, tenor banjo; Ramon DeArman, guitar/vocal, 2; Herbert Barnum, string bass; W. Lee O'Daniel, leader; vocal quartet, 3

Fort Worth, Apr. 25, 1935

FW-1215-	Fort Worth Rag	Vocalion unissued
FW-1216-	Doughboy Hop	Vocalion unissued
FW-1217-1	The Old Rugged Cross, -3	Vocalion 03064
FW-1218-1	There's No Disappointment In Heaven, -1,2	Vocalion 03064
FW-1219-	In The Garden	Vocalion unissued
FW-1220-	Whisper Your Mother's Name	Vocalion unissued
FW-1221-	The Cowboy's Dream, -3	Vocalion 03044

Clifford Gross, fiddle; Kenneth Pitts, fiddle; Doc Eastwood, tenor banjo; Curly
Perrin, guitar/vocal, 1; Ramon DeArman, guitar; Herbert Barnum, string bass;
vocal trio (DeArman, Perrin, Pitts), 2

Dallas, Sept. 20, 1935

DAL-105-2	My Blue Heaven, -1	Vocalion/OKeh 03141
DAL-106-1,-2	My Buddy	Vocalion unissued
DAL-107-2	Nobody's Darling But Mine, -1	Vocalion/OKeh 03065, Columbia 37604, 20203
DAL-108-1,-2	My Carolina Mountain Rose	Vocalion unissued
DAL-109-1	My Melancholy Baby, -1	Vocalion/OKeh 03141
DAL-110-2	Rural Rhythm, -2	Vocalion 03069
DAL-111-1	In A Little Gypsy Tea Room, -1	Vocalion 03069
DAL-112-1	The Waltz You Saved For Me, -1	Vocalion/OKeh 03065, Columbia 37604, 20203

Clifford Gross, fiddle; Kenneth Pitts, fiddle; Muryel Campbell, lead guitar;
Marvin Montgomery, tenor banjo; Dick Reinhart, guitar/vocal, 1; Bert Dodson,
string bass; vocal trio (probably Dodson, Reinhart and Pitts), 2; group vocal, 3

Fort Worth, Apr. 4, 1936

FW-1250-3	I'm A Ding Dong Daddy (From Dumas), -1	Vocalion 03239
FW-1251-	My Buddy, -2	Vocalion unissued
FW-1252-3	I Like Bananas (Because They Have No Bones), -3	Vocalion 03238
FW-1253-	The Wheel Of The Wagon Is Broken, -1	Vocalion unissued

Clifford Gross, fiddle; Kenneth Pitts, fiddle; Muryel Campbell, lead guitar;
Marvin Montgomery, tenor banjo; Dick Reinhart, guitar, probably vocal; Bert
Dodson, string bass

Fort Worth, Apr. 5, 1936

FW-1254-	Little Hillbilly Heart Throb	Vocalion unissued

Kenneth Pitts, fiddle, speech; Muryel Campbell, lead guitar; Marvin
Montgomery, tenor banjo, lead vocal, speech; Dick Reinhart, guitar; Bert
Dodson, string bass, speech; vocal quartet (Dodson, Reinhart, Pitts, Clifford
Gross)

Fort Worth, Apr. 5, 1936

FW-1255-3	Did You Ever Hear A String Band Swing	Vocalion 03239

Kenneth Pitts, fiddle; Clifford Gross, fiddle, 1; Muryel Campbell, lead guitar; Marvin Montgomery, tenor banjo, 2/tenor guitar, 3; Dick Reinhart, guitar; Bert Dodson, string bass, vocal

Fort Worth, Apr. 5, 1936

FW-1256-	Tonight I Have A Date,-2	Vocalion unissued
FW-1257-3	Saddle Your Blues To A Wild Mustang, -1	Vocalion 03238
FW-1258-2	Gloomy Sunday, -1,3	Vocalion unissued
FW-1259-	Memories	Vocalion unissued

Clifford Gross, fiddle; Kenneth Pitts, fiddle; Muryel Campbell, lead guitar; Dick Reinhart, mandolin, 1/guitar, 2/vocal, 3; Marvin Montgomery, tenor banjo, 4/tenor guitar, 5; Bert Dodson, string bass/vocal, 6; vocal trio (Dodson, Reinhart, Pitts), 7

Los Angeles, May 26, 1936

LA-1121-A	Little Hill-Billy Heart Throb, -2,3,4	Vocalion 03403
LA-1122-A	My Buddy, -1,5,7	Vocalion 03433
LA-1123-A	The Wheel Of The Wagon Is Broken, -2,3,5	Vocalion 03257
LA-1124-	Tonight I Have A Date, -2,4,6	Vocalion unissued
LA-1125-	Lost, -2,5,6	Vocalion 03257

Kenneth Pitts, fiddle; Clifford Gross, fiddle, 1; Muryel Campbell, lead guitar; Marvin Montgomery, tenor banjo, 2/tenor guitar, 3; vocal, 4; Dick Reinhart, guitar/vocal, 5; Bert Dodson, string bass/vocal, 6

Los Angeles, May 29, 1936

LA-1126-A	Uncle Zeke, -2	Vocalion 03310
LA-1127-A	All My Life, -1,3,6	Vocalion 03282
LA-1128-A	Jig In G, -1,2	Vocalion unissued
LA-1129-A	When The Moon Shines On The Mississippi Valley, -1,2,5	Vocalion 03403
LA-1130-A	I Have Found A Honey, -2,6	Vocalion 03433
LA-1131-A	It's Been So Long, -2,6	Vocalion 03282
LA-1132-A	Cross-Eyed Cowboy From Abilene, -2, 4	Vocalion 03310

Kenneth Pitts, fiddle/accordion, 1; Clifford Gross, fiddle; Muryel Campbell, lead guitar; Marvin Montgomery, tenor banjo; Dick Reinhart, guitar/vocal, 2; Bert Dodson, string bass/vocal, 3; vocal trio (Dodson, Reinhart, Pitts), 4; vocal quartet (Dodson, Reinhart, Pitts, Gross), 5

Fort Worth, Sept. 10, 1936

FW-1262-	I'd Love to Live In Loveland (With A Girl Like You), -2,3	Vocalion unissued
FW-1263-3	Happy Cowboy, -3,4	Vocalion 03345
FW-1264-	Blue Guitar	Vocalion unissued
FW-1265-	A Mug Of Ale	Vocalion unissued
FW-1266-	Sweet Georgia Brown	Vocalion unissued
FW-1267-3	Oh! Susanna, -1,3,5	Vocalion 03345
FW-1268-	The Strawberry Roan	Vocalion unissued
FW-1269-	The Big Corral	Vocalion unissued
FW-1270-	I Want A Girl (Just Like The Girl That Married Dear Old Dad), -2	Vocalion unissued
FW-1271-	When You Wore A Tulip (And I Wore A Big Red Rose), -2	Vocalion unissued

Kenneth Pitts, fiddle, 1/accordion, 2, piano, 3; Clifford Gross, fiddle, 4; Muryel Campbell, electric guitar; John W. "Knocky" Parker, piano/accordion, 5; Marvin
Montgomery, tenor banjo; Dick Reinhart, guitar/vocal, 6; Ramon DeArman, string bass/vocal, 7; vocal quartet (DeArman, Reinhart, Pitts, Gross), 8

Dallas, June 12, 1937

DAL-267-	Theme Song, etc. [*sic*]	Vocalion unissued
DAL-268-1	Emmaline,-1,6	Vocalion 03718
DAL-269-1,-2	Let Me Ride By Your Side In The Saddle	Vocalion unissued
DAL-270-1,-2	Tom Cat Rag	Vocalion unissued
DAL-271-1	Blues Guitars, -1	Vocalion/OKeh 03610
DAL-272-1	Dusky Stevedore, -3,4,5,6,7	Vocalion 03867
DAL-273-1	If I Don't Love You (There Ain't A Cow In Texas), -3,4,5,6	Vocalion 03718
DAL-274-2	Roll Along Jordan, -2,4,5,7,8	Vocalion 03867
DAL-275-1,-2	One Sweet Letter From You	Vocalion unissued
DAL-277-1,-2	Anna Lou	Vocalion unissued
DAL-276-1,-2	Song Of The Saddle	Vocalion unissued
DAL-278-1	Avalon, -3,4,5	Vocalion/OKeh 03610
DAL 279-1,-2	Little Girl Dressed In Blue	Vocalion unissued

Dallas, June 20, 1937

DAL-385-2	Gig-A-Wig Blues, -3,5	Vocalion 03926
DAL-386-1	In A Little Red Barn, -1,4,7	Vocalion 03645
DAL-387-1	Beaumont Rag, 4	Vocalion 03645
DAL-388-1	The Eyes Of Texas, -1,4,8	Vocalion/OKeh 03660, Columbia 37626, 20225
DAL-389-1	Washington And Lee Swing, -2,4	Vocalion/OKeh 03660, Columbia 37626, 20225
DAL-390	Stay On The Right Side Sister	Vocalion unissued
DAL-391-2	Just Once Too Often, -1,6	Vocalion 03926
DAL-392-	Stay Out Of The South (If You Want To Miss Heaven On Earth), -1,4,6	Vocalion unissued

Note: On this date, when the Doughboys recorded at 508 Park Avenue in Dallas, Mississippi blues singer Robert Johnson also recorded. Years later, after Johnson became a cult figure among white musicians, Montgomery said he didn't recall Johnson.

Kenneth Pitts, fiddle, 1/piano, 2/guitar, 3; Clifford Gross, fiddle, 4; Dick Reinhart, electric steel guitar, 5/electric guitar, 6/guitar, 7/vocal, 8; Muryel Campbell, electric guitar, 9/ guitar, 10; Knocky Parker, piano/accordion, 11; Marvin Montgomery, tenor banjo, 12/tenor guitar, 13; Ramon DeArman, string bass/ vocal, 14; Charles Burton, vocal, 15; vocal trio (DeArman, Reinhart, Pitts), 16; vocal quartet (DeArman, Reinhart, Pitts, Gross), 17; vocal with humming quartet (DeArman, Reinhart, Pitts, Parker Willson), 18

Dallas, May 14, 1938

DAL-529-1	Sitting On Top Of The World, -1,6,8, 10, 12	Vocalion/OKeh 04261
DAL-530-1	Weary Blues, 1,7,9,12	Vocalion 04921
DAL-531-1	Gulf Coast Blues, -1,7,8,9,12	Vocalion 04921
DAL-532-1	The Budded Rose, -1,4,7,9,12,14	Vocalion/OKeh 04825
DAL-533-1	I'll Get Mine, -1,4,7,8,9,12,17	Vocalion 04468
DAL-534-1	Blue Hours, -1,4,5,10,11,13	Vocalion 04326, Conqueror 9062
DAL-535-1	Three Shif-less Skonks,-1,4,7,9,12,14,17	Vocalion/OKeh 04261
DAL-536-1,-2	Kalua Loha	Vocalion unissued
DAL-537-1	Slow Down Mr. Brown, -1,7,8,9,12	Vocalion 04468
DAL-538-1	Beautiful Ohio, -1,4,7,9,12,15	Vocalion/OKeh 04158, Columbia 37722, 20299
DAL-539-1	Waiting For The Robert E. Lee, -2,4,7,8,9,11,12	Vocalion/OKeh 04216, Conqueror 9061
DAL-540-1	The Hills Of Old Wyomin', -1,7,9,12,15,18	Vocalion/OKeh 04158, Columbia 37722, 20299
DAL-541-1	Tom Cat Rag, -1,7,9,12,14,16	Vocalion/OKeh 05473
DAL-542-1,-2	Gig-A-Wig Blues, -1,4,7,9,12	Vocalion unissued

DAL-543-1	Knocky-Knocky, -1,7,9,12	Vocalion 04403
DAL-544-1	The Birth Of The Blues, -1,4,7,8,9,12	Vocalion/OKeh 04216, Conqueror 9061
DAL-545-1	Rockin' Alone (In An Old Rockin' Chair)	Vocalion unissued
DAL-546-2	Pretty Little Dear, -1,4,7,8,9,12,14	Vocalion/OKeh 05413, Conqueror 9411
DAL-547-1	Sweeter Than An Angel, -1,7,8,9,12	Vocalion 04403
DAL-548-1	Stumbling, -1,3,7,10,13	Vocalion 04326, Conqueror 9062
DAL-549-2	Clarinet Marmalade, -1,7,9,12	Vocalion/OKeh 05473

Kenneth Pitts, fiddle; Robert "Buck" Buchanan, fiddle, 1; John Boyd, electric steel guitar, 2; Muryel Campbell, electric guitar, 3/ guitar, 4; Knocky Parker, piano; Marvin Montgomery, kazoo, 5/tenor banjo, 6/tenor guitar, 7; Jim Boyd, guitar, 8/string bass, 9/vocal, 10; Ramon DeArman, guitar, 9/string bass, 8; humming trio (DeArman, Boyd, Pitts or Parker Willson), 11

Dallas, Nov. 30, 1938

DAL-641-1	It Makes No Difference Now, -1,2,3,7,8,10	Vocalion/OKeh 04559, Conqueror 9172
DAL-642-2	Blue-Eyed Sally, -1,3,6,8,10	Vocalion 04702
DAL-643-1	You're The Only Star (In My Blue Heaven), -1,4,7,8,10	Vocalion 04702
DAL-644-1	Baby, Give Me Some Of That, -1,3,6,8,10	Vocalion/OKeh 04638, Conqueror 9195
DAL-645-1	Dirty Dish Rag Blues, -3,6,8,10	Vocalion 04701
DAL-646-1	(New) Jeep's Blues. −1,3,6,8	Vocalion 04701
DAL-647-1	Zenda Waltz Song, -1,3,7,8	Vocalion/OKeh 04825
DAL-648-1,2	Grey Skies, -1,3,6,8,10	Vocalion unissued
DAL-649-1	Thousand Mile Blues, -1,3,5,6,8,10	Vocalion 04770
DAL-650-1	Gin Mill Blues,-1,3,7,9	Vocalion/OKeh 04560, Conqueror 9254
DAL-651-1,-2	Yancey Special, -1,3,6,8	Vocalion unissued
DAL-652-1	The Farmer's Not In The Dell, -1,3,6,8,10	Vocalion/OKeh 04638, Conqueror 9195
DAL-653-1	Foot Warmer, -1,3,6,9	Vocalion 04770
DAL-654-1	Troubles, -1,3,6,8,10,11	Vocalion/OKeh 04559, Conqueror 9172

Robert "Buck" Buchanan, fiddle; Muryel Campbell, electric guitar; Knocky
Parker, piano; Marvin Montgomery, tenor banjo, vocal, speech; Ramon
DeArman, guitar, vocal, speech, vocal effects; Jim Boyd, string bass, vocal;
Kenneth Pitts, vocal

Dallas, Nov. 30, 1938

| DAL-655-1 | Pussy, Pussy, Pussy | Vocalion/OKeh 04560, Conqueror 9254, Regal-Zonophone (Australian) G23970 |

Cecil Brower, fiddle; Kenneth Pitts, fiddle, 1/piano, 2/vocal, 3; Muryel
Campbell, electric guitar; Knocky Parker, piano/accordion, 4; Marvin
Montgomery, tenor banjo, 5/tenor guitar, 6/vocal, 7/speech, 8; Ramon
DeArman, guitar/ vocal, 9/speech, 10/vocal effects, 11; Jim Boyd, string bass/
vocal, 12/vocal effects, 13; Charles Burton, vocal, 14; Parker Willson, vocal,
15/speech, 16/vocal effects, 17; vocal trio (Willson, Boyd, DeArman), 18; vocal
quartet (DeArman, Boyd, Pitts, Willson), 19

Dallas, June 14, 1939

DAL-803-1	Let's Make Believe We're Sweethearts, -1,5,12	Vocalion 05269, Conqueror 9527
DAL-804-1	Thinking Of You, -2,4,5,9	Vocalion 04974, Conqueror 9350
DAL-805-1	If I Didn't Care, -1,6,14	Vocalion 04965
DAL-806-1	Mary Lou, -1,6,14	Vocalion 04965
DAL-807-1	In Ole' Oklahoma, -1,6,15	Vocalion 05308
DAL-808-1	She Gave Me The Bird, -1,3,5,7,8,9,11,12,13,15,17	Vocalion 05039
DAL-809-1	Three Naughty Kittens, -3,7,9,12,15,16,17	Vocalion 05269, Conqueror 9527
DAL-810-1	We Must Have Beer, -1,4,5,19	Vocalion 04973
DAL-811-1	Tea For Two, -1,6	OKeh 06016
DAL-812-3	Little Rock Getaway, -1,6	OKeh 06016
DAL-813-1	We Found Her Little Pussy Cat, -1,3,6,7,8,9,10,11,12,15,17	Vocalion/OKeh 05092
DAL-814-1,-2	Old November Moon, -1,5,12	Vocalion unissued
DAL-815-1	The Cattle Call, -1,5,12,18	Vocalion/OKeh 05413, Conqueror 9411
DAL-816-1	Texas Song Of Pride, 1,5,19	Vocalion/OKeh 05308

Note: "Little Rock Getaway" may have been recorded at the Burrus Mill studio in Saginaw, Texas

Cecil Brower, fiddle; Kenneth Pitts, fiddle, 1; Muryel Campbell, electric guitar; Knocky Parker, piano; Marvin Montgomery, tenor banjo/kazoo, 2; Ramon DeArman, guitar, 3/string bass, 4/vocal, 5; Jim Boyd, guitar, 4/string bass, 3/vocal, 6

Dallas, June 15, 1939

DAL-827-1	Two More Years (And I'll Be Free), -1,3,6	Vocalion 04974, Conqueror 9350
DAL-828-3	Mama Won't Let Me, -1,3	Vocalion 04973
DAL-829-1	All Because of Lovin' You, -1,3,5	OKeh 05867
DAL-830-3	Oh Baby Blues (You Won't Have No Mama At All), -1,3,6	Vocalion/OKeh 05201, Conqueror 9409, Columbia 37737, 20314
DAL-831-3	Beer Drinkin' Mama, -1,4,6	Vocalion/OKeh 05201, Conqueror 9409, Columbia 37737, 20314
DAL-832-1	Mama Gets What She Wants, -3,6	Vocalion 05039
DAL-833-1	My Gal's With My Pal Tonight, -1,3,6	OKeh 05968
DAL-834-1	I Had Someone Else Before I Had You (And I'll Have Someone After You're Gone), -1,3,6	OKeh 05968
DAL-835-1	You Got What I Want, -1,3,6	Vocalion/OKeh 05092
DAL-836-1	Jazzbo Joe, -1,2,3,6	Vocalion/OKeh 05357
DAL-837-1	If I Had My Way, -1,3,6	OKeh 05867

Cecil Brower, fiddle; Kenneth Pitts, fiddle, 1; Muryel Campbell, electric guitar, 2/guitar, 3; Marvin Montgomery, tenor banjo; Ramon DeArman, guitar, 4/string bass, 5/vocal, 6; Jim Boyd, guitar, 5/string bass, 4/vocal, 7

Saginaw, Texas, c. early Sept. 1939

| 25317-1 | I'll Keep On Lovin' You, -1,2,4,6 | Vocalion/OKeh 05120, Columbia 37736, 20313 |
| 25318-1 | Little Rubber Dolly, -3,5,6,7 | Vocalion/OKeh 05120, Conqueror 9306, Columbia 37736, 20313 |

Cecil Brower, fiddle; Kenneth Pitts, fiddle/vocal, 1; Muryel Campbell, electric guitar; Knocky Parker, piano; Marvin Montgomery, tenor banjo; Jim Boyd, guitar/vocal/horse effects, 2; Ramon DeArman, string bass/vocal, 3; Parker Willson, vocal, 4

Saginaw, Texas, c. late Oct. 1939

| 25525-1 | Harsie! Keep Your Tail Up! (Keep The Sun Out Of My Eyes), -1,2,3,4 | Vocalion/OKeh 05227, Conqueror 9349, Columbia 20452, Columbia (Canadian) C1137 |
| 25526-1 | Truck Driver's Blues | Vocalion/OKeh 05227, Conqueror 9349, Columbia 20452, Columbia (Canadian) C1137 |

Cecil Brower, fiddle; Kenneth Pitts, fiddle, 1/piano, 2/vocal, 3; Muryel
Campbell, steel guitar, 4/electric guitar, 5/guitar, 6; Knocky Parker, piano/
accordion. 7; Marvin Montgomery, tenor banjo, 8/tenor guitar, 9; Jim Boyd,
guitar and vocal; Ramon DeArman, string bass/vocal, 10

Saginaw, Texas, c. early Dec. 1939

25594-1	Green Valley Trot, -3,5,8,10	Vocalion/OKeh 05357, Conqueror 9410
25595-1	Marinita, -2,6,7,9	Vocalion/OKeh 05307
25596-1	Careless, -1,4,5,8	Vocalion/OKeh 05307
25597-1	Listen To The Mocking Bird, -4, 8,9,10	Vocalion unissued

Cecil Brower, fiddle; Leroy Millican, electric guitar; Babe Wright, piano; Marvin
Montgomery, tenor banjo; Paul Waggoner, guitar; Joe Ferguson, string bass/
vocal, 1; Ramon DeArman, vocal, 2; Kenneth Pitts, vocal, 3

Saginaw, Texas, Apr. 24, 1940

DAL-1054-2	Goodbye Little Darling, -1,2,3	Vocalion/OKeh 05535, Columbia 37745, 20322
DAL-1055-1	I Want A Feller, -2	Vocalion 05653
DAL-1056-2	Rainbow	Vocalion/OKeh 05610, Columbia 37746, 20323
DAL-1057-2	Alice Blue Gown, -1	Vocalion/OKeh 05535, Columbia 37745, 20322

Cecil Brower, fiddle; Leroy Millican, electric guitar; Babe Wright, piano; Marvin
Montgomery, tenor banjo; Paul Waggoner, guitar; Joe Ferguson, string bass/
vocal, 1; Ramon DeArman, vocal, 2; Kenneth Pitts, vocal, 3; Parker Willson,
vocal, 4

Saginaw, Texas, Apr. 26, 1940

DAL-1070-2	South	Vocalion/OKeh 05610, Columbia 37746, 20323
DAL-1071-1	She's Too Young (To Play With The Boys), -1,2,3,4	OKeh 05821
DAL-1072-2	Mean Mean Mama (From Meana), -1	OKeh 05752
DAL-1073-1	Cripple Creek −1,2,3,4	OKeh 05653
DAL-1074-2	Little Honky Tonk Headache, -1	OKeh 05752
DAL-1075-2	Good Gracious Gracie!, -1	OKeh 05821
DAL-1076-2	If You'll Come Back, -2	OKeh 05696
DAL-1077-1	Snow Deer	OKeh 05696

Cecil Brower, fiddle; Kenneth Pitts, fiddle/vocal, 1; Ted Daffan, electric steel
guitar, 2; Muryel Campbell, electric guitar; Frank Reneau, piano; Marvin
Montgomery, tenor banjo; J. B. Brinkley, guitar/vocal, 3; Joe Ferguson, string
bass/vocal, 4; Parker Willson, vocal, 5

Fort Worth, Feb. 27, 1941

DAL-1184-1	Too Late, -2,3,4	OKeh 06113, Conqueror 9865
DAL-1185-1	The Little Bar Fly, -3	OKeh 06621, V-Disc 280, V-Disc Navy 60
DAL-1186-1	It's Your Worry Now, -3	OKeh 06443
DAL-1187-1	Zip Zip Zipper, -1,3,4,5	OKeh 06594, V-Disc 439, V-Disc Navy 219
DAL-1188-1	The Bartender's Daughter, -3	OKeh 06621, V-Disc 280, V-Disc Navy 260
DAL-1189-1	Don't Lie To An Innocent Maiden, -4	OKeh 06216
DAL-1190, -1,-2	Little Honky Tonk Heart-throb, -3	OK unissued
DAL-1191-1	Five Long Years, -2,3	OKeh 06286, Conqueror 9866
DAL-1192-1	Sweet Sally, -3	OKeh 06594, V-Disc 439, V-Disc Navy 219
DAL-1193-1	Slufoot On The Levee	OKeh 06161
DAL-1194-1	Honky Tonk Shuffle	OKeh 06216

Cecil Brower, fiddle; Kenneth Pitts, fiddle/vocal, 2; Muryel Campbell, electric
guitar; Frank Reneau, piano; Marvin Montgomery, tenor banjo, 3/tenor guitar,
4/vocal, 5; J. B. Brinkley, guitar/vocal, 6; Joe Ferguson, string bass/vocal, 7;
Parker Willson, vocal, 8; Dolores Jo Clancy, vocal, 9

Fort Worth, Mar. 3, 1941

DAL-1207-1	Be Honest With Me, -1,3,6	OKeh 06113, Conqueror 9865'
DAL-1208-1	Bear Creek Hop, -2,3,6,7,8	OKeh 06349
DAL-1209-1	It's Funny What Love Will Make You Do, -1,3,6	OKeh unissued; Columbia Canada C4K47911 (CD)
DAL-1210-1,-2	Do You Ever Miss Me	OKeh unissued
DAL-1211-1	Won't You Wait Another Year, -1,3,6	OKeh 06286, Conqueror 9866
DAL-1212-1	I Want A Waitress, -1,2,3,5,6,7,8	OKeh 06349
DAL-1213-1	Can't Ease My Evil Mind, -1,3,6	OKeh 06161
DAL-1214-1	After You Said You Were Leaving, -1,4,9	OKeh 06443

Cecil Brower, fiddle; Kenneth Pitts, fiddle/vocal, 1; Muryel Campbell, electric guitar; Frank Reneau, piano; Marvin Montgomery, tenor banjo; J. B. Brinkley, guitar/vocal, 2; Joe Ferguson, string bass/vocal, 3; Parker Willson, vocal, 4

Fort Worth, Mar. 6, 1941

DAL-1229-1,-2	Big House Blues, -1,2,3,4	OKeh unissued
DAL-1230-1,-2	We Just Can't Get Along, -2	OKeh unissued
DAL-1231-1	Have I Lost Your Love Forever (Little Darling), -3	OKeh 06521
DAL-1232-1	Why Did You Lie To Me, -2	OKeh 06521
DAL-1233-1,-2	I'll Never Say Goodbye, 2	OKeh unissued

Light Crust Doughboys Sacred Quartet:

J. B. Brinkley, Joe Ferguson, Kenneth Pitts, Parker Willson, vocals; Frank Reneau, piano

Fort Worth, Mar. 6, 1941

DAL-1234-1,-2	Salvation Has Been Brought Down	OKeh unissued
DAL-1235-1,-2	I Shall See Him Bye And Bye	OKeh unissued
DAL-1236-1	I Know I'll See My Mother Again	Conqueror 9887
DAL-1237-2	Beyond The Clouds	Conqueror 9886

Fort Worth, Mar. 14, 1941

| DAL-1323-1 | This Life Is Hard To Understand | OKeh 06560, Conqueror 9886 |
| DAL-1324-1 | In The Morning | OKeh 06560, Conqueror 9887 |

The Little Ramblers

Roy Johnston, trumpet; Tommy Dorsey, trombone; Bobby Davis, clarinet, soprano and alto saxophones; Sam Ruby or Freddy Cusick, tenor saxophone; Adrian Rollini, baritone saxophone, couesnophone ("goofus"); Irving Brodsky, piano; Tommy Felline, banjo; Stan King, drums.

New York, July 14, 1925

| 140759-2 | Deep Elm | Columbia 432-D |

The Lone Star Cowboys

Joe Attlesey, mandolin and vocal; Leon Chappelear, guitar and vocal; Bob Attlesey, ukulele and vocal

Chicago, Aug. 4, 1933

| 76869-1 | Deep Elm Blues | Victor 23846, Bluebird B-6001, His Master's Voice (Indian) N4278 |

Note: The Lone Star Cowboys were sometimes identified as the Lone Star Rangers, but, contrary to some reports, "Deep Elm Blues" does not appear to have been released under this band name.

Ida May Mack

Mack, vocal; K. D. Johnson, piano

Memphis, TN, Aug. 29, 1928

45438-1, -2	Wrong Doin' Daddy	Victor V38532
45439-2	Sunday Mornin' Blues	Victor unissued
45442-1, -2	Elm Street Blues	Victor V38030
45443-2	Country Spaces	Victor unissued

Memphis, TN, Aug. 30, 1928

45446-1	Mr. Moore Blues	Victor 21690
45446-2	Mr. Moore Blues	Victor unissued; RCA (French) 86.430 (EP); Document DOCD 5321 (CD)
45447-1	When You Lose Your Daddy	Victor 21690
45447-2	When You Lose Your Daddy	Victor unissued; RCA (French) 86.430 (EP); BB 07863-60065-2, BBEu 07863-60065-2; Document DOCD 5163 (CD)
45450-1, -2	Mr. Forty-Nine Blues	Victor V38532
45451-1, -2	Good-bye, Rider	Victor V38030

William McCoy

McCoy, harmonica solo/speech

Dallas, Dec. 6, 1927

145334-2	Mama Blues	Columbia 14302-D, 15269-D
145335-1	Train Imitations And The Fox Chase	Columbia 14302-D, 15269-D

McCoy, harmonica solo; accompanied by possibly Sam Harris, guitar

Dallas, Dec. 7, 1928

147593-2	Just It	Columbia 14393-D
147594-1	How Long Baby	Columbia 14393-D

McCoy, vocal, harmonica; possibly Sam Harris on guitar; possibly Jesse Hooker on clarinet on "Out of Doors Blues"

Dallas, Dec. 8, 1928

147610-1, -2	Out of Doors Blues	Columbia 14453-D
147611-1	Central Tracks Blues	Columbia 14453-D

Peck Mills and His Orchestra

Mills, piano, unknown instrumentation and personnel

New York, Sept. 18, 1925

Deep Elm (You Tell 'Em I'm Blue)	Victor test (unnumbered)

Alex Moore

Moore, vocal, piano

Wiggle Tail (Rounder LP 1166-1209-1, CD 11559)

Dallas, Feb. 3, 1988

Wiggle Tail
Everybody Have a Good Time
Chasin' Rainbows
Newest Blue Bloomer Blues
Elephant Brain Man

Dallas, 1947, 1988

Then and Now: Untitled Piano Blues	Documentary Arts DA 105

Whistlin' Alex Moore

Moore, vocal, piano, whistling-1

Dallas, Dec. 5, 1929

149530-1	They May Not Be My Toes	Columbia 14596-D
149531-2	West Texas Woman	Columbia 14496-D
149534-2	Heart Wrecked Blues-1	Columbia 14518-D
149535-2	Ice Pick Blues-1	Columbia 14518-D

Moore, piano; possibly Blind Norris, guitar

Dallas, Dec. 6, 1929

149562-2	It Wouldn't Be So Hard	Columbia 14496-D
149563-2	Blue Bloomer Blues	Columbia 14596-D

Moore, vocal, piano; probably Andrew Hogg or Blind Norris, guitar; unknown vocal bass, possibly own vocal effects

Chicago, Feb. 18, 1937

61852-A	Blue Bloomer Blues	Decca 7288
61853-A	Come Back Baby	Decca 7288
61854-A	Bull Con Blues	Decca 7552
61855-A	Hard Hearted Woman	Decca 7552

Moore, vocal, piano

From North Dallas to the East Side   (Arhoolie CD 408)

Dallas, July 30, 1960

| Whistlin' Alex Moore's Blues |
| Pretty Woman with a Sack Dress On |
| Rubber Tired Hack |
| You Say I'm a Bad Feller |
| From North Dallas to the East Side |
| New Miss No-Good Weed |
| Black-Eyed Peas and Hog Jowls |
| Boogie in the Barrel |
| Going Back to Froggy Bottom |
| July Boogie |
| West Texas Woman |
| Frisky Gal |
| Chock House Boogie |

Dallas, 1947

| Miss No-Good Weed |
| Alex's Boogie |
| You Got Me Dissatisfied |
| Alex's Rag |
| Alex's Blues |
| Alex's Wild Blues |
| Sometime I Feel Worried |
| I Love You, Baby |

Stuttgart, Germany, Oct. 23, 1969

| Rock and Roll Bed |
| Boogiein' in Strasbug |

Bill Neely

Neely, vocal, guitar

Blackland Farm Boy (1974; Arhoolie LP 5014); *Texas Law & Justice* (2001, Arhoolie CD 496) includes additional material

| Satan's Burning Hell |
| Crying the Blues over You |
| Austin Breakdown |
| Lonely Mansion |
| Pflugerville Boogie |
| Law and Justice |
| Don't Waste Your Tears over Me |
| Blackland Farm |
| Big Yellow Moon over Texas |
| My Tennessee Home |
| Deep Elm Blues |
| Sun Setting Time in Your Life |

Washington Phillips

Washington Phillips, vocal and stringed instrument, possibly a Dolceola or zither

Dallas, Dec. 2, 1927

145304-2	Mother's Last Word to Her Son	Columbia 14369-D
145305-1	Take Your Burden to the Lord and Leave It There	Columbia 14277-D
145306-2	Paul and Silas in Jail	Columbia 14369-D
145307-2	Lift Him Up That's All	Columbia 14277-D

Dallas, Dec. 5, 1927

| 145330-1 | Denomination Blues, Part 1 | Columbia 14333-D |
| 145331-2 | Denomination Blues, Part 2 | Columbia 14333-D |

Dallas, Dec. 4, 1928

| 147569-2 | I Am Born to Preach the Gospel | Columbia 14448-D |
| 147561-1 | Train Your Child | Columbia 14448-D |

Note: "Train Your Child" is a long, spoken introduction followed by an instrumental.

Dallas, Dec. 5, 1928

| 147574-1 | Jesus Is My Friend | Columbia 14404-D |
| 147575-1, -2 | What Are They Doing In Heaven Today | Columbia 14404-D |

Dallas, Dec. 2, 1929

149500-2	A Mother's Last Word To Her Daughter	Columbia 14511-D
149501-1	I've Got the Key to the Kingdom	Columbia 14511-D
149502-2	The World Is in a Bad Fix Everywhere, Part 1	Columbia unissued
149503-2	The World Is in a Bad Fix Everywhere, Part 2	Columbia unissued
149504-2	You Can't Stop a Tattler, Part 1	Columbia unissued; Agram Blues AB2006 (LP) Document DOCD5054; Yazoo 2003, Roots 'n Blues CK46779, Roots 'n' Blues (Europe) 467890-2; Roots 'n' Blues (Japan) SRCS5511 (CDs)

149505-2	You Can't Stop a Tattler, Part 2	Columbia unissued; Biograph BLP 12027; Agram Blues AB2006 (LPs); Document DOCDT5054; Yazoo 2003, Roots 'n' Blues (Europe) 467890-2, Roots 'n' Blues (Japan) SRCS5511 (CDs)
149506-2	I Had a Good Father and Mother	Columbia 14566-D
149507-2	The Church Needs Good Deacons	Columbia 14566-D

Ben Pollack and His Orchestra

Harry James, Shorty Sherock, Charlie Spivak, trumpet; Bruce Squires, Glenn Miller, trombone; Irving Fazola, clarinet; Opie Cates, alto saxophone; Dave Matthews, tenor saxophone; Ray Cohen, violin; Freddy Slack, piano; Frank Frederico, guitar; Thurman Teague, string bass; Sammy Taylor, drums; Carol Mackay, Lois Still, vocal

Hollywood, Dec. 18, 1936

B-4373-B	Deep Elm	Variety 504, Vocalion 3769

Prairie Ramblers

Tex Atchison, fiddle; George "Bill" Thall, clarinet; Chick Hurt, mandola; Salty Holmes, guitar; Jack Taylor, string bass, vocal band, vocal; unidentified vocal

New York, Aug. 15, 1935

17963-2	Deep Elem Blues	ARC 5-11 51, Conqueror 8580

Alan Crockett, fiddle; Chick Hurt, mandola, vocal; Salty Holmes, guitar; Bob Long, guitar; Jack Taylor, string bass, vocal; band, vocal

Chicago, May 23, 1939

WC-2603-A	Just Because You're in Deep Elm	Vocalion 04899, Conqueror 9326

Willie Reed

Vocal, guitar

Dallas, Dec. 8, 1928

147600-2	Dreaming Blues	Columbia 14407-D
147601-1	Texas Blues	Columbia 4407-D

Dallas, Dec. 5, 1929

| 149544-1 | Leavin' Home | Columbia unissued; Historical Records ASC 17, HLP17, Roots RL335, Albatros VPA8187 (LPs); Document DOCD5161 (CD) |
| 149545-2 | Goin' Back To My Baby | Columbia unissued |

Dallas, Sept. 26, 1935

| DAL-166-2 | Some Low Down Ground-hog Blues | Vocalion 03093 |
| DAL-167-2 | White House on the Hill Blues | Vocalion unissued |

Dallas, Sept. 27, 1935

DAL-168-2	Lay My Money Down Blues	Vocalion unissued
DAL-169-2	Changing Time Blues	Vocalion unissued
DAL-170-2	All Worn Out and Dry Blues	Vocalion 03093
DAL-171-2	Boogie Woogie Mama Blues	Vocalion unissued

Dallas, Sept. 28, 1935

| DAL-176-2 | Central Avenue Blues | Vocalion unissued |
| DAL-177-2 | Rachel Lee Blues | Vocalion unissued |

Dallas, Sept. 30, 1935

| DAL 189-1 | Heart-Breakin' Mama Blues | Vocalion unissued |
| DAL-190-1 | Whose Muddy Shoes Are These? | Vocalion unissued |

Jimmie Revard & His Oklahoma Playboys

Ben McKay, fiddle; Emil "Bash" Hofner, electric steel guitar; Art Francis, piano; Cotton Cooper, tenor banjo; Adolph Hofner, guitar, vocal; Curly Williams, guitar or string bass; Jimmy Revard, guitar or string bass

San Antonio, TX, Feb. 26, 1937

| 07364-1 | Daddy's Got the Deep Elm Blues | Bluebird B-7061 |

Rhubarb Red

Les Paul, vocal, harmonica, guitar

Chicago, May 20, 1936

C-90734-A	Deep Elem Blues no. 2	Montgomery Ward 8013
C-90735-A	Deep Elem Blues	Montgomery Ward 8012

Willard Robison and His Orchestra

Unknown site, October 6, 1927

Deep Elm (You Tell 'Em I'm Blue)	Perfect 12387, Pathé 32308

Shelton Brothers

Joe Shelton, mandolin, vocal; Bob Shelton, guitar, vocal

Chicago, Feb. 22, 1935

C-9809-A	Deep Elem Blues	Decca 5009, 46008

Note: Decca 46008 apparently was issued in 1946.

New York, Dec. 19, 1935

60259-B	Deep Elem Blues No. 2	Decca 5198

Joe Shelton, mandolin and vocal; Bob Shelton, vocal; Harry Sorensen, accordion; Gene Sullivan, guitar; Slim Harbert, string bass

Dallas, Feb. 18, 1937

61839-A	Deep Elem Blues No. 3	Decca 5442

Bob and Joe Shelton, vocal duet; Cliff Bruner, fiddle; Bob Dunn, electric steel guitar; Leo Raley, electric mandolin; Dickie McBride, guitar; Hezzie Bryant, string bass

Houston, Mar. 4, 1939

65131-A	Just Because You're In Deep Elem	Decca 5665

Shelton brothers, vocal duet; Jimmy Thomason, fiddle; Billy McNew, electric steel guitar; Joe Shelton, electric mandolin; Merle Shelton, guitar; Slim Harbert, string bass; band, vocal

Houston, Apr. 7, 1940

92037-A	What's the Matter with Deep Elem	Decca 5898

Summer 1947

Deep Elm Boogie Woogie Blues	King 660

J. T. "Funny Paper" Smith (the Howling Wolf)

Vocal, guitar; unknown piano on some songs

Chicago, c. Sept. 18, 1930

C-6397	Hobo Blues	Vocalion unissued
C-6398	Old Rounder's Blues	Vocalion unissued

Chicago, Sept. 19, 1930

C-6404-A	Howling Wolf Blues no. 1	Vocalion 1558
C-6405-A	Howling Wolf Blues no. 2	Vocalion 1558

Chicago, c. Sept. 20, 1930

C-6408	Heart Bleeding Blues	Vocalion 1590
C-6409	Good Coffee Blues	Vocalion 1590

Chicago, c. Oct. 26, 1930

C-6451	Hobo Blues	Vocalion 1582
C-6452	Old Rounder's Blues	Vocalion 1582

Note: This recording apparently was either unissued or immediately withdrawn.

Chicago, c. Nov. 5, 1930

C-6494-A	Hard Luck Man Blues	Vocalion 1679
C-6495	God Bless Her Sweetheart	Vocalion unissued

Magnolia Harris, Smith, vocal duet; probably Smith, guitar

Chicago, c. late Dec. 1930

C-7100	Mama's Quittin' and Leavin', Part 1	Vocalion 1602, Melotone M12077
C-7101	Mama's Quittin' and Leavin', Part 2	Vocalion 1602, Melotone M12077

Note: Magnolia Harris may have been Texas singer Victoria Spivey.

Smith, vocal and guitar

Chicago, Jan. 10, 1931

C-7209-A	Howling Wolf Blues no. 3	Vocalion 1614
C-7210-A	Howling Wolf Blues no. 4	Vocalion 1614

Dessa Foster, Smith, vocal duet; Smith, guitar

Chicago, Jan. 19, 1931

C-7238-A	Tell It to the Judge no. 1	Melotone M12117, Polk P9013, Vocalion 02699
C-7239-A, -B	Tell It to the Judge no. 2	Melotone M12117, Polk P9013, Vocalion 02699

Smith, vocal, guitar

Chicago, Feb. 12, 1931

| VO-126 | Honey Blues | Vocalion 1633 |
| VO-127 | Corn Whiskey Blues | Vocalion 1633 |

Chicago, Mar. 10, 1931

| VO-130-A | Wiskeyhead [*sic*] Blues | Vocalion 1664 |
| VO-131-A | Forty-Five Blues | Vocalion 1664 |

Chicago, Mar. 11, 1931

| VO-132-A | County Jail Blues | Vocalion 1679 |

Chicago, July 10, 1931

VO-165-A	Hungry Wolf	Vocalion 1655
VO-166-A	Hoppin' Toad Frog	Vocalion 1655
VO-167-A	Fool's Blues	Vocalion 1674
VO-168-A	Seven Sisters Blues, Part 1	Vocalion 1641
VO-169-A	Seven Sisters Blues, Part 2	Vocalion 1641
VO-170-A	Before Long	Vocalion 1674

Smith, vocal and guitar; Black Boy Shine, piano, -1

Fort Worth, Apr. 21, 1935

FW-1175-2	Bed-Shaking Blues-1	Vocalion unissued
FW-1176-2	Life in Prison Blues-1	Vocalion unissued
FW-1177-1	Wee-Wee Toad Blues	Vocalion unissued
FW-1179-2	Lone Star Blues	Vocalion unissued
FW-1180-1	Shocking Blues	Vocalion unissued
FW-1181-2	Filly Blues	Vocalion unissued

Smith, vocal and guitar; "Little Brother" (Willie Lane), guitar

Fort Worth, TX, Apr. 22, 1935

FW-1189	Begging Blues	Vocalion unissued
FW-1190-2	V-8 Blues	Vocalion unissued
FW-1191	Pitching Blues	Vocalion unissued
FW-1192	Eight-Day Blues	Vocalion unissued
FW-1193	Champagne Woman Blues	Vocalion unissued
FW-1194-2	Waitin' for Me Blues	Vocalion unissued
FW-1195	Pork Chop Blues	Vocalion unissued

Smith, vocal and guitar

Fort Worth, Apr. 23, 1935

FW-1202	Waitin' on You Blues	Vocalion unissued
FW-1203-2	Howling Wolf Blues no. 5	Vocalion unissued
FW-1204-2	Howling Wolf Blues no. 6	Vocalion unissued
FW-1205-2	Servant House Blues	Vocalion unissued
FW-1206	Hot Plate Blues	Vocalion unissued

Southern Sanctified Singers

Apparently a Rev. D. C. Rice group; details unknown

Chicago, Mar. 9, 1929

| C-3087-C | Where He Leads Me I Will Follow | Brunswick unissued |
| C-3088-B | Soon We'll Gather at the River | Brunswick unissued |

Vocal group with unknown trumpet, trombone-1, piano, guitar, and drums

Chicago, c. Apr. 16, 1929

| C-3296 | Soon We'll Gather at the River | Brunswick 7074 |
| C-3297 | Where He Leads Me I Will Follow | Brunswick 7074 |

Dick Stabile and His Orchestra

Dick Stabile, clarinet, alto saxophone; Bunny Berrigan, Eddie Farley, trumpet; Mike Riley, trombone; Chauncey Gray, piano; unknown guitar, string bass, drums; Billy Wilson, vocal

New York, Jan. 29, 1936

| 60413-A | Deep Elem Blues | Decca 716, 25376, 28127 |

The Sunshine Boys

Jimmy Thomason, fiddle; Billy Mack (McNew), electric steel guitar; Aubrey "Moon" Mullican, piano; Merle Shelton, guitar; Grundy "Slim" Harbert, string bass, vocal; band, vocal

Saginaw, TX, May 4, 1940

| DAL-1134-1 | What's the Matter with Deep Elm | OKeh 05810, Conqueror 9728 |

Tennessee Tooters

Hymie Farberman or Harry Gluck, trumpet; Miff Mole, trombone; Chuck Muller, alto saxophone; Lucien Smith, tenor saxophone; Rube Bloom, piano; unknown banjo; Joe Tarto, brass bass; Harry Lottman, drums

New York, Aug. 13, 1925

| 1155 Deep Elm | Vocalion 15109, Guardsman (British) 7018 |

Note: Band identified as Pete Massey's All-Black Band on Guardsman.

Texas Jubilee Singers

Vocal group, including Laura Henton, lead singer; probably Arizona Dranes, piano and vocal

Dallas, Dec. 8, 1928

| 147604-2 | He's the Lily of the Valley | Columbia 14445-D |
| 147605-2 | He's Coming Soon | Columbia 14445-D |

Texas Wanderers

Grady Hester, fiddle; Anthony Scanlin, piano; J. D. Standlee, electric steel guitar; Leo Raley, electric mandolin; Johnny Thames, tenor banjo; Aubrey "Red" Greenhaw, guitar; Dickie McBride, guitar; Hezzie Bryant, string bass

Houston, Aug. 28, 1939

| 66311-A | Deep Elm Swing | Decca 5775 |

Jesse "Babyface" Thomas

Thomas, vocal, guitar

Dallas, Aug. 10, 1929

55324	Down in Texas Blues	Victor 23381
56325	My Heart's a Rolling Stone	Victor 23381
55326-1	Blue Goose Blues	Victor V38555
55327-2	No Good Woman Blues	Victor V38555

Note: This artist continued to record after 1943.

(Willard) Ramblin' Thomas

Thomas, vocal, guitar

Chicago, c. Feb. 1928

20334-2	So Lonesome	Paramount 12637
20335-3	Hard to Rule Woman Blues	Paramount 12670, Broadway 5087
20336-3	Lock and Key Blues	Paramount 12637
20337-2	Sawmill Moan	Paramount 12616
20338-1	No Baby Blues	Paramount 12670, Broadway 5087
20339-2	Ramblin' Mind Blues	Paramount 12616
20343-2	No Job Blues	Paramount 12609
20344-2	Back Gnawing Blues	Paramount 12609

Chicago, c. Nov. 1928

21017-4	Jig Head Blues	Paramount 12708, Tempo R51
21018-2	Hard Dallas Blues	Paramount 12708, Tempo R51
21019-4	Ramblin' Man	Paramount 12722
21020-4	Poor Boy Blues	Paramount 12722
21027-1	Good Time Blues	Paramount 12752
21028-2	New Way of Living Blues	Paramount 12752

Dallas, Feb. 9, 1932

70666-1	Ground Hog Blues	Victor 23332
70667-1	Shake It Gal	Victor 23332
70668-1	Ground Hog Blues No. 2	Victor 23365
70669-1	Little Old Mama Blues	Victor 23365

Bessie Tucker

Tucker, vocal; K. D. Johnson, piano

Memphis, Aug. 29, 1928

45436-2	Bessie's Moan	Victor V38526, Jazz Classic 514
45437-1, -2	The Dummy	Victor 21708
45440-1, -2	Fort Worth and Denver Blues	Victor 21708
45441-1	Penitentiary	Victor V38526
45441-2	Penitentiary	Victor V38526, Jazz Classic 514
45444-1	Fryin' Pan Skillet Blues	Victor unissued; Victor "X Vault" EVA8, HMV 7EG8085 (EPs); Victor "X Vault" LVA3016, Document DLP556 (LPs) DOCD5070 (CD)
45444-2	Fryin' Pan Skillet Blues	Victor V38018
45445-1	My Man Has Quit Me	Victor 21692

Memphis, Aug. 30, 1928

45448-1	Got Cut All to Pieces	Victor unissued; Victor "X Vault" EVA8, HMV 7EG8085 (EPs); Victor "X Vault" LVA3016, Doc DLP556 (LPs) DOCD5070 (CD)

| 45448-2 | Got Cut All to Pieces | Victor V38018 |
| 45449-2 | Black Name Moan | Victor 21692 |

Tucker, vocal; accompanied by K. D. Johnson, piano, presumably vocal-1; Jesse Thomas, guitar; unknown brass bass-2

Dallas, Aug. 10, 1929

55328-1, -2	Better Boot That Thing -1, -2	Victor V38542
55329-1, -2	Katy Blues-2	Victor V38542
55330-1, -2	Mean Old Jack Stropper Blues	Victor V38538
55331-1	Old Black Mary	Victor V38538

Tucker, vocal, accompanied by Jesse Thomas, guitar, K. D. Johnson, piano

Dallas, Oct. 17, 1929

56404-2	Key to the Bushes Blues	Victor 23385, BB B5128, Sunrise 3208
56405-1	Bogy Man Blues	Victor 23385, Bluebird B5128, Sunrise 3208
56406-1, -2	Mean Old Master Blues	Victor 23392
56407-2	Pick on Me Blues	Victor unissued

Dallas, Oct. 21, 1929

| 56447-1 | Whistling Woman Blues | Victor unissued; Document DLP556 (LP); DOCD5070, Bluebird 07863-60065-2, Bluebird Europe 07863-60065-2 (CDs) |
| 56448-2 | T. B. Moan | Victor 23392 |

Buck Turner (the Black Ace)

Turner, vocal, guitar

Fort Worth, Apr. 5, 1936

| FW-1260-1 | Bonus Man Blues | ARC unissued |
| FW-1261-2 | Black Ace Blues | ARC unissued |

Turner, vocal, guitar; unknown second guitar, possibly Andrew "Smokey" Hogg

Dallas, Feb. 15, 1937

61789-A	Trifling Woman	Decca 7281
61790-A	Black Ace	Decca 7281
61791-A	You Gonna Need My Help Some Day	Decca 7340
61792-A	Whiskey and Women	Decca 7340
61793-A	Christmas Time Blues (Beggin' Santa Claus)	Decca 7387
61794-A	Lowing Heifer	Decca 7387

Note: This artist's name was actually Babe Kyro Lemon Turner.

Paul van Loan and His Orchestra

Probably Paul van Loan, trombone; Allen McAllister, George Hall, trumpet; George Vaughn, Tom Kraus and Glen Wakeman, clarinet, soprano, alto and tenor saxophones; Joe Cirina, piano; Whitey Campbell, banjo; Ed Grier, brass bass; George Sterinsky, drums.

New York, c. Sept. 10, 1925

| 1623-C | Deep Elm (You Tell 'Em I'm Blue) | Cameo 820 |

Aaron "T-Bone" Walker

As Oak Cliff T-Bone, vocal, guitar; Douglas Finnell, piano

Dallas, Dec. 5, 1929

| 149548-1 | Trinity River Blues | Columbia 14506-D |
| 149549-2 | Wichita Falls Blues | Columbia 14506-D |

With Les Hite and His Orchestra: T-Bone Walker, vocal; Paul Campbell, Walter Williams, Forrest Powell, trumpet; Britt Woodman, Allen Durham, trombone; Les Hite and Floyd Turnham, alto saxophone; Quedellis "Que" Martyn, Roger Hurd, tenor saxophone; Sol Moore, baritone saxophone; Nat Walker, piano; Frank Pasley, guitar; Al Morgan, string bass; Oscar Bradley, drums.

New York, c. June 1940

| US-1852-1 | T-Bone Blues | Varsity 8391, Blue Note 530, Elite X10, Commodore 114 |

Note: Remaining titles from this session do not feature Walker.

With Freddie Slack and His Orchestra: T-Bone Walker: guitar; Charles Gifford, Clyde Hurley, John Letman, Bill Morris, trumpet; Bruce Squires, Gerald Foster, Bill Lawlor, trombone; Barney Bigard, clarinet, tenor saxophone; John Huffman, Willie Martinez, alto saxophone; Ralph Lee, Les Baxter, tenor and baritone saxophone; Freddie Slack, piano; George M. "Jud" De Naut, string bass; Dave Coleman, drums; Ella Mae Morse, vocal-1; Johnny Mercer, vocal-2

Hollywood, July 20, 1942

50	He's My Guy-1	Capitol 113
51-A	Mister Five by Five-1, -2	Capitol 115
52-A	The Thrill Is Gone	Capitol 115
53-A	Riffette	Capitol 129

Walker, vocal, guitar; Slack, piano; De Naut, string bass; Coleman, drums.

Hollywood, July 20, 1942

| 54-A | I Got a Break, Baby | Capitol 10033, 15033 |
| 55-A | Mean Old World | Capitol 10033, 15033 |

Walker, guitar, with Freddie Slack and His Orchestra (same personnel as above except add Margaret Whiting, vocal-3, and the Mellowaires, vocal group-4)

Hollywood, July 3, 1942

70	That Old Black Magic	Capitol 126
71	Old Rob Roy-1	Capitol 133
72	Waitin' for the Evening Mail -2	Capitol 137
73	Wreck of the Old 97-2	Capitol 122
74	Hit the Road to Dreamland -3, -4	Capitol 126
75-A	Get on Board, Little Children -1, -4	Capitol 133
76	I Lost My Sugar in Salt Lake City -2	Capitol 122

Note: This artist continued to record extensively while living in California after 1943.

Herb Wiedoeft and His Cinderella Roof Orchestra

Herb Wiedoeft, trumpet; Joseph Nemoli, cornet and viola; Jesse Stafford, trombone, baritone horn; Larry Abbot, Gene Siegrist, Fred Bibesheimer, clarinet, alto and tenor saxophones, oboe; Vincent Rose, piano; Jose Sucedo, banjo; Guy Wiedoeft, brass and string basses; Adolf Wiedoeft, drums, xylophone; Clyde Lucas, trombone, vocal; Dubbie Kirkpatrick, instrument unknown

New York, Oct. 14, 1925

| E-16701 | Deep Elm | Brunswick 2982 |

The Wilburn Brothers

Jan. 1956

| Deep Elem Blues | Decca 29887 |

Oscar "Buddy" Woods

Probably Woods and "Dizzy Head" (Ed Schaffer), also an African American guitarist, accompanying white vocalist Jimmie Davis

Memphis, May 20, 1930

| 59952-1 | She's A Hum Dum Dinger (From Dingersville) | Victor unissued; Bear Family BFX15285 (LP); Document (Austrian) DOCD5143 (CD) |
| 59952-2 | She's A Hum Dum Dinger | Victor V40286, Bluebird 1835 and B5005, Electradisk 1963, Sunrise S3128, Montgomery Ward M4283 |

With the Shreveport Home Wreckers: Ed Schaffer, guitar, kazoo, vocal; Woods, guitar

Memphis, May 21, 1930

| 59965-2 | Fence-Breakin' Blues | Victor 23275, Bluebird B5341, Sunrise S3422 |
| 59966-2 | Home-Wreckin' Blues | Victor 23275, Bluebird 5341, Sunrise S3422 |

Woods, guitar, 1/vocal, 2/speech, 3; Schaffer, guitar/speech, 5; Davis, vocal

Dallas, February 8, 1932

70656-1	Saturday Night Stroll, -2,4,5	Victor 23688,, Montgomery Ward M7363
70657-1	Sewing Machine Blues, -1	Victor 23703, Bluebird F5751
70658-1	Red Nightgown Blues, -1	Victor 23659, Bluebird B5699
70659-1	Davis's Salty Dog, -1,3	Victor 23674

Oscar and Eddie: Woods, guitar and vocal; Eddie Chafer (probably Ed Schaffer), guitar

Dallas, February 8, 1932

| 70660-1 | Nok-Em-All | Victor 23324 |
| 70661-1 | Flying Crow Blues | Victor 23324 |

Oscar Woods (The Lone Wolf), vocal and guitar

New Orleans, Mar. 21, 1936

60847-	Evil Hearted Woman Blues	Decca 7904
60848-A	Lone Wolf Blues	Decca 7219
60849-	Don't Sell It—Don't Give It Away	Decca 7219

With the Wampus Cats: Woods, guitar and vocal; Kitty Gray, piano; possibly Joe Harris, second guitar; unknown string bass

San Antonio, October 30, 1937

SA-2844-1	Muscat Hill Blues	Vocalion 03906
SA-2845-1	Don't Sell It (Don't Give It Away)	Vocalion 03906

With Kitty Gray and Her Wampus Cats: Kitty Gray, piano/vocal, 1; Woods, guitar; possibly Joe Harris, guitar; unknown string bass; unknown male vocal interjection, 2/vocal, 3

San Antonio, October 30, 1937

SA-2838-1	I Can't Dance (Got Ants In My Pants), -1,3	Vocalion 03992
SA-2839-1	Round and Round –1	Vocalion 03992
SA-1840-1	You're Standing On The Outside Now	Vocalion 04014
SA-2841-1	Swingology, -1,2	Vocalion 03869
SA-2842-2	The Joke Is On Me	Vocalion unissued
SA-2843-1	My Baby's Ways, -1	Vocalion 04121
SA-2846-1	Baton Rouge Rag	Vocalion unissued; Columbia CG33566, CBS (British) 88225, Document (Austrian) DLP517 (LPs), DOCD5143, DOCD5225 (CDs)
SA-2847-1	Weeping Willow Swing, -2	Vocalion 04014
SA-2848-1	Gettin' Away, -1, 3	Vocalion 04121

Kitty Gray, vocal, piano; Woods, guitar; unknown string bass, male vocal

San Antonio, October 31, 1937

SA-2853-1	Posin'	Vocalion 03869

Kitty Gray, vocal, piano; Woods, guitar; unknown trumpet, alto and tenor saxes, string bass and drums

Dallas, Dec. 4, 1938

DAL-700-1	Doing The Dooga	Vocalion 04629
DAL-701-2	You Keep Me Worried	Vocalion unissued
DAL-705-1	I'm Yours To Command	Vocalion 04629
DAL-706-2	As Long As You're Mine	Vocalion unissued

Buddy Woods and the Wampus Cats:Woods, vocal and guitar; Kitty Gray, piano; unknown trumpet, second guitar, string bass, drums

Dallas, Dec. 4, 1938

DAL-702-1	Jam Session Blues	Vocalion 04604
DAL-703-1	Low Life Blues	Vocalion 04745
DAL-704-1	Token Blues	Vocalion 04604
DAL-707-1	Come On Over To My House Baby	Vocalion 04745

Oscar (Buddy) Woods, vocal and guitar

Shreveport, Louisiana, Oct. 8, 1940

3989-A-1	Boll Weevil Blues	Library of Congress: Flyright-Matchbox FLYLP260 (LP), Travelin' Man TMCD09 (CD)
3989-A-2	Don't Sell It	Library of Congress: Flyright-Matchbox FLYLP260 (LP), Travelin' Man TMCD09 (CD)
3989-A-3	Sometimes I Get A-Thinkin'	Library of Congress: Flyright-Matchbox FLYLP260 (LP), Travelin' Man TMCD09 (CD)
3989-B-1	Sometimes I Get A-Thinkin'	Library of Congress: Flyright-Matchbox FLYLP260 (LP), Travelin' Man TMCD09 (CD)
3989-B-2	Look Here, Baby, One Thing I Got To Say	Library of Congress: Flyright-Matchbox FLYLP260 (LP), Travelin' Man TMCD09 (CD)

Bibliography

Books and Articles

Alyn, Glen (A. Glenn Myers). *I Say Me for a Parable: The Oral Autobiography of Mance Lipscomb, Texas Bluesman.* New York, W. W. Norton & Company, 1993.

Barlow, William. *Looking up at Down: The Emergence of Blues Culture.* Philadelphia: Temple University Press, 1989.

Basie, Count, as told to Albert Murray. *Good Morning Blues: The Autobiography of Count Basie.* New York: Random House, 1985.

Boyd, Jean A. *Dance All Night: Those Other Southwestern Swing Bands, Past and Present.* Lubbock: Texas Tech University Press, 2012.

———. *The Jazz of the Southwest: An Oral History of Western Swing.* Austin: University of Texas Press, 1998.

———. *"We're the Light Crust Doughboys from Burrus Mill": An Oral History.* Austin: University of Texas Press, 2003.

Brakefield, Jay F. "Birthday of a Bluesman: A Look Back at Life, Music of Blind Lemon Jefferson." *Dallas Morning News,* September 23, 1993, 5C.

Brewer, J. Mason. *Heralding Dawn: An Anthology of Verse.* Dallas: June Thompson Printing, 1936.

Brown, Roger S. "Recording Pioneer Polk Brockman." *Living Blues* 23 (1975): 31.

Business and Professional Directory of Colored Persons in Dallas, 1911. Dallas: Published under the auspices of the Dallas Negro Business League, 1911.

Carr, Patrick, ed. *The Illustrated History of Country Music.* New York: Doubleday, 1979.

Cartwright, Gary. "Benny and the Boys." *Texas Monthly,* October 1991: 134–139, 193–199.

Charles, Ray, and David Ritz. *Brother Ray: Ray Charles' Own Story.* New York: Dial, 1978.

Charters, Samuel. *The Bluesmen.* New York: Oak, 1968.

———. *The Country Blues.* New York: Rinehart, 1959.

Corcoran, Michael. *All over the Map: True Heroes of Texas Music.* Austin: University of Texas Press, 2005.

Cusic, Don. 2011. *The Cowboy in Country Music: An [sic] Historical Survey with Artist Profiles.* Jefferson, NC: McFarland.

Dance, Helen O. *Stormy Monday: The T-Bone Walker Story.* New York: Da Capo, 1990.

Daniels, Douglas Henry. *One o'Clock Jump: The Unforgettable History of the Oklahoma City Blue Devils.* Boston: Beacon, 2006.

Dempsey, John Mark. *The Light Crust Doughboys Are on the Air.* Denton: University of North Texas Press, 2002.

Dixon, Robert, and John Godrich. *Recording the Blues, 1902–1940.* New York: Stein and Day, 1970.

Doolin, Kaleta. *Fritos Pie: Stories, Recipes, and More.* College Station: Texas A&M University Press, 2011.

Driggs, Frank. "Budd Johnson, Ageless Jazzman." *Jazz Review* 3(9) (November 1960).

Enstam, Elizabeth York, ed. *When Dallas Became a City: Letters of John Milton McCoy, 1870–1881.* Dallas: Dallas Historical Society, 1982.

Evans, David. "Musical Innovation in the Blues of Blind Lemon Jefferson." *Black Music Research Journal* 20(1) (Spring 2000): 83–116.

———. "Ramblin.'" *Blues Revue Quarterly* 9 (Summer 1993): 16–18.

Fly, Everett L. "Pittman, William Sidney." *The Handbook of Texas Online,* Texas State Historical Association. http://www.tshaonline.org/handbook/online/articles/fpi32.

Ford, Shane. *Shine a Light: My Year with "Blind" Willie Johnson.* Lulu.com, 2011.

Foreman, Ronald Clifford. Jazz and Race Records, 1920–32: Their Origins and Their Significance for the Record Industry and Society. PhD diss., University of Illinois, 1968.

Fox, Ted. *Showtime at the Apollo.* New York: Holt, Rinehart and Winston, 1983.

Gazzaway, Don. "Conversations with Buster Smith." *Jazz Review.* Parts I, II, and III. (December 1959–February 1960).

Ginell, Cary. *Milton Brown and the Founding of Western Swing.* Urbana: University of Illinois Press, 1994.

Govenar, Alan. "Blind Lemon Jefferson: The Myth and the Man." *Black Music Research Journal* 20(1) (Spring 2000): 7–21.

———. "Buster Smith: Dallas Jazz Patriarch." *Parkway* (April 1983): 34–35.

———. *Daddy Double Do Love You.* Chicago: Jubilee, 1993.

———. "Hal Baker and the Gloomchasers." *Parkway* (May 1983): 31.

———. "Herbert Cowens: USO Drummer, Extraordinaire." *Legacies* 4 (Spring 1992): 32–36.

———. "The History of Deep Ellum." In program booklet for the Dallas Black Dance Theatre production of *Deep Ellum Blues,* December 4–6, 1986.

———. *Meeting the Blues: The Rise of the Texas Sound.* Dallas: Taylor, 1988.

———. *Portraits of Community: African American Photography in Texas.* Austin: Texas State Historical Association, 1996.

———. *Texas Blues: The Rise of a Contemporary Sound.* College Station: Texas A&M University Press, 2008.

———. "That Black Snake Moan: The Music and Mystery of Blind Lemon Jefferson." In *Bluesland: Portraits of Twelve Major American Blues Masters,* ed. Pete Welding and Toby Byron, 16–37. New York: Penguin, 1991.

———. "Them Deep Ellum Blues: A Street, a Sound, and a Time." *Legacies* 2 (Spring 1990): 4–9

———. "Variants of Texas Blues." *Texas Humanist* 7 (July–August 1985): 28–31.

———, Francis E. Abernethy, and Patrick B. Mullen. *Juneteenth Texas: Essays in African-American Folklore.* Denton: University of North Texas Press, 1996.

Govenar, Alan, and Phillip Collins, eds. *Facing the Rising Sun: Freedman's Cemetery.* Dallas: African American Museum and Black Dallas Remembered, 2000.

Greene, A. C. *Dallas USA.* Austin: Texas Monthly Press, 1984.

Hall, Michael. "The Soul of a Man: Who Was Blind Willie Johnson?" *Texas Monthly* (December 2010). Accessed online May 24, 2012. http://www.texasmonthly.com/2010-12-01/feature3.php.

Hardman, Peggy, and Laurie E. Jasinski. "Johnson, 'Blind Willie.'" *The Handbook of Texas Online,* Texas State Historical Association. http://www.tshaonline.org/handbook/online/articles/fjoaw.

———. *Dallas Morning News,* January 16, 1994, 44A.

Harlan, Louis R. *Booker T. Washington: The Wizard of Tuskegee, 1901–1915.* New York: Oxford University Press, 1983.

Haslam, Gerald A., with Alexandra Haslam Russell and Richard Chon. *Workin' Man Blues: Country Music in California.* Berkeley: University of California Press, 1999.

Heilbut, Tony. *The Gospel Sound: Good News and Bad Times.* New York: Simon and Schuster, 1971.

Hester, Mary Lee. "Texas Jazz Heritage." *Texas Jazz* (June 1979).

Holmes, Maxine, and Gerald D. Saxon, eds. *The WPA Dallas Guide and History.* Denton: University of North Texas Press, 1992.

"Honest Joe Goldstein, Pawn Shop Owner, Dies." *Dallas Morning News,* September 4, 1972.

Johnson, Idella Lulamae. *Development of the African American Gospel Piano Style (1926–1960): A Socio-Musical Analysis of Arizona Dranes and Thomas A. Dorsey.* PhD diss., University of Pittsburgh, 2009.

Jones, George William. *Black Cinema Treasures: Lost and Found.* Denton: University of North Texas Press, 1991.

La Chapelle, Peter. *Proud to Be an Okie: Cultural Politics, Country Music, and Migration to Southern California.* Berkeley: University of California Press, 2007.

Laird, Ross. *Brunswick Records: A Discography of Recordings, 1916–1931.* Westport, CT: Greenwood, 2004.

———, and Brian Rust. *Discography of OKeh Records, 1918–1934.* Westport, CT: Praeger, 2004.

Lederer, Katherine. "And Then They Sang a Sabbath Song." *Springfield* (April–June 1981): 24–28, 33–36, 24–26.

Lindsley, Philip. *History of Greater Dallas and Vicinity,* vol. 1. Chicago: Lewis, 1909.

Lippman, Laura. "Blind Lemon Sang the Blues: Wortham Man Recalls His Memories of Musician." *Waco Tribune-Herald,* June 2, 1983, 11A.

Lornell, Kip, and Charles Wolfe. *The Life and Legend of Leadbelly.* New York: HarperCollins, 1992.

Malone, Bill C. *Country Music U.S.A.* Austin: University of Texas Press, 1985.

McDonald, William L. *Dallas Rediscovered: A Photographic Chronicle of Urban Expansion* 1870–1925. Dallas: Dallas Historical Society, 1978.

Minutaglio, Bill. "The Buried Past." *Dallas Life Magazine, Dallas Morning News,* September 5, 1993.

Monge, Luigi. "The Language of Blind Lemon Jefferson: The Covert Theme of Blindness." *Black Music Research Journal* 20(1) (Spring 2000) 35–81.

———, and David Evans. "New Songs of Blind Lemon Jefferson." *Journal of Texas Music History* 3(2) (Fall 2003): 8–28.

Morris, Mark N. *Saving Society through Politics: The Dallas, Texas, Ku Klux Klan in the* 1920s. PhD diss., University of North Texas, December 1997. Ann Arbor, MI: UMI Dissertation Services, 1999.

Murray, Albert. *Stomping the Blues.* New York: Random House, 1982.

Negro Business Bulletin. Dallas: Negro Business Bureau, 1925.

Nixon, Bruce. "The Sounds of Deep Ellum." *Dallas Times Herald,* September 23, 1983.

Oakley, Giles. *The Devil's Music.* New York: Harcourt, Brace, Jovanovich, 1976.

Obrecht, Jas, ed. *Blues Guitar: The Men Who Made the Music.* San Francisco: Miller Freeman, 1993.

Official Souvenir of Klan Day at the State Fair of Texas, Dallas, October 24, 1923. Dallas: Standard American Publishing House.

Oliphant, Dave. *Jazz Mavericks of the Lone Star State.* Austin: University of Texas Press, 2007.

———. *Texan Jazz.* Austin: University of Texas Press, 1996.

Oliver, Paul. *Blues off the Record.* New York: Da Capo, 1988.

Payne, Darwin. *Dallas, an Illustrated History.* Woodland Hills, CA: Windsor, 1982.

Pearson, Nathan W., Jr. *Goin' to Kansas City.* Urbana: University of Illinois Press, 1987.

Pittman, Ophelia. *Por você, por mim, por nós.* Rio de Janeiro: Editora Record, 1984.

Price, Sammy. *What Do They Want? A Jazz Autobiography.* Urbana: University of Illinois Press, 1990.

Rogers, John William. *The Lusty Texans of Dallas.* New York: Dutton, 1951.

Russell, Ross. *Jazz Style in Kansas City and the Southwest.* Berkeley: University of California Press, 1971.

Russell, Tony. *Country Music Originals: The Legends and the Lost.* New York: Oxford University Press, 2010.

———. *Country Music Records: A Discography,* 1921–1942. New York: Oxford University Press, 2004.

Rust, Brian. *The American Dance Band Discography,* 1917–1942. New Rochelle, NY: Arlington House, 1975.

————. *Jazz Records* 1897–1942, fifth ed. Chigwell, Essex: Storyville, 1986.

Sampson, Henry T. *Blacks in Blackface: A Source Book on Early Black Musical Shows.* Metuchen, NJ: Scarecrow, 1980.

Sanders, Barrot Steven. *Dallas, Her Golden Years.* Dallas: Sanders, 1989.

Schuller, Gunther. *The Swing Era: The Development of Jazz,* 1930–1945. New York: Oxford University Press, 1989.

Schuller, Tim. "The Buster Smith Story." *CODA* (December–January 1987–1988), 4–5.

Soltes, William. "A Little Story of My Life in America." Unpublished manuscript, 1967.

Spivey, Victoria. "Blind Lemon Jefferson and I Had a Ball." *Record Research* 78 (May 1966): 9.

Stackhouse, Houston. "*Living Blues* Interview: Houston Stackhouse." Interview by Jim O'Neal. *Living Blues* 17 (Summer 1974): 20–36.

Steinberg, Richard U. "See That My Grave Is Kept Clean." *Living Blues* 83 (1982): 24–25.

Stewart, Ruth Ann. *Portia: The Life of Portia Washington Pittman, the Daughter of Booker T. Washington.* Garden City, NY: Doubleday, 1977.

Stricklin, Al, with Jon McConal. *My Years with Bob Wills.* San Antonio: Naylor, 1976.

"T-Bone Blues: T-Bone Walker's Story in His Own Words." *Record Changer* (October 1947): 5–6, 13.

Townsend, Charles R. *San Antonio Rose: The Life and Music of Bob Wills.* Urbana: University of Illinois Press, 1986.

Uzzel, Robert L. "Music Rooted in Texas Soil." *Living Blues* 83 (1982): 24–25.

Willoughby, Larry. *Texas Rhythm, Texas Rhyme: A Pictorial History of Texas Music.* Austin: Texas Monthly Press, 1984.

Wilonsky, Robert. "Knights' Tale: Another Historic Emblem of Black Dallas Stands on the Brink." *Dallas Observer,* December 20, 2007. http://www.dallasobserver.com/content/printVersion/833827/.

Interviews and Letters

Albert, Don. Interview with Nathan Pearson and Howard Litwak, April 17, 1977.

Bedford, Louis. Interview with Jay Brakefield, December 5, 1992.

Boyd, Jim, and Marvin Montgomery. Interview with Alan Govenar and Jay Brakefield, January 29, 1992.

Bruner, Cliff. Interview with Jay Brakefield and Allan Turner, June 7, 1981.

Callahan, Homer (Bill). Interview with Jay Brakefield, December 6, 1993.

Carter, Hobart. Interview with Alan Govenar, June 7, 1999.

Cody, Joe. Interview with Jay Brakefield, June 18, 1992.

Cokes, Curtis. Interview with Jay Brakefield, August 7, 1992.

Conley, Anna Mae, and Lucille Bosh McGaughey. Interview with Jay Brakefield and Alan Govenar, October 3, 1992.

Cowens, Herbie. Interviews with Alan Govenar, January 20, 1992, and February 5, 1992.

Cox, Quince. Interviews with Alan Govenar March 18, 1987, and June 7, 1999.

Doran, Ed. Interview with Jay Brakefield, April 24, 1992.

Edwards, C. W. ("Gus"). Interview with Jay Brakefield, May 1, 1992.

Emory, Emerson. Interview with Jay Brakefield, December 5, 1992.

Feldman, Label. Interview with Jay Brakefield, May 20, 1992.

Fields, Jimmy. Interview with Alan Govenar, January 23, 1994.

Freed, Joe. Interview with Jay Brakefield, May 6, 1992.

Gimble, Johnny. Interview with Alan Govenar, September 22, 1994.

Goldstein, David, and Isaac ("Rocky") Goldstein. Interview with Jay Brakefield, March 22, 1992.

Goldstein, Dora. Interviews with Jay Brakefield, February 28, 1992, and May 1, 1992.

Goldstein, Eddie. Interview with Jay Brakefield, April 3, 1992.

Goldstein, Isaac ("Rocky"). Interviews with Jay Brakefield, March 22, 1992, and May 21, 1992.

Holland, Lurline. Interview with Alan Govenar, May 15, 1999.

Howard, Theaul. Interviews with Jay Brakefield, October and November 1993.

Howze, Harmon. Interview with William Howze, October 10, 1984.

Hurd, Charlie. Interview with Jay Brakefield, November 1993.

Kirkes, Walker. Interview with Alan Govenar, June 9, 1994.

Lipscomb, Mance. Interview with Glen Myers, Center for American History Collection, Austin, Texas.

Luterman, Sam. Interview with Jay Brakefield, August 19, 1992.

McCormick, Mack. Interview with Jay Brakefield, July 29, 1989.

McGowan, Alto. Interview with Jay Brakefield, April 15, 1992.

McMillan, Rudolph. Interview with Jay Brakefield, April 9, 1993.

Montgomery, Marvin. Interviews with Alan Govenar, July 31, 1996; August 1, 1996; August 2, 1996; March 12, 1998; and March 18, 1998.

———. Interview with Jay Brakefield and Alan Govenar, July 15, 1996.

Moore, Alex. Interviews with Alan Govenar, April 9, 1982; November 5, 1988; and November 8, 1988.

Moss, John H. Interview with Alan Govenar, August 12, 1993.

Neely, Bill. Interview with Alan Govenar, August 29, 1984.

———. Interview with Jay Brakefield, June 1989.

Parker, John "Knocky." Interview August 28, 1963. Reel 1, pp. 2–4. Hogan Jazz Archive, Howard-Tilton Memorial Library, Tulane University, New Orleans.

Pittman, Eliana. Interview with Jay Brakefield, August 8, 1996.

Porte, Masha. Interview with Alan Govenar, March 4, 1992.

Price, Sammy. Interview with Alan Govenar, September 27, 1984.

———. Interview with Jay Brakefield, June 7, 1991.

Prince, Robert. Interview with Jay Brakefield, January 1993.

Putnam, Ernestine. Interview with Alan Govenar, September 10, 1993.

Richardson, Jack ("Ghost"). Interview with Jay Brakefield, May 23, 1992.

Sampson, Albert. Interview in Hogan Jazz Archive, Howard-Tilton Memorial Library, Tulane University, New Orleans.

Smith, Henry ("Buster"). Interviews with Alan Govenar, December 14, 1982, and January 10, 1983.

Smith, Junious, and Jay Smith. Interview with Jay Brakefield, July 11, 1992.

Stillman, Sam. Interview with Jay Brakefield, March 2, 1992.

Stout, Bret. Interview with Jay Brakefield, June 1993.

Sullivan, Robin ("Texas Slim"). Interview with Jay Brakefield, April 22, 2012.

Tuck, Sam. Interview with Jay Brakefield, June 15, 1992.

Wackwitz, Hank. Letter to Alan Govenar, March 1992.

Walker, Julius. Interview with Jay Brakefield, August 1, 1992.

Watson, Willard. Interview with Jay Brakefield, July 16, 1992.

Williams, Danny. Letter to Alan Govenar, September 30, 1996.

Wilonsky, Herschel. Interviews with Jay Brakefield, May 5, 1994, and February 20 and 21, 2012.

Wilson, Will. Interview with Jay Brakefield, May 15, 1993.

Wright, Margaret. Letter to Alan Govenar, March 20, 1992.

Wyll, Max. Interview with Jay Brakefield, March 25, 1992.

Newspapers

Brotherhood Eyes (Dallas, TX)
Dallas Express (Dallas, TX)
Dallas Morning News (Dallas, TX)
Dallas Times Herald (Dallas, TX)
Freeman (Indianapolis, IN)

Albums, Tapes, CDs, and Films

Alex Moore: Then and Now. Audiocassette. Dallas: Documentary Arts, DA 105.

Black on White/White and Black. Documentary film. Dallas: Documentary Arts, 1989.

Briggs, Keith. Liner notes to *Jesse Thomas, 1948–1958*. Document BDCD-6044.

Calt, Stephen. Liner notes to *Blind Lemon Jefferson: King of the Country Blues.* Yazoo 1069.

———, Woody Mann, and Nick Perls. Liner notes *to Funny Papa Smith: The Original Howling Wolf.* Yazoo L-1031.

Charters, Samuel. Liner notes to *The Complete Blind Willie Johnson.* Columbia 52835.

Corcoran, Michael. *Here Is My Story: The Sanctified Soul of Arizona Dranes* (liner notes). Tompkins Square Recoreds, 2012.

Doering, Teddy. Liner notes to *J. T. "Funny Paper" Smith, 1930–1931.* 1991. Document BDCD-6016.

Evans, David. Liner notes to *Blind Willie Johnson: Sweeter as the Years Go By.* Yazoo 1078.

Funk, Ray. Liner notes to *Preachin' the Gospel: Holy Blues.* Columbia Legacy CK 46779.

Garon, Paul. Liner notes to *Texas Blues: The Complete Recorded Works of Coley Jones, "Bo" Jones, Little Hat Jones, Willie Reed, Oak Cliff T-Bone (Walker) 1927–1935.* 1993. Document DOCD-5161.

Govenar, Alan. Liner notes to *Alex Moore: Wiggle Tail*. Rounder 2091.

Groom, Bob. Liner notes to *Ramblin' Thomas & the Dallas Blues Singers: Complete Recorded Works 1928–1932 in Chronological Order*. 1992. Document DOCD-5107.

Harrison, Ken. *Prince Albert Hunt* (originally *Memories of Prince Albert Hunt*), documentary film. Dallas: Moonlight Productions, 1974. http://www.youtube.com/watch?v=QnWKK8NPA6M. http://www.folkstreams.net/film,180. Transcription at http://www.folkstreams.net/context,314, accessed April 4, 2012.

Lornell, Kip. "Blind Lemon Meets Leadbelly." *Black Music Research Journal* 20(1) (Spring 2000): 23–33.

———. Liner notes to *Gene Campbell: Complete Recorded Works 1929–1931*. 1993. Document DOCD-5151.

———. Liner notes to *Texas Black Country Dance Music, 1927–1935*. 1993. Document DOCD-5162.

———. Liner notes to *"Texas Slide Guitars": Complete Recorded Works 1930–1938 in Chronological Order. Oscar Woods & Black Ace*. Document DOCD-5143.

McCormick, Mack. "Biography of Henry Thomas: Our Deepest Look at Roots." Liner notes to the album *Henry Thomas: Ragtime Texas*. Herwin 209.

Miner, Gregg, and Kelly Williams. "The Instruments of Washington Phillips." http://www.minermusic.com/dolceola/phillips_instruments.htm.

Oliver, Paul. Liner notes to *Whistling Alex Moore: From North Dallas to the East Side*. Arhoolie CD 408.

Romanski, Ken. Liner notes to *Arizona Dranes: Complete Recorded Works in Chronological Order 1926–1929*. Document BDCD-6031.

———. Liner notes to *The Complete Recorded Works of Reverend F. W. McGee in Chronological Order 1927–1929*. Document BDCD-6031.

Shaw, Malcolm. Liner notes *for Arizona Dranes, 1926–1928*. Herwin 210.

Waltz, Bob. "Remembering the Old Songs: Black Bottom Blues/Deep Elem Blues." Originally published in *Inside Bluegrass*, November 1998. http://www.lizlyle.lofgrens.org/RmOlSngs/RTOS-BlackBottom.html.

Index

Other titles in the John and Robin Dickson Series
in Texas Music: